Liberalism
at the Crossroads

Liberalism at the Crossroads

An Introduction to Contemporary Liberal Political Theory and Its Critics

Second Edition

Edited by
Christopher Wolfe

ROWMAN & LITTLEFIELD PUBLISHERS, INC.
Lanham • Boulder • New York • Oxford

ROWMAN & LITTLEFIELD PUBLISHERS, INC.

Published in the United States of America
by Rowman & Littlefield Publishers, Inc.
A Member of the Rowman & Littlefield Publishing Group
4501 Forbes Boulevard, Suite 200, Lanham, Maryland 20706
www.rowmanlittlefield.com

PO Box 317
Oxford
OX2 9RU, UK

British Library Cataloguing in Publication Information Available

Library of Congress Cataloging-in-Publication Data

Liberalism at the crossroads : an introduction to contemporary liberal
political theory and its critics / edited by Christopher Wolfe.—2nd ed.
    p. cm.
Includes bibliographical references and index.
   ISBN 0-7425-3270-4 (cloth : alk. paper)—ISBN 0-7425-3271-2 (pbk. : alk. paper)
   1. Liberalism. I. Wolfe, Christopher.
   JC574.L53753 2003
   320.51'3—dc21   2003001507

Printed in the United States of America

∞™ The paper used in this publication meets the minimum requirements of American
National Standard for Information Sciences—Permanence of Paper for Printed Library
Materials, ANSI/NISO Z39.48-1992.

Contents

Acknowledgments

The papers on which this book is based were presented at a conference of the American Public Philosophy Institute on "The Crisis of Contemporary Liberalism," which was made possible by a generous grant from the Homeland Foundation and by the support and encouragement of Lewis Lehrman.

Much of the editorial work to transform the conference papers into a book was undertaken by Christopher Wolfe with the help of a summer grant from the Marquette University Bradley Institute for Democracy and Public Values. John McAdams and Stephen Hollingshead were generous in sharing their computer expertise.

Gratefully acknowledged are the following publishers for their kind permission to reprint excerpts from their works: Cambridge University Press, for quotations from Michael Sandel's *Liberalism and the Limits of Justice* and from Richard Rorty's *Contingency, Irony, and Solidarity;* Oxford University Press, for quotations from Joseph Raz's *The Morality of Freedom;* and the University of Notre Dame Press, for quotations from Alasdair MacIntyre's *After Virtue.* The diagram on page 36 is reprinted by permission of the publisher from *A Theory of Justice* by John Rawls (Cambridge, Mass.: Belknap Press of Harvard University Press, © 1971 by the President and Fellows of Harvard College).

Chapter 9, "The Unorthodox Liberalism of Joseph Raz," by Robert George, appeared earlier in *The Review of Politics* 53, no. 4 (fall 1991). Reprinted by kind permission of the *Review of Politics*.

Preface to the Second Edition

The essays in the first edition of *Liberalism at the Crossroads* were written a decade ago, and, unsurprisingly, the vigorous debates among liberal theorists, and between liberal theorists and their critics, have not diminished in the intervening years. So it seems worthwhile to revisit the debate in two ways: adding several new chapters that expand the scope of the volume, and updating the original chapters.[1]

Three new chapters grace this volume, extending its reach to include representatives of liberal feminism, law and economics, and natural law. As with the original chapters, the most important goal of these additions is to provide a summary exposition of the major tenets of these authors, while secondarily offering brief critical comments.

Celia Wolf-Devine contributes a chapter on Susan Moller Okin, a feminist liberal. She describes Okin's attack on the distinction between what is private and what is public and her attempt to extend the liberal political principles of justice developed by Rawls into the family itself. She has a special interest in family structures because she believes the family to be the "linchpin" of the whole gender structure, so that genderless families would ultimately result in a genderless society. Wolf-Devine then discusses Okin's own positive position, aiming at establishing a "gender-free society," and she describes how Okin's position—which is characterized as "hegemonic liberalism"—would justify almost limitless governmental interference in the internal workings of families and religious communities in order to safeguard the autonomy of the children being educated in them. That would be a rather paradoxical conclusion for a genuinely liberal theorist.

Jack Wade Nowlin gives an account of the pragmatic theory of Richard Posner, one of the founders of the law and economics movement. (Because this theory can be characterized as another variant of "right-wing" liberalism, it is inserted after the chapter on Robert Nozick.) Posner's approach to questions of law, justice, sexuality, aging, and other social matters is most fundamentally an empirically oriented, instrumental, and interdisciplinary (though heavily eco-nomic) social science approach. He is a self-described classical or Millian lib-eral: a libertarian who supports both the free market and the legal recognition of a very broad sphere of personal autonomy. He is highly critical of the theoreti-cal enterprise he describes pejoratively as "academic moralism" (e.g., the work of John Rawls, Ronald Dworkin, and John Finnis). Posner's pragmatism rejects the moral realist-rationalist project of attempting to discern through reasoned ar-gument the requirements of an "objective" morality, including the ultimate moral-political ends to which even "pragmatic" policies are directed. Posner's pragmatism extends beyond the moral-political sphere to the legal and constitu-tional sphere. As a legal pragmatist, Posner is a critic of legal formalism, legal positivism, and ambitious legal theories that seek to inform legal reasoning by reference to "theory" or "academic moralism." He advocates a pragmatic adju-dication that recognizes the necessity and legitimacy of granting judges some limited decisional freedom to inquire into social consequences of the legal recognition of a particular claim—a judicial role that is itself pragmatically jus-tified by its broader social consequences. Nowlin gives us a number of reasons, however, to question whether Posner can really distinguish his own theorizing from the academic theories he criticizes.

Joseph R. Reisert contributes a chapter on the "new natural law theory" of John Finnis. Although Finnis is critical of liberal/conservative political labels, Reisert argues that there are reasonable grounds for describing his position as a form of liberalism. He gives an account of Finnis's natural law theory of practical reasoning, which provides objectively true normative princi-ples governing ethical and political life. Like Rawls, Finnis believes that some form of public reason is capable of identifying inviolable human rights, but he rejects the contractarian understanding of public reason and the aspiration to dis-cover principles of political right that can be affirmed independently of claims about the good. His own understanding of public reason is that it corresponds to the universally accessible principles of practical reason that constitute the natu-ral law. According to this view, the political community is capable of identifying and facilitating the attainment of basic human goods.

Two features of Finnis's approach, in particular, can be viewed as placing it in the liberal tradition: first, the common good is understood (*contra* clas-sical thinkers such as Aristotle), not as an intrinsic good but as an instrumen-tal good, and second, government must be understood as limited in very im-portant ways by the demands of practical reasonableness, which, for Finnis, includes intentional killing and deliberate deception (such as capital punishment and nuclear deterrence). Like Raz and Galston, Finnis shows that more perfectionist forms of liberalism can provide alternatives to the currently dominant antiperfectionist liberalism.

All of the book's original essays have been revised or extended substantially. The opening chapter on Rawls has been substantially rewritten to account more fully for the reformulation of his theory in *Political Liberalism.* The chapter on Ronald Dworkin briefly describes several recent works, especially *Sovereign Virtue,* which organizes his efforts to formulate an ethical foundation for liberalism. A brief addendum to the chapter on Robert Nozick highlights his participation in the so-called philosophers' brief in the Supreme Court's assisted-suicide case. The discussion of Michael Sandel is expanded substantially to include his elaboration of a public philosophy of civic republicanism in *Democracy's Discontent.* The chapter on Alasdair MacIntyre includes more extended analysis of his earlier works, *Whose Justice? Whose Rationality?* and *Three Rival Versions of Moral Inquiry,* as well as consideration of the more recent *Dependent Rational Animals,* all of which have reflected his deepened commitment to Thomism. The chapter on Richard Rorty adds discussion of his recent *Achieving Our Country,* noting its deeply secular and passionate and more serious humanism. William Galston's recent work is described as emphasizing the need for maximum feasible accommodation of diverse ways of life, limited only by the minimum requirements of civic unity, and defending "value pluralism" against classical or theological ideals of a single, generally valid model of human flourishing on the one hand, and against relativism on the other.

Ten years after the first edition of *Liberalism at the Crossroads,* American public philosophy remains at the same crossroads: whither liberalism? In the footsteps of the antiperfectionist liberalism developed by Rawls and refined and defended by others? In the direction pointed out by other "comprehensive" (rather than "political") liberals? Down paths recommended by more perfectionist strands of liberalism? Making the decision about which direction to take requires that we first understand what the alternative paths are. This second edition of *Liberalism at the Crossroads* hopes to carry on the first edition's contribution to that understanding.

NOTE

1. Other commitments precluded revision of two chapters in the first edition of *Liberalism at the Crossroads:* John Hittinger's essay on David A. J. Richards and Russell Hittinger's essay on Roberto Unger. These essays therefore are not included in this second edition. Readers are encouraged to read these excellent chapters in the first edition.

Introduction to the First Edition

Christopher Wolfe and John Hittinger

The political theory of liberalism has long been dominant in Anglo-American legal and political thought, even during periods, such as the recent past, when conservatism seemed ascendant in American politics. The aim of this book is to provide the general reader with a nontechnical introduction to the ideas of leading participants in the contemporary philosophical debate about liberalism. Each chapter provides an exposition and analysis of the thought of an influential contemporary liberal thinker or leading critic of liberalism. Although the book is primarily expository, many contributors also suggest lines of criticism of the writers whose views are presented.

The key questions that form the context of each chapter are: what is liberalism, what is its current condition, what is the best statement of its theoretical foundations, what are its greatest weaknesses, and how can it best cope with the most important criticisms leveled against it (if it can do so at all)? Of course, not all the essays address themselves to all these questions, but they form the core concerns of the book.

Classical liberalism is usually identified with the thought of John Locke (1632–1704), although some of its most essential features appear in the earlier thought of Thomas Hobbes (1588–1679). In Hobbes and Locke there is a fundamental shift in conceptions about the origin and purposes of political life. Ancient political philosophers such as Plato and Aristotle considered the political community to be a natural development from prepolitical communities—natural not only in the sense that it was "normal," but, more important, in the sense that it was necessary for the complete flourishing of natural human capacities. The ultimate purpose of the political community was to foster a certain way of life, some idea of what it meant to be truly and fully human, some form of human excellence. If political practice did not often live up to these elevated notions, still they provided the ideal in light of which the political life of a community was evaluated.

The coming of Christianity brought with it an inevitable and substantial modification of ancient political thought. Political life was radically "demoted." The highest form of human life—the supernatural life of grace—was, after all, to be attained not through the political community, which reflected the weakness and malice of fallen human nature, but in the transpolitical community of the Church. Political life was, for the most part, confined to more limited, temporal goods. But medieval political thought still saw politics in its highest reaches as oriented toward the ultimate human good, because the political community had the duty of acknowledging and revering the Creator and Redeemer and of being guided by the eternal law and by man's participation in it, the natural law.

Hobbes and Locke broke with ancient and medieval conceptions of the origin and purpose of political life. Their starting point was a state of nature in which the first law was derived from the most fundamental passion, the desire for self-preservation. Various unpleasant aspects of this state of nature induced men to leave it, by establishing civil society. In so doing they gave up their own executive power to enforce their own self-preservation and transferred it to the government. The government's purpose was limited to protecting the fundamental rights that it had been created to protect more effectually: life, liberty, and property. This meant that it would put to the side the various conceptions of human good that had occasioned interminable wrangling among men—most recently, in the form of religious warfare.

Hobbes was convinced that the only kind of authority that could accomplish this purpose was an absolute ruler who could awe men into submission. Locke considered this a fundamental mistake, because an absolute ruler himself would threaten the rights of man. He opted instead for a mixed form of government, in the belief that it would be less likely to endanger the rights it was created to protect—above all, the right to property (which, in a certain sense, included the others). The focus of government had thus shifted from making men good to making them secure.

But the break with ancient and medieval philosophy on this point—the concern of the political community with the moral qualities of its citizens—was not complete, however, because classical liberalism was not completely indifferent to character formation. Classical liberals believed that liberalism required certain kinds of citizens and that government might, out of a concern for its own self-preservation, encourage what was essential for (a minimal form of) civic virtue. For example, Locke could write the *Letter Concerning Toleration,* advocating a strikingly broad toleration of religious views, but still assume that atheism undermined the foundations of government and therefore government could proscribe it. This was, however, a decidedly subordinate theme of liberalism, given its emphasis on the securing of human rights. Classical liberalism was primarily a theory of the state, a limited state, with little attention to the question of what is good for individual human beings, other than the protection of negative rights.

A major nineteenth-century figure who revealed some of the ambiguities of liberalism was John Stuart Mill (1806–1873). Probably his best-known work in America is *On Liberty,* in which he argued for very sharp limits on the power of government to intervene in individual lives, above all, with respect to conduct that does not relatively immediately and tangibly impinge on the lives of others. Each individual is the one most interested in the way of life he lives and should have the power to choose his way of life, unhampered by others, as long as he respects their like rights. This might be called the "antiperfectionist" strain of Mill: government, in particular, has no authority to undertake the perfecting of its citizens by coercion.

Yet there were other strains in Mill, too. First, he assumed that certain conditions had to be met, to enable society to adopt his norms. A country must be a "civilized" one, in which "mankind have become capable of being improved by free and equal discussion" (Hackett edition, p. 10). Second, Mill's argument for liberalism was in great measure based on the fact that it conduces to the better formation of human beings. For example, chapter two of *On Liberty* argues that free speech leads men more effectively to truth, and chapter three argues that freedom to act and the positive fostering of a person's "individuality" are essential for "the highest and most harmonious development of his powers to a complete and consistent whole" (p. 55). Mill would surely have found it very strange had someone called him an "antiperfectionist."

Despite his individualism, Mill's doctrine of liberty rested on explicitly utilitarian moral foundations. In defending his doctrine, Mill claimed to forgo any advantage to his argument to be gained by appeal to "abstract right." Utility, he declared, should be the final arbiter on all matters of moral consequence. This utilitarianism, whether in the blunter form adopted by Mill's father and Jeremy Bentham or in the more refined form adopted by John Stuart Mill, became the standard framework for liberalism.

Post-Millian liberalism understood itself as a reforming public philosophy. Liberals concerned themselves with improving the lot of mankind by placing social institutions on a more "rational" or "scientific" basis. Reform-minded liberals sought to replace the "religious" or "metaphysical" ideas that had informed many social institutions (e.g., the idea of retributive punishment in criminal law) with "enlightened" social goals (e.g., the rehabilitation of offenders and the elimination of the "causes" of crime).

Late-twentieth-century liberals continue to admire Mill's libertarianism. Many, however, have come to question the adequacy of utilitarianism as a foundation for civil rights and liberties. Fearing that the philosophy of "the greatest happiness of the greatest number" will justify the sacrificing of individual interests to the collective welfare, various contemporary liberal thinkers have sought to devise nonutilitarian forms of liberalism. At the same time, most liberals' growing commitment to economic equality, to be achieved through active interventionist government, seems to call for a more explicit and principled defense of egalitarianism.

The appearance of John Rawls's *A Theory of Justice* in 1971 marked a key event in contemporary liberal political theory. Reacting against the dominant utilitarianism in twentieth-century Anglo-American political and legal theory, Rawls aimed to revive social contract theory, firmly rooting it in Kant. He sharply distinguished between "the right" and "the good," identifying justice with the former and demanding "neutrality" of the state on the latter. A central feature of Rawls's project was to bring the egalitarian ambitions of liberalism into harmony with its libertarian commitments. In this respect Rawls's contractarianism diverges from the more classical liberalism of Locke. Most contemporary liberal theorists are either trying to develop and apply the basic approach of *A Theory of Justice* or devote considerable attention to criticizing it as a preliminary to the presentation of alternative views.

This thumbnail sketch of Anglo-American liberalism provides the context for the essays in this book, which begin with an account of Rawls, and of the development and application of his "antiperfectionist" theory in legal philosophy by Ronald Dworkin. Antiperfectionists argue that political communities should, as far as possible, refrain from taking a stand on "the morally good life" as such. They hold that governments may not legitimately attempt to perfect citizens according to some notion of what is the best life for them to lead, but should leave questions of "the good" to individual deliberation and choice. The role of government is primarily to provide a protective framework of rights for these essentially private or personal decisions.

Michael Pakaluk's essay deftly summarizes Rawls's monumental work *A Theory of Justice* and more briefly indicates some later explications and modifications of its major points. Rawls's starting point is the goal of social cooperation among persons who are free and equal. By means of a thought experiment (in which people in the "original position" select principles of justice "behind a veil of ignorance"), Rawls attempts to establish two "lexically ordered" fundamental principles of justice. First, each person has the right to equal basic liberties. Second, social and economic inequalities must satisfy two conditions, that is, they must be open to all under conditions of equality of opportunity, and they must be to the greatest benefit of the least-advantaged members of society.

The next chapter introduces a legal thinker who was significantly influenced by Rawls's antiperfectionism: Ronald Dworkin. Christopher Wolfe's chapter on Dworkin briefly describes Dworkin's early work and then devotes considerable attention to his more recent defenses of the foundations of liberalism. Like Rawls, Dworkin has somewhat modified his claim that liberalism is neutral with respect to various conceptions of the good life. In fact, he has recently argued that the foundations of liberalism lie precisely in central insights about the good life that we (or at least most of us) share. Most important, he maintains that a good life is defined not by its effects or consequences, but by skillful performance in facing the challenge of living. He attempts to show how such an understanding leads to a form of political liberalism that is fundamentally rooted in a certain conception of human equality.

The following essay, by R. George Wright, completes our picture of antiperfectionist liberalism by examining a "right-wing" liberal, Robert Nozick. Nozick's *Anarchy, State, and Utopia* is the leading contemporary theoretical defense of the minimal or the "night-watchman" state. Nozick begins from the premise of a general moral right of individuals to be free of theft, force, fraud, and coercion, in an individualistic, reasonably benign anarchistic society. He then shows how a series of evolutionary steps to deal with violations of these rights can lead to the minimal state. Nozick reminds us that earlier forms of liberalism were not identified with egalitarianism, as today's liberalism is, and that the logic of antiperfectionist premises can be carried out in quite different political directions.

The next section of the book describes the response to antiperfectionist liberalism. Terry Hall provides a chapter on Michael Sandel's trenchant critique of Rawls's liberal individualism, which is representative of a group of loosely related critics typically referred to as "communitarians." Sandel rejects Rawls's postulate of the "original position" as a device for identifying sound principles of justice. According to Sandel, the "unencumbered selves" whom Rawls places in the original position (i.e., persons stripped of the identities that are supplied by prior attachments and commitments made in the relational contexts of the communities to which they belong) are unequipped for the task Rawls sets for them. Sandel rejects Rawls's identification of the self with the *capacity* to make individual "choices" (about, e.g., what kind of life is morally valuable) and argues that the self is in fact *constituted* by the ends it chooses. Ultimately, in Sandel's judgment, Rawls's "deontological" liberalism (in which "the right" has priority over "the good") fails because the "unencumbered selves" in the original position lack the moral ties or commitments needed to conduct moral deliberation. Sandel argues that we must reconceive the self as essentially constituted by its attachments and values and as fulfilling itself in meeting the requirements of the common good. Apparently, Sandel wants to rehabilitate liberalism rather than supersede it. In any event, it is unclear how far he may be willing to go in the direction of more traditional (preliberal) forms of political philosophy.

Alasdair MacIntyre's work represents another influential strand of the communitarian critique of liberalism. One might call it a more "conservative" strand, not so much in the narrowly political sense but in the sense that MacIntyre's thought has gradually evolved in the direction of more traditional philosophical positions such as Thomism. David Wagner presents MacIntyre's description of liberalism as a tradition inaugurated by the Enlightenment, which attempted to construct a tradition-independent form of moral discourse. According to MacIntyre, all liberalism has managed to do, however, is to inaugurate a *new* tradition characterized by a cacophony of moral theories without a rational set of criteria to adjudicate among them (a tradition subjected to powerful criticism by Nietzsche, among others). Current antiperfectionist liberalism is a logical culmination of the Enlightenment's hostility to the idea of tradition-based moral inquiry, but it has its own conception of the human good: preserving the conditions of the tradition-free (and inconclusive) search for the human good. In his later work, MacIntyre expresses sympathy for certain preliberal philosophical positions (especially Augustinianism and Thomism), finding that they meet the best test available for deciding between opposing traditions of moral enquiry. This is a robustness test: Which traditions have historically demonstrated the greatest capacity to overcome "epistemological crises" and carry on, strengthened rather than weakened by the challenges they have faced?

Gerard Bradley describes "pragmatic liberalism," a renewed assertion of antiperfectionism in the face of these criticisms, through an analysis of the social theory of Richard Rorty. Rorty's antirealist epistemology leads to a world of incommensurable vocabularies with no rational criteria for adjudicating among them. Sharing many of Unger's existentialist assumptions, Rorty argues that if there is a basis for human "solidarity," it is our common experience of pain, with the imperative to avoid cruelty. Rorty's ideal society is held together by our conviction that everyone should have a chance at self-creation to the best of his or her abilities. Ultimately, however, Rorty concedes that he and other liberal intellectuals are "ironists" whose beliefs have no greater claim to "truth" than the views of those whom they criticize.

The final two essays take up an entirely different response to the theoretical crisis of contemporary liberalism: the attempt to develop and defend a "perfectionist" liberalism. Robert George describes Joseph Raz's rejection of antiperfectionist "neutrality" (as neither desirable nor even possible) and analyzes Raz's claim that the goal of political action is to encourage pursuit of what is truly good and discourage pursuit of what is morally unworthy. Despite this strong perfectionist claim, Raz's political philosophy gives pride of place to individual liberty, or autonomy, which he considers to be intrinsically valuable. One exercises autonomy in choosing among a plurality of (other) human goods. Nonetheless, Raz forthrightly denies the value of autonomy used to choose what is morally bad and says that society has no reason to protect worthless, much less morally evil, options. Raz is more conventionally liberal, however, in espousing a version of J. S. Mill's "harm principle," arguing that a due regard for autonomy rules out government use of coercive means to discourage "victimless" immoralities. George raises serious questions, however, about whether Raz's strong perfectionism (of which George approves) can support his principled rejection of "morals legislation."

Finally, Brian Benestad's chapter considers the quasi-Aristotelian perfectionist liberalism of William Galston. Like Raz, Galston rejects antiperfectionist neutrality and insists that liberal society must embrace a conception of the human good. Galston observes that if the good is unknowable, we are led not to liberal neutrality but to unconstrained struggle. Moreover, even antiperfectionist liberal theorists assume a substantive view of the good (treating human life and human purposiveness and rationality, for example, as goods). In his most recent work, Galston attempts to spell out and defend more fully his liberal conception of the good. The key factor that preserves Galston's claim to be a liberal is his respect for a pluralism of ends that limits his position to a "minimal perfectionism." Benestad is less optimistic than Galston that the liberal tradition itself (e.g., in its Lockean, Kantian, or Romanticist forms) provides an adequate foundation for virtue.

The emergence of the forms of perfectionist liberalism described in the chapters on Raz and Galston manifests the possibility of, and helps to create the opportunity for, a much more substantial dialogue between proponents of natural law thinking—especially as applied to the pluralistic circumstances of the modern world—and advocates of liberalism. The encouragement of that dialogue is precisely the goal of the American Public Philosophy Institute, under whose auspices the chapters of this book were written. Our primary purpose in writing this book has been to provide an accessible and fair presentation of the thought of major contemporary liberal thinkers and their critics. At the same time, we hope that it will help readers to see the formidable theoretical problems that liberalism faces today, and that they will begin to suspect, as we do, that the future of liberalism lies, not in a working out of the antiperfectionist impulse, but in a dialogue with more traditional and "perfectionist" philosophical positions (such as Aristotelian natural right and Thomistic and contemporary natural law theories).

1

The Liberalism of John Rawls: A Brief Exposition

Michael Pakaluk

John Rawls's career as a political philosopher is defined by two books, his *Theory of Justice,* published in 1971,[1] and his *Political Liberalism,* published in 1993, with an important second edition published in 1996.[2] *Political Liberalism* is in significant respects a repudiation of *A Theory of Justice.* For this reason it is accurate to speak of two periods in Rawls's political thought. Following a common terminological expedient in philosophy, let us refer to these as "early Rawls" and "late Rawls."

EARLY RAWLS

A Theory of Justice is ambitious, grand, and magisterial. It aimed to revive what Quentin Skinner has called "grand theory" in the social and political sciences, and it did.[3] It begins with the high-sounding phrase that "justice is the first virtue of social institutions, as truth is of systems of thought"[4] and ends by claiming that anyone who looks at the world from the standpoint of Rawls's theory is viewing it from almost a God's-eye point of view: "to see our place in society from the perspective of this position is to see it *sub specie aeternitatis:* it is to regard the human situation not only from all social but also from all temporal points of view."[5] The exalted moral tone of the book is truly breathtaking.

A Theory of Justice is a presentation of contract theory in order to justify liberal principles of constitutional government. (By "liberal" understand at this point, roughly the classical liberalism of the American founders, as embodied in the U.S. Constitution and Bill of Rights.) Rawls's philosophical "opponents" in *A Theory of Justice* are utilitarianism (J. S. Mill would be the classical proponent of this) and perfectionism (Plato and Aristotle would be the classical proponents of this). Sometimes it is said that Aristotle, Mill, and Kant exhaust the important range of alternatives for moral theory. The view that Rawls favors in *A Theory of Justice* is broadly Kantian; thus the book may correctly be understood as arguing for a Kantian understanding of political association, over the other alternatives. It is concerned, we might say, with what kind of moral theory might most appropriately be adapted to give the best account of political association.

Let us understand utilitarianism as the theory that states an action is right which maximally contributes to the aggregate general welfare. Utilitarianism was originally developed as a moral theory for individual choice; we might wonder then whether it can be extended and made to justify liberal constitutional arrangements or charters of human rights. It would seem not. A basic problem with utilitarianism, long sensed, is that one may easily conceive of circumstances in which the oppression of some small class of people would contribute maximally to the aggregate general welfare. For instance, it is relatively easy to think of circumstances in which aggregate welfare would be maximized by enslaving or even killing off a few people. We might find utilitarianism obnoxious for that reason, but our feelings of moral repugnance are not yet an argument against it.

Let us understand perfectionism, on the other hand, as any theory which defines first what the highest good for a human being is, and which then holds that laws are just insofar as they promote the citizens' attainment of this good. Plato's *Republic* is a good example of a perfectionist theory: Plato sets down an end, by giving an outline of what an ideally virtuous human being would be, and all the institutions and laws of the society are tailored to the realization of that ideal. One difficulty long felt with perfectionism is that it is not easily reconciled with limited government; a perfectionist regime apparently tends toward totalitarianism. Now this, too, is morally repugnant; but, again, our feelings of repugnance do not yet count as an argument against perfectionism.

The genius of *A Theory of Justice,* and the reason why it was received as a kind of vindication of liberalism, is that it presents a novel and apparently self-contained *argument* for constitutional government. It thereby moved liberalism beyond the realm of hunches and intuitions. Moreover, it did so using ideas and devices taken from economics and the theory of rational choice. This last point is important, since a large reason for the prestige of *A Theory of Justice* was its appearance of having all of the rigor of the more technical social sciences: "The theory of justice," Rawls went so far as to state, "is a part, perhaps the most significant part, of the theory of rational choice."[6] That it have this kind of rigor was necessary for it to provide a true alternative to utilitarianism, which has continued to exercise an appeal to intellectuals, in spite of its counterintuitive structure and results, precisely because it is at least an ethical theory which is clearly stated and which allows for quantification and calculation.[7]

The central intuition of *A Theory of Justice* is contained in Rawls's notion that justice amounts to fairness, hence the tag for his theory, "justice as fairness."[8] Fairness, in turn, amounts to reciprocity and shared consent; it means cooperation based upon complete agreement, not coercion or force. A system of rules that governs coordinated action is just if those rules are acceptable, whatever position you take in the association. For instance, in chess, the rules apply equally to white and black: there is equality in the initial position; reciprocity in moving (white gets to move first, but players alternate playing white or black); and similar powers for their pieces. So the game is fair. In contrast, to the extent that someone in an association is forced to do something against his reasonable objections, to that extent he is being treated unjustly: for instance, white insists that black play without one of his rooks, even though white is the stronger player. Note that we must add this caveat, namely, that fairness means that no one can *reasonably* object to the arrangement. We cannot define fairness simply as what people *do* or *would* accept; for it to be at all plausible, we must define it as what they can reasonably accept. So, then, to give the notion of "justice as fairness" any force, we have to say something more definite about what counts as a reasonable or unreasonable objection to a set of rules or system of laws. As we shall see, this is where the philosophical work needs to be done, which inevitably will be controversial.

What would it be for the rules or laws governing a political association to be just in the sense of being fair? Obviously, that they be agreeable to all; that all citizens would accept them insofar as these citizens were ideally reasonable. Well, how can we determine this? Rawls says: Imagine a group of ideally reasonable people who do not yet belong to any political society but who wish to form a political society together. Imagine their meeting together to propose and agree upon a constitution and the basic laws for their society. What character must those laws have for the laws to be the sort of thing that everyone involved might reasonably accept in advance? If you answer this question, Rawls says, then you answer the question of what laws governing a political association would be fair and therefore just. So we see how Rawls's contractarian approach falls directly out of his identification of justice as involving fairness.

In order to answer the question just stated, Rawls fills out a bit more this thought experiment of a social contract among ideally reasonable people. He calls this thought experiment the "argument from the original position." The original position is simply Rawls's description of the nature of these ideally reasonable people and their circumstances of negotiation. Note that this kind of contractarianism is "constructivist" rather than "historical." Rawls is not making any historical claim about there actually having been any time when people lived outside of political society and contracted into it, leaving their descendants apparently bound by the terms of the contract they had made—a notion that has various problems of its own. Rather, he regards the social contract as something hypothetical and always present to us, precisely as something hypothetical. By adopting the right point of view here and now we can enter in thought into the original position and arrive by ourselves at the basic terms of the social contract.

Rawls makes three controversial points in his argument from the original position. First, he claims that we must imagine the participants as being placed under a "veil of ignorance," as he calls it. This veil blocks them from knowing what position they will occupy in the society that they will enter upon; moreover, it blocks them from knowing what philosophical or religious views they will have. Rawls insists that the veil must extend this far, since otherwise the participants might regard themselves as immune from the bad effects of the laws they are about to agree upon. Second, Rawls claims that the participants will use what economists call the "maximin" principle of selection; that is, they will settle upon those laws that guarantee that the worst position they might have to occupy society is as desirable as possible. (They aim to *maximize* the desirability of the *minimal* positions in society.) Third, Rawls claims that the participants in the original position will not be altruistic—they will be primarily and minimally self-interested—yet neither will they be influenced by envy.

Each of these assumptions has been the subject of controversy, and it is important to be clear on the nature of the controversy. We need to ask: What is it that should determine for us how the original position is to be filled out? It would seem at first that there are only two possible approaches, which we may identify as "objective" as opposed to "pragmatic."[9] The objective approach presumes that there really is such a thing as ideal human nature: we then fill out the original position by including in it features that we believe express what is essential in human nature. Thus, if we think that ideal human nature is not envious, then we exclude envy from the makeup of the participants in the original position. If we think that human personhood or personality is something independent of a person's identification with a particular religious group, then we exclude knowledge of one's own religious beliefs from the original position. The pragmatic approach, on the other hand, holds that we should fill out the original position with simply those elements that are needed in order to get the desired result. That is, we look first to the kind of contract that strikes us antecedently as fair, and we then construct the original position in such a way that it ensures that the participants decide upon a contract having that form. In the objective approach, the notion of human nature seems most basic, whereas the terms of the contract are derived; in the pragmatic approach, the terms of the contract seem most basic, since they are antecedently identified, and the original position therefore appears to be something derived.

It is common to reason that Rawls could not, of course, be taking the pragmatic approach, because, after all, he intends to *argue* for liberal principles of government, and you cannot assume what you wish to argue for. Yet, on the other hand, his depiction of the original position is unattractive and seems faulty if it is taken as an idealization of human nature: we are not self-interested; we are envious; and we are not so risk averse as to be guided fundamentally by the maximin principle of choice. However, such criticisms are off the mark. Rawls wishes to take neither the objective nor the subjective approach. He intends, rather, that both the specification of the original position, and the terms of the social contract that are settled upon, constitute a single whole, which captures our best intuitions about what justice is. His theory is meant to be a single, coherent whole, which we accept or reject all at once.[10]

With the "original position" specified as mentioned, Rawls now imagines that its participants are presented with a kind of menu of forms of political association. We ask the participants: which of the following would you prefer? Would you prefer to enter a society in which the laws are determined by the utilitarian principle? Or a society in which the laws are fixed by some perfectionist account of the human good? Or a society in which the laws are determined by what Rawls calls the two "principles of justice"?

We should pause a moment and look more carefully at the "principles of justice," since these are Rawls's important encapsulation of what he regards as the basic themes of a liberal democracy. Although in the course of his career Rawls adjusts slightly their exact form, we may well enough quote here the form in which he states them in his later work:

a. Each person has an equal claim to a fully adequate scheme of equal basic rights and liberties, which scheme is compatible with the same scheme for all. . . .

b. Social and economic inequalities are to satisfy two conditions: first, they are to be attached to positions and offices open to all under conditions of fair equality of opportunity; and second, they are to be to the greatest benefit of the least advantaged members of society.[11]

Rawls intends these principles to apply in the first instance merely to what he calls the "basic structure" of society, which is something like the broadest social framework of a nation, within which various voluntary associations operate. According to Rawls, the basic structure consists of the political constitution, the

Michael Pakaluk

judiciary, forms of property, and the general structure of the economy. It apparently does not include business enterprises, households, churches, universities, and the family.[12]

The principles, furthermore, are rank-ordered: the first principle has priority over the second, in the sense that it needs to be satisfied first, and this then places constraints upon the satisfaction of the second principle. Rawls explains this concretely by relating each principle to a different part of the basic structure: the first principle is intended to govern the drawing up of the constitution of a society; the second principle is intended to govern the legislative activity of a society conforming to such a constitution.[13]

The first principle is sometimes called that of "Equal Basic Liberties"; the first clause of the second principle is known as "Fair Equality of Opportunity," and the second clause of the second is referred to as the "Difference Principle." The Difference Principle holds that any deviations from strict equality in the status and advantages of citizens is just only if the condition of the least advantaged persons, given this deviation, is better than it would have been, had strict equality been maintained. It is supposed to be a principle of solidarity, in the sense that, if it is observed, then it is possible for all citizens to view themselves as beneficiaries of a system of joint cooperation. Note that the Difference Principle presupposes that there is some standard of what counts as "advantage" in a society. Rawls therefore has to develop a theory of what he calls "primary goods" which he thinks provides a rough but serviceable index of relative advantage.[14]

Let us return, then, to the argument from the original position. Rawls argues that the deliberators in the original position will reject utilitarianism, if there is some better alternative. Why? Because, as we saw, utilitarianism leaves it open that it might work out best for society as a whole if some small group of persons is oppressed. Since you cannot rule out, in the original position (because of the veil of ignorance) that you will end up in this class, and since you are using the maximin rule of choice, you cannot accept utilitarianism, if there is some better alternative open to you. The best worst condition will be very bad, if there is a slave class or oppressed group in society.

Similarly, the deliberators in the original position will reject perfectionism. Why? Since they do not know what religious or philosophical views they will hold in society (again, on account of the veil of ignorance), they will not freely consent to living in a society the laws of which are fixed by some particular religious or philosophical view, with which they will perhaps deeply disagree. The constant offense to their conscience will be too onerous. The best worst condition will be very bad, in a state governed in some totalitarian way by a uniform ideal of human perfection. Thus, they cannot accept perfectionism, if there is some better alternative.

But there is a better alternative forthcoming, Rawls says, namely, a society shaped by the two "principles of justice." That everyone have as much liberty as is compatible with a like liberty enjoyed by others is obviously something that anyone can accept. The idea seems eminently consistent with the core intuitions of reciprocity and fairness. Furthermore, that everyone be equal unless inequalities work out for the good of the least fortunate seems similarly acceptable to all, since only someone who was envious would resent another person's greater prosperity, when this is linked directly to being better off oneself—and envy has been excluded from the original position. Thus, the principles of justice are acceptable to deliberators in the original position, in the way that utilitarianism and perfectionism are not. Therefore, only a society whose constitution and basic laws are dictated by the principles of justice will be a fair and therefore a just society. It would be a society, Rawls maintains, the laws of which no person could reasonably reject.

This is the basic argument of *A Theory of Justice*. It can be stated in a few pages. The book is as long and intricate as it is because Rawls aims to make the argument as rigorous as possible; he also attends at some length to some minor technical problems (like his account of "primary goods"); and he aims to anticipate and respond to objections.[15]

It should be noted that *A Theory of Justice* contains a distinctive understanding of what justification amounts to in moral and political theory. We might think at first that to justify a political theory, one needs to begin from intuitive or self-evident, true premises and argue deductively from there. Rawls rejects this notion of justification. Rather, he regards a political theory as justified if it can sustain what he calls "reflective equilibrium." Rawls describes reflective equilibrium in a manner that seems appealing at first.[16] He says that, in ethics and political philosophy, the only decisive evidence we can rely upon is our "considered judgements" as to what is right and wrong. These play a role similar to observations in science. Just as a good scientific theory is one that best matches and accounts for observations, so a good theory of justice is one that best matches and accounts for our considered judgments as to right and wrong. It might seem to us that Rawls's story of the original position and a hypothetical contract under the veil of ignorance is a fantastic story that simply builds in from the start what one wishes to prove. Rawls replies, in effect, that we can do more than this. The story that he tells matches our considered judgments; we can ask no more than this in moral and political philosophy; thus, it is the correct theory.

For the purposes of better understanding the later development of Rawls theory, it is important to pay attention to the emphasis in *A Theory of Justice* that Rawls places on the idea of what he calls "publicity," which resembles the notion of "Nash equilibrium" used by economists. A law or principle of government satisfies the condition of publicity, Rawls says, if it determines the constitution and laws of a society, and people generally know that it determines things thus, and, furthermore, people generally know that others know that this is so.[17] We may understand the publicity condition as a kind of analogue, on the political scale, of friendship: in fact, it is a kind of condition of civic friendship. Just as, in a friendship where we have some agreement about how we are to act reciprocally, you and I both know that this is so, and we know that each of us knows it, so, in a political society in which everyone may truly be said to be acting together cooperatively, the publicity condition is met. Rawls considers it essential to his principles of justice that their acceptance involve publicity. But he regards it as not essential to utilitarian or perfectionist principles that they satisfy publicity, and he takes this to be an additional mark in favor of his principles, since the publicity of the principles governing the basic structure makes that system of cooperation more stable.[18] The reason why publicity need not be satisfied in the other cases, Rawls argues, is that utilitarianism and perfectionism are concerned principally with outcomes (that the general welfare be maximized, that the true human good be reached), rather than with the processes for getting there.

LATE RAWLS

Political Liberalism, Rawls's second magnum opus, published in 1993, marks a radical break with *A Theory of Justice*. In fact, it repudiates *A Theory of Justice*. Here is why such a repudiation becomes necessary.

Although the basic argument and intuitions of *A Theory of Justice* are simple, nonetheless, the full defense of the theory, against eager supporters of alternative views, involves many controversial, subtle, and difficult moves. In fact, as we have seen, even the basic argument of *A Theory of Justice* incorporates controversial assumptions, for example, the extent of the veil of ignorance; the motivations of the participants in the original position; the appropriateness of the maximin principle. Now, in *A Theory of Justice,* because of the requirement of publicity, Rawls imagines that a just society will be one in which there is consensus, not only about the principles of justice but also about the justification of those principles.[19] That is, there has to be consensus that the principles are justified by the argument from the original position, and that the argument should and does proceed in a particular way.

However, the wrangling among scholars over *A Theory of Justice* in the years following its publication was itself sufficient proof that the argument was not so cogent as immediately or inevitably to gain even widespread assent. Furthermore, that it should be generally accepted in a just society was a view in contradiction with the argument of *A Theory of Justice* itself. For the participants of the original position under a veil of ignorance would not know whether, in the society in which they were about to enter, they would be Rawlsians, or utilitarians, or Aristotelians, or Islamic fundamentalists. They would not therefore consent to principles which carried along with them a certain mode of justification that they could not accept.[20]

We might put the crucial point in this way. In *A Theory of Justice,* Rawls assumes that, in a just society, everyone will accept liberal principles of justice, and on Rawlsian grounds. But by the time he writes *Political Liberalism,* Rawls comes to see that this second requirement is too restrictive. He thinks there is no reason why allegiance to the principles of justice might not be secured on a variety of different grounds. So Rawls sees that he now must "justify" his principles of justice in a way that prescinds from the controversial social contract argument of *A Theory of Justice.* Rawls in the period between *A Theory of Justice* and *Political Liberalism* is a principled liberal in search of a politically serviceable justification for his principles; in *Political Liberalism* he thinks he has found the (minimal) justification that his principles need.

In a sense—and to anticipate—the justification that Rawls now advances is no justification at all. Rawls presumes that his theory is addressed to persons who are already successfully participating in a form of association which might be identified as "political liberalism." They have a sense of fairness, and they have at least an untutored sense of what it would be for the "basic structure" of society to be fair. That is, they already have a grasp of what Rawls comes to call the "fundamental intuitive idea" of political liberalism, namely, "political society as a system of fair terms of cooperation among free and equal persons."[21] What such persons need is not justification so much as clarification. The aim of the later philosophy of Rawls is simply to get clearer about what form of association is implied by this fundamental intuitive idea. Rawls does not try to convince others to accept it, since he thinks that most of us accept it already. As for those who do not accept it, even after all the relevant distinctions are made clear to them: well, they are being unreasonable, illiberal, undemocratic. Therefore, one can't reason with them; one can only constrain them by law as necessary and hope that liberalism is found appealing enough generally to win the day.[22] It has never been part of Rawls's project to devise arguments capable of convincing or converting fanatics.

The first step of clarification that Rawls attempts is to draw a distinction between what he calls a "political conception" and a "comprehensive doctrine."[23] Yet it must be said that this distinction is not particularly clear. Rawls says that a comprehensive doctrine is a view of "everything": a grand philosophical system or a religious viewpoint. A political conception, in contrast, is a view of how large-scale political society should be organized. Once he has made this distinction, Rawls thinks he can separate out from *A Theory of Justice* a political conception of liberalism that is independent of the comprehensive conception that is developed in the book, expressed in the social contract argument. Rawls takes the political conception to be captured in the fundamental intuitive idea of "political society as a system of fair terms of cooperation among free and equal persons."

It is fair to say that what Rawls is constrained to do is to find analogues for the elements of the argument of *A Theory of Justice,* where these analogues are commonsensical and acceptable to all. So, for instance, whereas in the argument from *A Theory of Justice,* the veil of ignorance keeps people from knowing what political or religious views they actually hold in society, in *Political Liberalism* Rawls introduces instead what he calls "the fact of reasonable pluralism." This is the claim that, in a society that has sufficient freedom to be livable, people will inevitably arrive at widely differing philosophical views. That they will do so inevitably Rawls explains by the notion of "the burdens of judgment." He means by this that these matters are difficult and involve close calls, so that different judges will adopt different views, in the same way that we might expect even skilled critics in music or art to form differing judgments about the merits of a performance or work.[24] We then have an argument of sorts based on "the fact of reasonable pluralism," which is an analogue of the argument from the original position: if you wish to associate with others fairly, you have to have their consent, but you cannot reasonably expect them to consent to matters at odds with, or that go beyond, the "comprehensive doctrines" they hold—and you should not coerce them to accord with your comprehensive doctrine in these matters, just as you would not wish for them to coerce you to accord with theirs.[25]

Once those matters on which people might be expected reasonably to disagree have been set aside, we might wonder what are the guarantees that there will be any basis for association at all. Nothing guarantees it, but, as was said, Rawls is convinced that it exists all the same. He would say that it is simply a fact, observable in the liberal political tradition, that people of various religious and philosophical persuasions are all capable of affirming the two principles of justice. It is this fact that they can do so which Rawls refers to as the "overlapping consensus": the same principles of association are justified in different ways from within different philosophical and religious grounds. For example, a Catholic might affirm the principles of justice as something deducible from natural law; an Aristotelian scholar, as implied by Aristotle's discussion of the best form of government practically attainable; an Evangelical Protestant, as required by our all being created in the image of God; a Muslim, as dictated by divine law, the Shari'a.[26]

Rawls thinks that political liberalism is a distinct and recognizable form of association, which has an inherent stability, and which is capable of being appreciated for its own sake. It has a stability because it tends to alter and curb the character of the allegiance that people have to the comprehensive doctrines they hold. Political liberalism has a liberalizing effect: those who perhaps initially profess a lack of regard for liberalism, if they live over time in liberal political society, will come to alter their views, to make them coincident with political liberalism. In doing so, as Rawls understands it, they are becoming "reasonable," able to cooperate fairly with others.[27]

Rawls believes that, historically, this transformation in religious communities has taken place in two stages. First, religious zealots were moved to separate church and state on essential pragmatic grounds, rather than on principled grounds. Rawls says that this state of affairs is one in which the various component groups of a society ostensibly organized on liberal principles accepts those principles only as a modus vivendi. To say this is to say that each holds that, if it could get the upper hand in power, then it would revoke liberal principles of association. In that case, liberal government amounts to no more than a truce, arrived at by groups of roughly equal power, weary of strife. However, once the truce is adopted, the originally contending groups come to recognize that they have, as if by accident, stumbled upon a form of association that is desirable in its own right. They see the appeal and attractiveness of respecting one another's equality and freedom through fair terms of association. Consequently, since their comprehensive doctrines are ones that lead them to affirm and endorse things that they regard independently as good, those doctrines themselves get transformed. The result is that the various religious groups now accept political liberalism as the inherently right basis for their joint association.[28]

So far we have been discussing the grounds of acceptance of the two principles of justice in a pluralistic society, as Rawls conceives it. But principles need to be applied once they are accepted. The two principles of justice are given rather abstractly. How exactly are they to be interpreted and applied, especially in difficult or controversial cases? It should be noted that in general Rawls has avoided discussion of applications of his principles. [29] In *A Theory of Justice* he describes the stages in which they should be deployed, arguing that they imply a constitution similar to that of the United States, and a bill or charter of rights.[30] Yet this takes us, as it were, only to where the United States was at its founding, which is not of very great help. We might think that the application of the principles of justice is not so great a problem within the context of *A Theory of Justice,* since there we have available a "comprehensive doctrine," which presumably could give guidance as to application. But when the principles are separated out of *A Theory of Justice* and considered only within a narrow "political conception," what then can guide their application?

This explains the importance of Rawls controversial notion of "public reason,"[31] which is the requirement that any development or application of the principles of justice (e.g., the balance or adjudication of claims of right; extensions or limitations of rights) be justified only on the basis of reasons that, like the political conception of society in the first place, are independent of the comprehensive doctrines held by the various constituent groups in political society.[32] It would appear that the only available reasons of this sort are ones that are implicit within, or consistent with any reasonable interpretation of the conception of society as involving "fair terms of association among free and equal persons."

We might put the need for some notion such as public reason in this way: just as there would be a contradiction in society's *adopting* the principles of justice on, so to speak, sectarian grounds, so there would be a contradiction in society's *applying* those principles on "sectarian" grounds.

It is understandable, then, why "public reason" has been the subject of controversy. It is where Rawls's theory comes into contact with political practice. Its difficulties seem to encapsulate felt difficulties in Rawls's political philosophy generally. We should do well, then, to get clear about it.

Rawls rather carefully qualifies and circumscribes his claims about public reason, and indeed some common objections to public reason carry weight only if these restrictions are ignored. The restrictions are as follows:

1. public reason applies only to the issues arising as regards the "basic structure" of political society, not those involving the internal affairs of voluntary associations within political society;
2. it applies, furthermore, only to constitutional matters as regards this basic structure;
3. it applies only to deliberations conducted by citizens acting as citizens, not to discussions in popular culture generally (it is not intended as a restriction on freedom of speech); and
4. even as regards such deliberations, it requires only that the essential core of such deliberations consist of "public reasoning."[33]

This last point Rawls refers to as "the proviso." He is concerned not to articulate a notion of public reason that would have kept, say, Martin Luther King, Jr., from referring to New Testament scripture when leading crusades against segregation. The proviso is that people are free, even when addressing one another as citizens speaking to citizens, to make use of ideas peculiar to their own "comprehensive doctrines," so long as at some point they translate the essentials of what they wish to say into ideas that they take to be capable of persuading any "reasonable" person whatsoever.

It is difficult to see, however, how public reason, thus delineated, has sufficient content to serve as the sole means by which serious disagreement in society is resolved. Public reason seems to be essentially a political version of the Golden Rule in its negative formulation, namely, do *not* do unto others, as you would *not* have them do unto you. But then it will have all of the infirmities usually, and correctly, attributable to the view that the Golden Rule, understood as a merely formal rule for ethical decision, is sufficient all by itself. Notoriously, the Golden Rule yields no determinate results without substantive assumptions about the human good.[34]

Furthermore, public reason, like any attempt at a purely formal or procedural rule of conduct, is incapable in itself of settling questions concerning those to whom, properly, the rule is to apply: the notorious difficulty of the "subjects of justice." Yet disputes of this sort have historically been among the most contentious and divisive. Are Jews, or black Africans, or South American Indians, or unborn children, or the comatose elderly, among those to whom public reason should be understood as applying? Must they be regarded as "free and equal persons"? Public reason itself cannot say: this requires, rather, a substantive view about what confers dignity on a being, that is, it requires a "comprehensive doctrine," in Rawls's sense.

The absence of content in the notion of public reason is manifest, also, in how Rawls handles the topic of human rights. In *A Theory of Justice,* human rights were regarded as secondary constructs. The primary notion at work was that of "the most extensive basic liberty compatible with a similar liberty for others"—as the first principle of justice is stated in *A Theory of Justice*[35]—as though liberty were some kind of uniform "stuff" to be maximized, and charters of rights were merely ad hoc ways of describing a sufficient maximization of this stuff. Rawls was forced to abandon this view, as a result of some searching criticisms brought against *A Theory of Justice* by the Oxford legal philosopher, H. L. A. Hart.[36] In *Political Liberalism,* Rawls rather conceives of human rights as given or arrived at simply through a list—like that in the U.S. Declaration of Independence and Bill of Rights, or in international declarations of rights. He even reconceives the argument from the original position so that the deliberators now are asked to consider the two principles of justice, where the first principle simply incorporates some received statements of rights. The problem here, of course, is that declarations of rights historically have been motivated by and developed within "comprehensive doctrines," and certainly attempts to balance claims of rights have historically involved comprehensive doctrines. So what content there *is* in the notion of public reason is not obviously something that could survive a thorough disentanglement of public reason from comprehensive doctrines.[37]

Furthermore, the setting of boundaries to public reason, as is necessary, will inevitably require violations of the strictures set by public reason. The delineation of public reason requires something more than public reason, since a comprehensive doctrine is needed to decide whether a viewpoint is a comprehensive doctrine or not.[38] Likewise, what counts as the basic structure cannot be settled by public reason alone. For example, does the family count as part of the basic structure of political society? (If it does, then the liberal political principles of "freedom and equality" may be enforced within the family.) This question cannot be decided without a comprehensive doctrine about the character of the family. If, say, the family is by nature prior to political society, then it is not straightforwardly part of the basic structure, in which case it cannot consistently in law be handled as though it is, without reliance on some comprehensive doctrine that rules out its being prior by nature.[39]

We might say that the doctrine of public reason raises afresh all of the worries about "reasonability" which, as we saw, led to Rawls's argument from the original position. If we grant that justice involves fairness, and we accept that fairness means cooperation on principles to which none of those concerned could reasonably object, we have achieved nothing unless we can give some account of what reasonability amounts to. The argument from the original position attempted to do this, with some success. But when that argument is jettisoned in Rawls's later adoption of "political liberalism," the problem breaks out all over again.

Public reason in some respects resembles the idea, from economics, of market equilibrium: prices for goods become settled and agreed upon across the market by the negotiation of competing demands. However, claims of right are typically not negotiable, as are marketplace demands. It is natural to conceive of public reason as the seeking of common ground by mutual compromise, since it seems to involve civility and a willingness to accept only a view that the other person can accept as well. But of course many disputes involving rights ought not be resolved through compromise: rather, they should be resolved by the finding that one of the rights supposedly in conflict is spurious or misconceived. When, then, is a refusal to compromise uncivil, and when is it principled? The Northern abolitionists were regarded as unyielding and antidemocratic by the South, and yet we can see now, as the abolitionists in their time could presumably see as well, that they were principled, and that it was the South that ought to have yielded in its claim of a right to "self-government" as comprising a right to own slaves. Public reason, and Rawlsian political philosophy generally, seems incapable of giving reliable guidance in such matters.[40]

FULFILLMENT OF PROMISE OR DISAPPOINTMENT?

Rawls's early papers in the 1950s were written in the style of conceptual analysis, then the dominant manner of practicing analytic philosophy: Rawls seemed to be proposing an analysis of the concept of justice, just as others had given analyses of the concept of number (Frege and Russell), the concept of mind (Ryle), and so on. Rawls began his 1958 paper, "Justice as Fairness," as follows: "It might seem at first sight that the concepts of justice and fairness are the same. . . . In this paper I wish to show that the fundamental idea in the concept of justice is fairness; and I wish to offer an analysis of the concept of justice from this point of view."[41] However, in the preface to *A Theory of Justice,* Rawls says that he has been persuaded, by reflecting on the views of W. V. Quine, that "the notions of meaning and analyticity play no essential role in moral theory as I conceive it."[42] This signals a turn to outright pragmatism, in the path of Quine. This pragmatism was hidden by certain features of *A Theory of Justice* which we have already seen: its ideal of rigor; its attempt to imitate the best characteristics of formal social science; its talk of deductive arguments; and its high moral rhetoric, which made it appear to resemble the deeply metaphysical views of an Aristotle or a Kant. It is in his 1980 Dewey lectures, "Kantian Constructivism in Moral Theory,"[43] that Rawls's pragmatism is first unambiguously articulated. By the time of *Political Liberalism,* this pragmatism is given an explicitly political rather than a philosophical motivation: the point of Rawls's political philosophy is not to report on the truth about justice, prior to convention; or to give an analysis of some independent concept of justice; but, rather, simply to hold up for us an available manner of association which, Rawls thinks, is the best hope for the peaceable coexistence of people who will inevitably hold widely disparate views about the human good, morality, and religion.[44]

What counts for pragmatism is the result. Once Rawls explicitly adopts pragmatism, he becomes free to jettison his preferred means to the end, so to speak, if that will make the end easier of attainment. He becomes free to reject the argumentative structure of *A Theory of Justice,* if that will secure better the result aimed at therein, and, on his own terms, that rejection becomes necessary in the political forum, since his view is simply one among others. Robert Frost once quipped that a liberal is someone who won't take his own side in an argument. Rawls's philosophical career is that of a philosopher who progressively works himself free from taking his own side. In a sense, the chief task of later Rawls becomes that of explaining how Rawls's principles of justice may be accepted without accepting Rawls.

But this freedom from metaphysics has its risks. *Political Liberalism* is discursive and intuitive. It draws distinctions, gives descriptions, and clarifies misconceptions, but it contains few deductive arguments, and it certainly does not aspire to the ideal of "moral geometry." Its power and prestige seem derivative upon that of *A Theory of Justice,* which, however, it repudiates. Disengaged entirely from *A Theory of Justice,* the view it proposes appears to be little more than counsel, in need of further elaboration, simply to get along with others. The path of Rawls's political philosophy, then, traces out a dilemma: it presents us with a choice between a rich philosophical view, which must, however, remain controversial and incapable of winning widespread assent, and a narrowly drawn political view, on which indeed we can all agree, but simply because to agree to it is to agree, so far, to nothing.

NOTES

1. John Rawls, *A Theory of Justice* (Cambridge, Mass.: Harvard University Press, 1971).
2. John Rawls, *Political Liberalism* (Cambridge, Mass.: Harvard University Press, 1993, 2nd ed., 1996).
3. Quentin Skinner, ed., *The Return of Grand Theory in the Human Sciences* (Cambridge: Cambridge University Press, 1990).
4. Rawls, *Theory of Justice,* 3.
5. Rawls, *Theory of Justice,* 587.
6. Rawls, *Theory of Justice,* 16.
7. Rawls is explicit about the ideal of rigor he sets for himself: "The argument aims eventually to be strictly deductive. To be sure, the persons in the original position have a certain psychology, since various assumptions are made about their beliefs and interests. These assumptions appear along with other premises in the description of this initial situation. But clearly arguments from such premises can be fully deductive, as theories in politics and economics attest. We should strive for a kind of moral geometry with all the rigor which this name connotes." On the drive for rigor in moral theory, see Charles Taylor, "The Diversity of Goods," in *Utilitarianism and Beyond,* ed. Amartya Sen and Bernard Williams (Cambridge: Cambridge University Press, 1982), 129–44.
8. See John Rawls, "Justice as Fairness," *Philosophical Review* 67 (April 1958): 164–94.
9. These terms, "objective" and "pragmatic," are my own and are not used by him in his exposition of his theory.
10. Rawls, *Theory of Justice,* 121–22.
11 John Rawls, *Political Liberalism,* 2nd ed. (New York: Columbia University Press, 1996), 5–6.
12. Rawls, *Theory of Justice,* 83–90, 274–84.
13. Rawls, *Theory of Justice,* chap. 4.
14. Rawls, *Theory of Justice,* 90–95.

15. Hence some observers prefer Rawls's early article, "Justice as Fairness," over *Theory of Justice,* on the grounds that it contains the same basic argument, but in a more perspicacious form.

16. Rawls, *Theory of Justice,* 46–53.

17. Rawls, *Theory of Justice,* 133.

18. Rawls, *Theory of Justice,* 15, 177–82.

19. As we have seen, if we reject the distinction between "objective" and "pragmatic" approaches to the argument from the original position, then that argument and the principles of justice together constitute a single, unified whole. The two must apparently be taken together or rejected together.

20. In a late essay Rawls describes the change in his thought as follows: "I end by pointing out the fundamental difference between *A Theory of Justice* and *Political Liberalism.* The first explicitly attempts to develop from the idea of the social contract, represented by Locke, Rousseau, and Kant, a theory of justice that is no longer open to objections often thought fatal to it, and that proves superior to the long dominant tradition of utilitarianism. a theory of justice hopes to present the structural features of such a theory so as to make it the best approximation to our considered judgements of justice and hence to give the most appropriate moral basis for democratic society. Furthermore, justice as fairness is presented there as a comprehensive liberal doctrine (although the term 'comprehensive doctrine' is not used in the book) in which all the members of its well-ordered society affirm that same doctrine. This kind of well-ordered society contradicts the fact of reasonable pluralism and hence *Political Liberalism* regards that society as impossible." See "The Idea of Public Reason Revisited," in John Rawls, *Collected Papers* (Cambridge, Mass.: Harvard University Press, 1999), 614.

21. Rawls, *Political Liberalism,* 16ff.

22. The element of "faith" and "hope" is important in Rawls's philosophy. One might say that it replaces what, in more classical political theory, is accomplished by the notion of "nature." Since political liberalism is not based upon or grounded in human nature, or the nature of things, nothing guarantees its continued existence, except our aspiring that it continue, which is this "faith." Thus, it is common in Rawls and his disciples to speak in phrases such as the following from Sam Freeman's introduction to his *Collected Papers:* "It is a career guided by a reasonable faith that a just society is realistically possible"(xii). Note also that, in spite of the rhetoric, political liberalism is not infinitely tolerant and plastic to alternative points of view. It is prepared, sooner or later, to find a view at odds with itself to be "unreasonable" and therefore undeserving of consideration.

23. See, e.g., John Rawls, "Justice as Fairness: Political not Metaphysical," *Philosophy and Public Affairs* 14 (1985): 223–52; *Collected Papers,* 388–414.

24. Rawls, *Political Liberalism,* 35–57. Rawls's need to find this sort of analogue of the veil of ignorance explains his preoccupation with the sixteenth-century wars of religion. He evidently believes that the threat of religious conflict is the greatest danger facing liberal democracy, and not, say, the threat of apathy, general scepticism, or a lack of conviction in moral truth. See *Political Liberalism,* xiv–xvii.

25. Note how reasoning that roughly takes the shape of the Golden Rule becomes decisive for Rawls, once the hypothesis of the original position is put to the side.

26. But only when the Shari'a is understood, Rawls says, in the manner of a supposed earlier and more authoritative Mecca period of Muhammed. See note 46 in "The Idea of Public Reason Revisited," *Collected Papers,* 590, where Rawls favorably cites the revisionist interpretation of Shari'a proposed by Abdullahi Ahmed An-Na'im.

27. Rawls sees the decree on Religious Liberty (Dignitatis humanae) from Vatican II as an example of this. He quotes approvingly from David Hollenbach, S.J., who writes: "And though the Church resisted the liberal discovery of modern freedoms through much of the modern period, liberalism has been transforming Catholicism once again through the last half of our own century." See "The Idea of Public Reason Revisited," note 52, CP 592–93. The "reasonable faith that a just society is realistically possible" is therefore also a faith that religious communities will transform themselves in the appropriate ways.

28. Rawls, *Political Liberalism,* xxxixf., xlii, lviii.

29. The ostensible reason for this is methodological, and a matter of philosophical temperament. Rawls is a peaceable philosopher who likes to avoid controversy and to gain agreement where he can; he also thinks that it is proper in philosophy to discuss central and more easily resolvable cases first, and only after agreement has been reached there, to move on to less central or more controversial matters.

30. See, again, Rawls, *Theory of Justice,* chap. 4.

31. Rawls, *Political Liberalism,* 212–54.

32. It is because public reason involves the application of principles of justice that Rawls points to the collective body of U.S. Supreme Court decisions since the Founding as exhibiting a kind of supreme exercise of public reason: *Political Liberalism,* 231–40.

33. See John Rawls, "The Idea of Public Reason Revisited," in *Collected Papers,* 573–615.

34. For example, a thief might reason that robbery should not be prosecuted, as he should not like to be prosecuted; a pedophile can reason that child molestation should be legal, just as he would not like to be regarded as a second-class citizen. In each case, the Golden Rule is used inappropriately because it is used to generalize desires and dispositions that need to be judged, on other grounds, to be against the human good.

35. Rawls, *Theory of Justice,* 60.

36. See John Rawls, "The Basic Liberties and Their Priority." Originally in *The Tanner Lectures on Human Values,* III, ed. Sterling M. McMurrin (Cambridge: Cambridge University Press, 1982), 1–87; also in *Collected Papers.*

37. That Rawls cites U.S. Supreme Court jurisprudence as an eminent example of public reason would seem to show that there is no notion of public reason sufficiently rich to resolve important disputes, but which does not rely on "comprehensive doctrines," since "comprehensive doctrines" are everywhere presupposed by U.S. Supreme Court decisions. See, for instance, Michael J. Sandel, *Democracy's Discontent* (Cambridge, Mass.: Harvard University Press, 1996). Rawls evidently believes

that Supreme Court jurisprudence since, say, 1970, is similarly a supreme example of public reason; this in itself casts serious doubt on coherence of the notion of public reason.

38. Rawls gives an inadequate response to similar criticism at *Political Liberalism,* 29n.

39. Rawls's changing views on the family are worth a chapter themselves. Early Rawls in *A Theory of Justice* looks upon the family suspiciously, as upon an inherently unequal institution (see 511ff.), and thus it must be, since if, in political society, we act as free and equal persons, then it must be the case that, to the extent that we associate differently from political association, to that extent we are not free and unequal. Late Rawls is much more explicit on the matter: he contemplates apparently a radical overhaul of the family, since the family is now a part of the basic structure of society: "The Idea of Public Reason Revisited," in *Collected Papers,* 597–600.

40. See the exchange between Christopher Wolfe and Stephen Macedo in *Natural Law and Public Reason,* ed. Robert George and Christopher Wolfe (Washington, D.C.: Georgetown University Press, 2000).

41. Rawls, "Justice as Fairness" (1958), 164; *Collected Papers,* 47.

42. Rawls, *A Theory of Justice,* xi.

43. "Kantian Constructivism in Moral Theory," *Journal of Philosophy* 77 (1980): 515–72. *Collected Papers,* 303–58.

44. See, again, Rawls, "Justice as Fairness: Political Not Metaphysical."

2

The Egalitarian Liberalism of Ronald Dworkin

Christopher Wolfe

Ronald Dworkin, it is safe to say, is one of the leading figures today in Anglo-American jurisprudence. He is the successor to H. L. A. Hart as Professor of Jurisprudence at Oxford University and is also Professor of Law at New York University, having taught previously at Yale Law School. He has degrees from Harvard College, Oxford, and Harvard Law School, and served as clerk to Judge Learned Hand.

A CHRONOLOGY/INTELLECTUAL TOPOGRAPHY OF DWORKIN'S WORK

Dworkin's first major book, based on articles published in law reviews (Chicago, Yale, Harvard) and in the *New York Review of Books* between 1966 and 1976, was *Taking Rights Seriously*.[1] In it, Dworkin proposed to define and defend a new liberal general theory of law, one sharply critical of the ruling theory, which has its roots in Jeremy Bentham. Bentham's analysis has been developed, in its conceptual part (i.e., the part that says what law is), by H. L. A. Hart's version of positivism, and, in its normative part, by utilitarian economic analysis. The most important ground for Dworkin's critique of the ruling theory and its major critics on the right and the left is that they reject the idea that individuals can have rights against the state that are prior to the rights created by explicit legislation. Dworkin's theory places a concern for individual rights at the center of legal philosophy, although it shares with the ruling theory a rejection of earlier, metaphysically based conceptions of natural rights. Dworkin develops a theory of adjudication that is both conceptual

and normative in his chapter on "Hard Cases." Through an analysis of John
Rawls's *A Theory of Justice,* he develops a theory of legislative rights based
on the fundamental and axiomatic right of equality, or equal concern and respect. Finally, he provides a theory of compliance, which embraces theories
regarding the nature and limits of a citizen's obligation to obey the law and
norms for enforcement and punishment.[2]

Dworkin's ambitious enterprise was continued in *A Matter of Principle,*
based on essays in various journals and books between 1978 and 1983.[3] This
book is essentially a refinement, extension, and application, through discrete
essays, of the basic views described in *Taking Rights Seriously.* Dworkin's
most recent book, *Law's Empire,* systematized what was done through discrete essays in the first two books, setting out a theory of law in full-length
form.[4] He argues that "legal reasoning is an exercise in constructive interpretation, that our law consists in the best justification of our legal practices as
a whole, a narrative story that makes of these practices the best they can be"
(p. vii). In this book, Dworkin locates this theory of law's "foundations in a
more general politics of integrity, community, and fraternity, . . . track[ing] its
consequences for abstract legal theory and then for a series of concrete cases
arising under the common law, statutes, and the Constitution" (p. viii). Its systematic character precludes excessively detailed examination of specific
points (for which Dworkin refers his readers to *A Matter of Principle*).

Dworkin's subsequent work included a series of four articles on equality,
an article on "Liberal Community," and especially his Tanner Lectures on
Human Values, delivered at Stanford in 1988, entitled "Foundations of Liberal Equality."[5] It represents a movement in Dworkin's work from writing in
which the center of gravity is specifically legal theory to writing that focuses
on broader moral and political philosophy. The articles on equality attempt to
flesh out Dworkin's definition of his version of liberalism, "liberal equality,"
and to show the interconnectedness and consistency, indeed the fundamental
unity, of its different parts (relative to issues of distribution of resources, personal liberty, and political rights). In "Liberal Community," he argues that
liberal tolerance not only is not incompatible with community but that it also
supplies the best interpretation of the idea that people should identify their
own interests with those of their political community. Dworkin's aim in the
Tanner Lectures is "to find ethical foundations for liberalism." He eschews an
attempt to find self-evident axioms from which liberal principles flow, con-
tenting himself with showing "how liberalism as a political philosophy connects with another part of our intellectual world, our ideas about what a good
life is" (p. 3). Dworkin rejects the most typical liberal strategy for explaining
to people why they should be liberals, a strategy of "discontinuity," which requires them to set aside their convictions about the good life when they act

politically. He tries to construct and defend a competing strategy which argues that liberalism is continuous with the best personal ethics, with the right philosophical view of the good life. The heart of his argument is that most people's ethical intuitions are best explained by a view of ethics that focuses not on the impact or consequences of a life but rather on meeting the challenge of living skillfully, and that this "challenge model" supports the ideal of liberal equality.

Having provided a brief outline of Dworkin's developing work in legal and political philosophy, in the rest of this chapter I want to do three things: first, describe the major points of his constructive theory of law; second, lay out his particular understanding of the content of liberalism ("liberal equality"); and third, summarize his argument about the ethical foundations of liberalism.

THE CONSTRUCTIVE THEORY OF LAW

Dworkin distinguishes between empirical disagreement about law (whether the legislature really passed a statute forbidding something) and theoretical disagreement (the grounds of law—what makes a particular proposition of law true, even if there is no empirical disagreement about what statutes and precedents have said). But legal philosophers often evade this distinction, he says, and argue that theoretical disagreement is an illusion. This "plain-fact" view holds that disagreement is a result of empirical mistakes or of disputes over what the law *should* be, issues of law and morality. In its popular form, this view is reflected mainly in the focus on whether or not judges have been "faithful" to the law, although some people take the view that judges ought to improve the law whenever they can. Academics, who are less likely than laypeople to assume that what is in the law books is decisive, have a different plain-fact view: The law is silent and judges inevitably must exercise discretion and make new law. (They vary over how this discretion should be exercised, democratically or adventurously.)[6]

Yet concrete hard cases involving common law, statute, and constitution all seem to focus on what the law is, not just what it should be. How do academic adherents of the plain-fact view explain this? They do so by what Dworkin calls semantic theories, which hold that lawyers and judges do use the same criteria in deciding when propositions of law are true. The dominant theory is legal positivism, which emphasizes specific historical events.[7]

If positivism is right, and disagreement is only on what legal institutions have actually decided in the past, rather than the theoretical question of what the criteria for law are, why do judges and lawyers seem to argue about not merely whether to be faithful to the law or what the law should be but about what the law is? Some positivists say it is a pretence, given public belief that there is always law and that judges follow it. Others argue that "law" has a standard meaning, but is used differently with regard to some marginal cases. And yet the differences seem to arise not just in "borderline" cases but also in "pivotal" ones. Why deny theoretical disagreement then? Positivists think that is the only way to avoid nihilism.[8]

Dworkin proposes a different account of theoretical disagreement, using as an example the case of a community with shared practices and traditions whose members make and dispute claims about what is the best way to interpret them. Interpretation of a social practice and artistic interpretation are examples of "creative interpretation" of entities people have not made themselves, in contrast to interpretation of ordinary conversation, which focuses on intentions. Creative interpretation is not conversational, but constructive, and it is concerned not with the purposes of the author, but the purposes the interpreter imposes on an object or practice to make it the best possible example of the form or genre to which it is taken to belong. The interpreter cannot do whatever he wants for he is constrained by the history and shape of the practice or object.[9]

Dworkin refines the notion of constructive interpretation by noting various stages of interpretation: the preinterpretive stage, in which the rules and practices that provide tentative content to the practice are identified; the interpretive stage, at which the interpreter settles on some general justification for the main elements of the practice identified earlier; and the postinterpretive stage, at which the interpreter adjusts his sense of what the practice really requires so as better to serve the interpretive justification. Dworkin also distinguishes between concept, the core idea of a practice, and conception, the competing ways of spinning it out; and he notes the importance of certain paradigms, concrete examples that any interpretation must fit.[10]

Law, then, according to Dworkin, is an interpretive concept, and general theories of law are constructive interpretations, trying to show legal practice in its best light to achieve equilibrium between legal practice as the interpreter finds it and the best justification of that practice. Dworkin argues that the most abstract and fundamental point of legal practice is to guide and constrain the power of government, by insisting that force not be used or withheld, no matter how useful, except as licensed or required by individual rights and responsibilities flowing from past political decisions about when collective force is justified. More particular conceptions of law refine this concept by answering three questions: Is there any point to requiring public force to be used only in this way? If so, what is it? And what notion of "consistency with past decisions" best serves it?[11]

The three main rival conceptions Dworkin identifies are conventionalism, legal pragmatism, and law as integrity.[12] Conventionalism says that there is a point to the law's constraint of coercion (the predictability and procedural fairness the constraint supplies) and that rights or responsibilities flow from past political decisions only when they are explicit or can be made so in conventionally accepted ways. Legal pragmatism answers the first question negatively (there is no point) and offers the interpretation that judges do whatever seems to them best for the community's future, not counting consistency with the past as valuable. Law as integrity accepts law and legal rights, but says that the point is not merely predictability or procedural fairness but the securing of an equality among citizens that makes their community more genuine and improves its moral justification for exercising the political power it does. It says that rights and responsibilities flow from past decisions not only when they are explicit but also when they follow from the principles of personal and political morality that the explicit decisions presuppose by way of justification.

Dworkin examines each of these three conceptions, evaluating it for fit (how well does it explain our legal practice?) and then for how well it justifies those practices. Conventionalism can make a plausible initial case for fit, but it is inadequate in the end because, paradoxically, it does not take conventional sources of law seriously enough (judges are grappling with law long after its explicit extension has run out) and because over time there have been so many dramatic changes in legal practice that cannot plausibly be considered the result of convention. Does conventionalism's ideal of protected expectations justify our legal practice as a whole? One argument is that it is necessary to prevent parties being surprised because that is unfair. But because the explicit extension of convention runs out fairly quickly, conventionalism authorizes judges to make law at that point, so that will allow surprises too. (If strict conventionalism or unilateralism—that the defendant should win in the absence of an explicit extension of convention—denies that, it does not remotely fit with our practices.) Thus, a new justification—the need for a blend of predictability and flexibility—is necessary. But conventionalists cannot make a persuasive case that they provide such a blend better than pragmatist do.

Pragmatism, for the very reasons conventionalism fails, seems as if it might offer a more adequate account of our legal practice. But Dworkin argues that it too fails on the first count. It requires us to ignore or treat as deception the judicial opinions that grapple with problematical statutes as if consistency with the past really mattered. Is pragmatism attractive as a political justification of state coercion? Pragmatism is a skeptical conception of law, rejecting the idea that rights are trumps over what would otherwise be the best future, properly understood. Legal rights are only instruments for the best future. Although there are some advantages to this, Dworkin argues that such a conception is incompatible with the claims of integrity.

Ordinary politics shares certain goals with utopian political theory (fairness, justice, procedural due process), but it also has a further ideal: the virtue of political integrity, by which government must act in a principled and coherent manner toward all its citizens, extending to everyone the substantive standards of justice or fairness it uses for some. In a society in which people disagree about justice, it is important to be able to recognize that other people's acts can express a conception of fairness or justice or decency even when we do not endorse that conception ourselves. This ability is an important part of our more general ability to treat others with respect, and it is therefore a prerequisite of civilization. Integrity as a distinct political virtue provides a basis for recognizing legal rights, for it justifies a commitment to consistency in principle for its own sake. Dworkin finds in our instinctive rejection of "checkerboard solutions" (arbitrary internal compromises, such as compromise on abortion that would allow it for pregnant women born in even years but not for those born in odd years) evidence that integrity is recognized as a virtue in our political life. A long argument grounding the attractiveness of integrity ends in the conclusion that the problem of legitimacy is best resolved in a true community of principle. A community of principle, which takes integrity to be central to politics, assimilates political obligations to the general class of associative obligations (responsibilities attaching to our membership in some biological or social group). A community with a general commitment to integrity meets the requirements for legitimate associative obligations because it expresses a concern by each for all that is sufficiently special, personal, pervasive, and egalitarian.

Law as integrity insists that legal claims are interpretive judgments and therefore combine backward- and forward-looking elements. They interpret contemporary legal practice seen as an unfolding political narrative. The adjudicative principle of integrity instructs judges to identify legal rights and duties, as far as possible, on the assumption that they were all created by a single author—the community personified—expressing a coherent conception of justice and fairness. Propositions of law are true, then, if they follow from the principles of justice, fairness, and procedural due process that provide the best constructive interpretation of the community's legal practice.

The image of law as integrity that Dworkin gives is a chain novel, in which one author writes a chapter, then passes it on to another whose obligation is to continue the novel, making it the best that it can be. The writing can be judged on two dimensions. First, it must fit the parts that have been written previously, that is, provide an interpretation that has general explanatory power and flows throughout the whole text (although there may be no interpretation that fits on all points). Second, when more than one interpretation fits the bulk of the text, the writer should judge which of the eligible readings, all things considered, makes the work best.

Judges who accept law as integrity decide hard cases by trying to find, in some coherent set of principles about people's rights and duties, the best constructive interpretation of the political structure and legal doctrine of their community. Convictions about fit will provide a rough threshold requirement. When more than one interpretation fits, then the judge must choose between them by asking which shows the community's structure and decisions in a better light from the standpoint of political morality.

LIBERAL EQUALITY

Having described the more formal aspects of Dworkin's legal theory, let us move on to its substantive political content: liberal equality.[13] The most efficient exposition of liberal equality, says Dworkin, begins with an account liberalism gives of the just distribution of property, that is, control over resources. The ideal distribution is achieved only when the resources different people control are equal in the "opportunity costs" of those resources (i.e., the value they would have in the hands of other people). The economist's envy test—this is not a psychological usage of the term envy—is thus the test for ideal equality: Equality is perfect when no member of the community envies (would prefer to have) the total set of resources under the control of any other member. (This test can be met even when welfare or happiness or well-being are unequal: for example, if my ambitions are more expensive or difficult to achieve but I still would not trade my resources for yours.) Under certain assumptions, this envy test would be met if we all started with an equal number of auction tokens and bid for all resources and kept the auction going until no one wanted it run again.

The problem with this approach is that people have two kinds of resources, personal and impersonal. Impersonal resources—things that can be owned and transferred—can be bid for, but personal resources—physical and mental health, strength, talent—cannot. Another problem is that some people have more luck than others. To deal with these problems, liberal equality insists on compensatory strategies to repair the inequalities in personal resources and luck. Redistributive schemes financed by general taxation can be modeled on hypothetical insurance markets to achieve at least substantial advances toward equality.

This analysis of distributional equality suggests how liberal equality connects equality and liberty. An egalitarian society, in this sense, must be a free society. Invasions of liberty (e.g., criminal laws prohibiting certain ways of life) are invasions of equality as well, unless they can be justified as necessary to protect an egalitarian distribution of resources and opportunities by providing security of person and property or in some other way. Because no laws based on personal morality could pass that test, liberal equality supports liberal tolerance in matters of personal morality.

Liberal equality in political matters does not consist in equality of impact or influence over the community's decisions (political power not being treated as a private resource). Rather, it is a matter of distributing the vote and protecting political liberties so as to serve the other goals of liberal equality: the distributive goals already mentioned, but also participatory goals. For example, liberal equality supposes that a worthwhile life includes political activity as an extension of moral experience and insists that the opportunity for genuine political engagement be available to all who are willing to take it up. This means more than just a formal opportunity to vote: it means that politics must be organized so that it can be a theater of moral argument and commitment based on the responsibilities of community rather than only another market for discovering passive revealed preferences. The familiar liberal political rights (e.g., freedom of speech and religion), embedded in a political culture of expression and reason, are at least as important as full suffrage. This brief sketch shows how liberal equality fuses together equality, liberty, and community into an overall political ideal. Dworkin emphasizes that liberal equality sharply distinguishes between personality and circumstance. People are to be equal in resources, so far as possible (including personal resources), but they are not to be equal in their welfare. They take responsibility themselves for their tastes and projects and ambitions and other features of personality in virtue of which one person may count his life better or worse than another who has identical resources. (No one has a right to more resources just because his tastes are more expensive, for example.)

Dworkin also emphasizes that liberal equality requires tolerance: it insists that government must be neutral in ethics; it may not forbid or reward any private activity on the ground that one set of substantive ethical values (one set of opinions about the best way to lead a life) is superior or inferior to others.

These main points in Dworkin's definition of liberal equality will be developed further in his arguments in defense of liberal equality.

THE ETHICAL FOUNDATIONS OF LIBERALISM

The Rejection of Discontinuous Strategies

Traditional, contractarian liberal theories from John Locke onward (Dworkin expresses doubt about calling Thomas Hobbes a liberal) have used a "discontinuous" strategy to defend liberalism, that is, one in which a person adopts two different, unrelated perspectives in matters of personal life and in political life. The perspective in personal life includes concerns rooted in two different departments of ethics: well-being (personal preferences and beliefs about what life is good for oneself) and morality (how to respond to others' needs and ambitions). The liberal political perspective, on the other hand, seems to command that we set aside our notions of well-being, our convictions about the good life, and make political decisions with a certain kind of impartiality. In the personal arena, people are committed and attached; in the political arena, they should be neutral and impartial. How is liberalism to deal with this apparent conflict between liberal politics and ordinary ethics?[14]

Social contractarians, in proposing a "discontinuous strategy," note that in contractual situations people are typically driven by the first set of considerations (the personal perspective that emphasizes self-interest) and they try to provide a similar motive for the political contract. Rawls is interesting especially because he tries to base the contract at least partly on morality and not just on self-interest. This would make the social contract theory more palatable to many and improve the discontinuity strategy. This strategy has promise in terms of the political requirement of consensus, getting people with very different substantive views to agree on some political theory as a basis of government. Its main problem is that, in addition to consensual promise, theories of justice also need "categorical force," a moral basis or ground for collective responsibility other than consent (because liberals argue that certain political acts *ought* to be done even before consent has been secured). Dworkin surveys some contemporary liberal thinkers (oriented toward the discontinuity strategy) and concludes that they cannot provide the categorical force liberalism claims, and cannot thereby reconcile the two perspectives.[15]

Dworkin proposes a strategy of continuity, which provides a more integrated moral experience in which peoples' politics match their personal convictions about what it means to live well. This effort to provide new ethical foundations for liberalism requires him to undertake an excursion into philosophical ethics.[16] In particular, he must show how, in a strategy of continuity, political neutrality can grow out of ethical commitment. His answer lies in a distinction between philosophical ethics, where liberalism takes sides, and more substantive levels of ethics, where the side it takes at the philosophical level dictates neutrality. Liberal ethics must be abstract enough not to rule out conceptions of the good life likely to be popular in our community, yet it must be sufficiently distinctive and muscular to lead those who embrace it to liberal politics. According to liberal ethics, our views of the good life are not "bracketed" and placed to the side when we engage in politics (as they are in discontinuous strategies for defending liberalism)—in fact, liberal politics gives full effect to our most comprehensive and philosophical convctions about them.

Critical Interests and Some Anxieties

Dworkin starts out by distinguishing between volitional and critical interests. Volitional interests are what I want and critical interests are what I should want (what my not wanting would make my life worse).[17] Liberal ethics requires us to concentrate on critical, as distinct from volitional, well-being.[18] Dworkin then elaborates a series of worries and puzzles about critical interests, points on which our intuitions seem often to be inconsistent.[19] They include the following:

Significance: People who are self-conscious about the question of living well treat that question as a matter of capital importance. What are the grounds for this? A single human life is such a small point in the universe.

Transcendent or Indexed?: Are ethical values transcendent (everywhere and always the same) or are they indexed in some way to culture and ability and resource and other circumstances, so that the best life for a person in one situation is very different from the best life of a person in another? If we reject the transcendent view, can ethics be more than merely subjective?

Ethics and Morality: What is the connection between self-interest and morality? Is living well wholly independent of living justly (e.g., Cezanne dodging the draft out of a desire to paint)? Or is justice a component of critical well-being, but still not the whole story? Or is there no conflict, because one can never lead a critically better life through unjust acts, as Plato thought? (Critical interests are, after all, supposed to be normative.)

Additive or Constitutive?: Must a person recognize experiences or relationships or events as good for them to count as components of a good life? The additive view says that one can judge a person's life good or bad apart from his opinion of its value. (For example, wouldn't Adolph Hitler have been better off if he had been locked up in adolescence?) The constitutive view says that no component may contribute to the value of a person's life without his endorsement. (For example, coerced religious acts cannot improve the value of a life.)

Ethics and Community: Finally, what is the unit of ethical value, that is, the entity whose life ethics aims to make good? The individual (because we consider ethics entirely personal) or the community (does the community have an ethical life of its own on which the critical success of an individual's life depends to some degree, as some contemporary Germans feel responsibility for the Holocaust)?

Models of Critical Value

These puzzles arise because our ethical instincts and impulses reflect two distinct models of value, which are interpretations of ethical experience rather than efforts to offer any general argument of ethical value from the ground up.[20] They respond not so much to general doubt about ethics as a whole (external skepticism) but to doubts about how to organize the various ethical intuitions most of us have (internal skepticism), by showing how most of our convictions, at least, can be saved by looking at them in a certain light.

The Impact Model: This model holds that the value of a good life consists in its product, that is, in its consequences for the rest of the world, for example, discovering cures or composing great music or benefiting a race or country. (The model abstracts from the specific question as to what good consequences are.) Although it finds support in some ethical intuitions, it makes some popular views about critical interests seem silly and self-indulgent, for example, those who focus on doing something well just to do it, apart from any consequences it may have (e.g., learning to play a musical instrument). Examples of the impact model that Dworkin gives are aestheticism (producing great works of art), theological anthropocentrism (pleasing God), and hedonistic anthropomorphism (adding to human pleasure, on some utilitarian calculus).[21]

The Challenge Model: This model argues that the value of a good life lies in the inherent value of a skillful performance of living. Living a life is itself a performance that demands skill. It is the most comprehensive and important challenge we face, and our critical interests consist in the achievements, events, and experiences that mean we have met the challenge well. It assumes we have convictions about how to live, but it does not judge these. It tells us that we will understand our ethical life better if we see our convictions as opinions about the skillful performance of a self-assignment rather than just as opinions about how we can change the world for the better. This model is said to have dominated Greek ethics, espcially Aristotelian ethics, and in the modern period it has played a crucial part—in distinct battle with ethical skepticism—in the development of humanist ethics.[22]

Dworkin then engages in a long and complicated effort to show how the two models respond to the various puzzles of ethics.[23] The upshot of that discussion is that interpreting the convictions that we have as convictions about a skillful response to a complex challenge gives them more sense and coherence than the alternate general interpretation, that they are convictions about having the best impact.

No systematic summary of this complicated argument is possible in a brief chapter, but it is important to note several of the conclusions Dworkin draws in this discussion. The impact model treats all our circumstances as limitations on the quality of life we can lead. The challenge model treats some circumstances as limitations, but others as parameters that help define what a good performance of living would be. Some of these parameters are normative, defining our ethical situation not as it is but as it should be; that is, our lives can go badly not just because we are unwilling or unable to respond to the circumstances we have, but also because we have the wrong circumstances and cannot face the right challenge. (For example, most of us treat the inevitability of death as a parameter rather than a limitation, yet dying young—before the typical life span with its variety of challenges—is treated as a tragedy). Some parameters are hard (their violation makes life a total failure), whereas others are soft (they only reduce the value of a life; for example, Mozart's life was reduced by an early death, but was still brilliant).[24]

Justice is a normative parameter, according to Dworkin. If living well consists in responding in the right way to the right challenge, then life goes worse when the right challenge cannot be faced because of injustice. (Even the person who is given more than what is just faces the wrong challenge and thereby has a worse life.)[25]

With some limited exceptions, the challenge model leads to a rejection of paternalism regarding critical interests because the challenge model fuses ethical value and choice (the principle of ethical integrity). Nothing can improve the critical value of a person's life unless it is seen as an improvement by the person whose life it is. (This does not make ethics subjective because living out of conviction requires reflection, coherence, and openness to the examples of others. I must want to live a really good life and not merely one I think is good.) The challenge model also rules out conceptual paternalism (educational devices for removing bad options from a person's view) because that view assumes an independent, transcendent picture of ethical value that the model begins by rejecting.[26]

Ethical Liberals and Liberal Equality

The final part of Dworkin's argument is that the ethical roots of political liberalism are found in the challenge model of ethics. He sets up a thought experiment, trying to show how conversation among ethical liberals (i.e., those who, despite very great substantive differences, accept the challenge model) would lead to their acceptance of liberal equality.[27]

Again, through a long and complicated argument, Dworkin shows that ethical liberals would come to the following conclusions.

1. They would define justice in terms of resources rather than in terms of welfare. Welfare-based theories suggest a two-step procedure: first, each citizen decides what level of well-being he would reach under different proposed arrangements, and second, officials select those arrangements that divide things in the fairest way under the version of

justice adopted. This approach seems more oriented toward volitional than critical interests or toward critical interests on the impact model. But it makes no sense for the challenge model, according to which ethics and justice are dynamically interrelated. Ethical liberals accordingly need an account of justice in which resources enter ethics as normative parameters, which only a resource-based view of justice provides. Moreover, another reason for ethical liberals to reject welfare-based views is that the two-step procedure has officials trying to ensure that people lead lives that are equally good. Even if they could do so (which is doubtful) this would undermine the challenge of living (which includes the identification by each person of what life is good for himself). Government's task under the challenge model is to help people live good lives by trying to make circumstances what they should be.[28]

2. Ethical liberals will agree that the just share of resources is an equal share. They must treat the question of justice as a part of ethics, deciding what share of resources each should have by deciding what parameters it is appropriate for each person to accept as defining the character of a life good for himself. Suppose they begin with a presumption that all members of a community start with the same abstract ethical challenge and therefore deserve an equal share of resources? What counterarguments are available? Eliminating arguments that do not acknowledge justice as a parameter of ethics, the only counterarguments left are those that appeal to the inherent difference or worth of different people or groups. But ethical liberals cannot accept that society's institutions predefine different challenges in living for different people, because each person is to decide his own ethical identity. It obscures and demeans the stark challenge of ethics, the categorical force of the imperative to live well, to locate its source in anything more contingent than our being persons with lives to live. Nonegalitarian theories demean ethics by supposing it is the job of politics rather than people to construct the parameters of ethical identity. Thus, the challenge model supports equality of resources directly, as flowing from people's sense of their own best interests critically understood. Moreover, this reinforces the fact that justice is a parameter of ethics: Living well has a social dimension, and I live less well in community with others if they treat my efforts to lead a good life as unimportant. Indeed, everyone is insulted by a political and economic system dedicated to inequality, even those who profit in resources from injustice, because a structure of community that assumes the challenge of living is hypothetical and superficial denies the self-definition that is part of dignity.[29]

3. Ethical liberals have no difficulty harmonizing the partiality of the personal perspective (I care more about my friends than about strangers)

with the equality of the political perspective on which they have now decided. Welfare-based theories carry the problem that politics is committed to reestablishing the equal welfare that private individuals undo by their efforts to live better. But equality of resources is not undone by the partiality of my personal choices and the effects of my private efforts. Equality of resources licenses partiality.[30]

4. Ethical liberals agree not to include among the personal resources to be made equal various features of personality (e.g., preferences, tastes, convictions, predilections, ambitions, attachments). The alternative line to draw between what is compensable and what is not would be whether differences between people are voluntary. (Handicaps are compensated, a cultivated taste for caviar is not.) But that distinction breaks down because tastes are cultivated in response to higher-order ambitions that are not deliberately cultivated. So all tastes, and so forth would be part of circumstances and compensated, and equality of circumstances would collapse back to equality of welfare. Liberal equality does not assume that people choose their beliefs, but only supposes that they reflect on them and choose how to act on the basis of those reflections. Liberal equality aims to make people equal in their circumstances, for example, talents and handicaps. But convictions and preferences are plainly not opportunities or limitations in identifying and pursuing what a person deems to be a good life, but rather essential components of his view of the good life; they cannot be limitations because the person would be worse, not better off, without them. The distinction between handicaps and convictions is arbitrary only from the voluntarist perspective that assumes all people want at bottom the same thing: utility or pleasure. But voluntarist ethics is untrue to most people's actual ethical experiences, according to which our deep (perhaps unattainable) ambitions are not obstacles to living the life we most want to lead.[31]

5. Ethical liberals would agree on liberal tolerance or neutrality. Neutrality has two forms: neutrality in appeal (the ability to be accepted by a great variety of ethical traditions) and neutrality in operation (tolerance, even general tolerance of illiberal bigots).[32] The contractarian tradition begins in the ambition to make liberalism ecumenical or neutral in appeal and urges toleration (neutrality in operation) to that end. Dworkin (who once embraced that view but has changed his position) argues that liberalism based on a continuity strategy begins in ethics and comes upon neutrality in the course of its argument, as theorems (not axioms). Dworkin agrees that liberal ethics is not neutral in appeal or ecumenical in the strong sense that it can be drawn from convictions almost everybody already holds. He settles for the weaker sense that liberal ethics

could be generally accepted without people having to abandon what they believe is important to them, that is, their convictions of ethical identity and their substantive views about living a life well, given that ethical identity. No one would have to abandon his first-person ethical views. People would have to abandon views requiring them to force other people to act rightly—the "third-person beliefs" involved in coercive critical paternalism. Thus, liberal equality gives promise of consensus, because it is far less utopian to hope that people will give up their third-person than their first-person beliefs. That does not apply, of course, to the fanatic who thinks that God will punish him, for eternity, unless he kills us. We must not turn our backs on him, or to his luggage, but he cannot be part of our liberal community.[33]

A liberal community embraces neutrality in operation (or toleration), denying the legitimacy of outlawing a kind of life because it is demeaning or corrupt, although it is conceded not to be unjust. Dworkin acknowledges that liberal equality is not ethically neutral in its effects, because some lives will be more difficult or expensive in a liberal society—but that is not in virtue of a condemnation of those lives but is due to liberalism's conception of justice.[34]

How is it that ethical liberals, who hold very different substantive ethical views passionately, can accept tolerance, rather than letting their personal ethics be carried over to politics? Liberal equality permits them to do so, but denies them one weapon: they may not forbid someone to live a life simply because they think his ethical convictions wrong. The conclusive reason ethical liberals have for that is that they accept an account of justice demanding equality of circumstances, and laws are a part of people's circumstances. This does not require ethical liberals to bracket their ethical convictions, but gives full force to them. They cannot make their own lives better by ignoring limits justice sets to their power, and they cannot make others' lives better because, on the challenge model, someone's life cannot be improved against his own steady convictions.[35]

Liberal equality then demands tolerance, but one short of what some of its critics think liberalism aims at. It will have the result that some lives are more difficult to live. It leaves room for short-range educational paternalism that looks forward to genuine endorsement. And liberalism's tolerance is not global because it must disapprove other theories that dispute its principles. (Therefore, liberal neutrality is not compromised when a thief whose idea of the good life is theft is punished, or when a racist whose life mission is to promote white supremacy is thwarted.) In one general respect, then, liberal equality is not neutral, namely, in regard to third-person ethics, or first-person ethics that are parasitic on third-person ethics.[36]

In summary, then, adopting the challenge model of ethics leads people to see that their own personal convictions are parasitic on justice; that they therefore must accept a resource-based view of justice; that the only appropriate resource-based conception for ethical liberals is egalitarian; that the liberal conception of justice condemns ethical intolerance; and that the paternalistic objection (based on the view that people's lives can be made better against their own convictions) is mistaken.

DWORKIN'S RECENT WORK

Dworkin has published three major books since 1993. *Life's Dominion: An Argument about Abortion, Euthanasia, and Individual Freedom*[37] examines arguments on both conservative and liberal ends of the political spectrum and attempts to show that there is greater ground for agreement than might be thought. He does not sugarcoat these issues, conceding that fetuses are human lives, indeed that they are sacred in some sense. Their value, however, comes not from being persons with rights but from the intrinsic (but nonabsolute) good of human life. The frustration of life—"the waste of the natural and human creative investments that make up the story of a normal life"—varies with the stage and quality of life; it can be as much by lack of opportunity to live a successful life in given circumstances (justifying abortion of children whose life chances seem dim) as by premature death. Dworkin sifts through popular convictions (e.g., views of people who oppose abortion, but see it as less than murder, and who justify abortion in the "hard cases" such as a threat to the life of the mother and rape) to show that conservatives, too, weigh the value of the life of the child against other interests, justifying the liberal allowance of abortion on considerations of the quality of life of the future child and of the mother and family. Euthanasia is also defended, largely on the grounds that a person has a critical interest in the way he dies (and that decisions can be made on behalf of those who are no longer competent, in light of their earlier views).

Freedom's Law: The Moral Reading of the American Constitution[38] is a compilation of articles (almost all of them written for the *New York Review of Books*). Their common strand is his continuing defense of the proposition that the Constitution should be read by judges and lawyers in light of what they take to be justice: this is the "moral reading" of the U.S. Constitution. Within the confines of two principles (that they start with what the framers said, and that they abide by the requirement of integrity—that is, their moral readings must be consistent with the Constitution's structural design and with dominant lines of past constitutional interpretation), judges should read constitutional provisions—understood very broadly—according to the best moral principles available. Dworkin rejects the majoritarian premise that political decisions should conform to what an informed majority would want. A better "constitutional conception" of democracy is that collective decisions be made by political institutions that treat all members of the community with equal respect. The book then works out the implications of this approach by applying it to many timely subjects, such as abortion, euthanasia, race, libel, pornography, and the controversies involving the Supreme Court nominations of Robert Bork and Clarence Thomas.

The most important of Dworkin's recent works is *Sovereign Virtue: The Theory and Practice of Equality,*[39] which brings together some of the articles discussed earlier, especially those relating to equality and to the foundations of liberalism. Dworkin believes that the principle of equality—the "sovereign virtue" of equal concern for all people—is under assault and seeks to vindicate it. He provides what he calls the beginning of an argument (to be developed more fully in a book based on his John Dewey Lectures) that

> a theory of political morality, such as the theory developed in this book, should be located in a more general account of the humane values of ethics and morality, of the status and integrity of value, and of the character and possibilities of objective truth.[40]

He sets himself explicitly against the work of two leading contemporary liberals, Isaiah Berlin and John Rawls. Berlin's value pluralism emphasized the conflicts between important values such as liberty and equality, whereas Dworkin's project seeks to integrate them. Rawls's political liberalism attempts to insulate political morality from ethical assumptions about the character of the good life and controversies about them, while Dworkin's project seeks to ground liberalism in them.

The book rests especially on two assumptions of ethical individualism, Dworkin says. The first is the principle of equal importance, according to which it is equally important that all lives be lived successfully rather than being wasted. The second is the principle of special responsibility, according to which all should recognize the equal objective importance of the success of a human life, but one person has a special and final responsibility for that success, namely, the person whose life it is. These two principles require that government should work to see that, as far as possible, a person's fate should not be sensitive to who they are (their economic backgrounds, gender, race, or particular set of skills and handicaps) and that it is sensitive to the choices they have made.

Within this framework, the first part of the book discusses various theoretical issues of equality, liberty, and community, and the second part of the book discusses more specific issues of public policy, such as health care, welfare, campaign finance reform, affirmative action, genetic experimentation, euthanasia, and homosexuality. (Dworkin notes, however, that the second part makes important contributions to the theoretical elaboration of principles of political morality). While not exactly embracing the notion of a "third way" between conservatism and liberalism, Dworkin allows that his argument can be seen as sharing the "old egalitarian" commitment to collective responsibility to show equal concern, without its failure to define equal concern in terms of citizens' personal responsibilities, and as sharing conservatives' emphasis on personal responsibility, without ignoring collective responsibility.

CONCLUSION

It still remains for Dworkin to develop the philosophical grounds of his legal theory, especially a more substantial argument for the superiority of the "challenge model" of ethics. In particular, he will have to construct a much more plausible alternative model than the "impact model," which appears to be something of a straw man. For example, no one argues that a person's ethical life is good simply because it produces good extrinsic results, entirely apart from the disposition or intention of the person. The challenge model too will need further development because it may be doubted that the challenge of living can be divorced from the question of objective human ends as thoroughly as Dworkin separates them. His citation of Aristotle as an example of the challenge model suggests this problem: on Aristotle's own self-understanding it would be absurd to cite his approach to ethics while divorcing it from a specific conception of human ends. The search for formalistic agreement in ethics (divorced from substantive content) may be necessary for an antiperfectionist liberal ethics, but it seems unlikely to provide a solid foundation for political life and community.

NOTES

1. Ronald Dworkin, *Taking Rights Seriously* (Cambridge, Mass.: Harvard University Press, 1977).

2. John Rawls, *Theory of Justice* (Cambridge, Mass.: Harvard University Press, 1971), vii–xv.

3. Ronald Dworkin, *Matter of Principle* (Cambridge, Mass.: Harvard University Press, 1985).

4. Ronald Dworkin, *Law's Empire* (Cambridge, Mass.: Harvard University Press, 1986).

5. The four articles on equality are: "What Is Equality? Part 1: Equality of Welfare," *Philosophy & Public Affairs* 10 (1981): 185–246; "What Is Equality? Part 2: Equality of Resources," *Philosophy & Public Affairs* 10 (1981): 283–345; "What Is Equality? Part 3: The Place of Liberty," *Iowa Law Review* 73 (1988): 1–73; and "What Is Equality? Part 4: Political Equality," *University of San Francisco Law Review* 22, no. 1 (1987): 1–30. "Liberal Community" appears in *California Law Review* 77 (1989): 479–504. "Foundations of Liberal Equality" is in *Tanner Lectures on Human Values,* vol. 2 (Salt Lake City: University of Utah Press, 1990), 1–119.

6. Dworkin, *Law's Empire,* 3–9.

7. Dworkin, *Law's Empire,* 31–35. Other semantic theories include (1) natural law theories, which argue that the criteria for law are not factual, but to some extent moral, and (2) legal realism, which argues that law depends on context, and in particular on certain kinds of predictions about what judges will do or how the law will develop.

8. Dworkin, *Law's Empire,* 37–44.

9. Dworkin, *Law's Empire,* 46–65.

10. Dworkin, *Law's Empire,* 65.

11. Dworkin, *Law's Empire,* 87–94.

12. Dworkin deals with conventionalism in *Law's Empire,* chapter 4, with legal pragmatism in *Law's Empire,* chapter 5, and with law as integrity in *Law's Empire,* chapters 6–7.

13. Dworkin, *Tanner Lectures,* 36–42.

14. Dworkin, *Tanner Lectures,* 16–22.

15. Dworkin, *Tanner Lectures,* 22–35.

16. Dworkin, *Tanner Lectures,* 42–88.

17. This is not simply the distinction between subjective and objective well-being. My volitional interests are not simply my possibly mistaken judgments about my critical interests; for example, I can reasonably want some things that are not critical interests. No more inclusive category of well-being can adjudicate conflicts between them.

18. Dworkin, *Tanner Lectures,* 42–47.

19. Dworkin, *Tanner Lectures,* 47–53.

20. Dworkin, *Tanner Lectures,* 53–55.

21. Dworkin, *Tanner Lectures,* 55–57.

22. Dworkin, *Tanner Lectures,* 57–58.

23. Dworkin, *Tanner Lectures,* 59–88.

24. Dworkin, *Tanner Lectures,* 66–71.

25. Dworkin, *Tanner Lectures,* 71–75.

26. Dworkin, *Tanner Lectures,* 77–86. The community may, however, collectively endorse and recommend ethical ideals not adequately supported by the culture and it may provide for compulsory education if it is sufficiently short-term and noninvasive and likely to be genuinely endorsed. That flows from the central, constitutive role the challenge model assigns to reflective or intuitive judgment.

27. Dworkin, *Tanner Lectures,* 88–118.

28. Dworkin, *Tanner Lectures,* 93–98.

29. Dworkin, *Tanner Lectures,* 98–104. In his article on "Liberal Community," Dworkin relies heavily on the notion that facing the challenge of living well requires

having the right circumstances (including the circumstances of living in a just society, as defined by liberal equality, in which, for example, one has neither more nor less than the resources to which one is entitled).

30. Dworkin, *Tanner Lectures,* 104–106.

31. Dworkin, *Tanner Lectures,* 106–10.

32. Dworkin, *Tanner Lectures,* 110–11.

33. Dworkin, *Tanner Lectures,* 111–13.

34. Dworkin, *Tanner Lectures,* 113–14.

35. Dworkin, *Tanner Lectures,* 114–16.

36. Dworkin, *Tanner Lectures,* 117–18.

37. Ronald Dworkin, *Life's Dominion: An Argument about Abortion, Euthanasia, and Individual Freedom* (New York: Knopf, 1993).

38. Ronald Dworkin, *Freedom's Law: The Moral Reading of The American Constitution* (Cambridge, Mass.: Harvard University Press, 1996).

39. Ronald Dworkin, *Sovereign Virtue: The Theory and Practice of Equality* (Cambridge, Mass.: Harvard University Press, 2000).

40. Dworkin, *Sovereign Virtue,* 4.

3

The Hegemonic Liberalism of Susan Moller Okin

Celia Wolf-Devine

To try to classify Susan Moller Okin simply as either a liberal or as a critic of liberalism is to approach her in a way that obscures what motivates and guides her work. Her primary commitment is to feminism (and to one particular brand of feminism at that), and this commitment serves as a yardstick against which every political theory, ancient or modern, is to be measured. Whether her own position should be characterized as liberal or not is an open question. While her policy recommendations in *Justice, Gender, and the Family* are designed to allow those who prefer gender-structured marriages to choose them (although she wants to discourage them from doing so), this may be merely a tactical concession that does not stem from a principled respect for other people's consciences. In her recent essays in *Is Multiculturalism Bad for Women?* she has become less tolerant of traditional religions and cultures, and more ready to use the power of the state to make it harder for them to educate children in their own tradition—at least at any point at which their practices are "sexist." Since she has a very broad definition of "sexist," and regards virtually all the world's major religions as such, this throws her liberal credentials into serious doubt. For freedom of religion requires allowing people to pass on their religion to their children.

Whether Okin ultimately comes out as a liberal, however, is not what is most important from the point of view of the future of liberalism. What is more important is the fact that she is struggling with a problem that all liberals must face, namely, how liberal societies ought to deal with associations such as the family or religious institutions that exist within a broader liberal society but are not themselves organized according to liberal principles. The standard liberal position, adopted by Rawls in the *Theory of Justice,* has been to confine the application of their liberal principles to the public realm and to leave a significant private sphere immune to governmental surveillance. Okin, in *Justice, Gender and the Family,* rejects the private/public distinction and attempts to extend the sort of political principles of justice developed by Rawls into the family itself, and her subsequent work moves increasingly in the direction of what could be called "hegemonic liberalism."

Hegemonic liberals wish to extend liberal principles to every sphere of life, even private associations such as the family and churches. When pushed all the way, of course, hegemonic liberalism ceases to be liberal at all, since it fails to accord any respect to the preferences and consciences of noncompliant persons. On the other hand, a liberalism which is endlessly accommodating of associations based on nonliberal principles would also cease to be liberal in any meaningful sense. So the challenge for liberals is to draw the lines in the right places.

In part I below, I focus on Okin's treatment of Rawls. Her purpose is to draw out the feminist potential in Rawls's theory of justice; one of the section headings in her chapter on Rawls is entitled "Rawls's Theory of Justice as a Tool for Feminist Criticism." This sort of overtly instrumental approach to political theory sometimes leaves the reader with the impression that Okin is hiding the ball—that what is important has happened somehow off the page. And in a sense it has. Her ideal of the "genderless" society is one that she has adopted from feminist theorists, and she does very little to provide arguments for it that would persuade those not already convinced. For, by "gender," she means the "deeply entrenched institutionalization of sexual difference"(JGF 6),[1] and her concept of "institutionalization" is extremely broad, so that a society without gender (if possible at all) would be a very radical departure from the one we now have. "A just future would be one without gender. In its social structures and practices, one's sex would have no more relevance than one's eye color or the length of one's toes" (JGF 171). Her special interest in family structures, then, stems from the fact that she believes the family to be the "linchpin" of the whole gender structure, so that genderless families would ultimately result in a genderless society. Critics, I think, tend to overlook how radical her proposals are and take her to be saying something milder than she is, such as that we ought to end sexual discrimination in employment, or that more equal parenting by fathers and mothers would be a good thing for children, and so forth. *Justice, Gender, and the Family* is an important book, then, because in it she makes an attempt to break out of the rather ingrown world of feminist theory and connect her views with more mainstream political philosophy. The central question to be addressed in part I is whether or not she has succeeded in showing that Rawls's principles have the implications she believes they do.

I begin by briefly discussing Rawls's views on the family in the *Theory of Justice*. I then explain what Okin finds attractive about Rawls's principles, and the way in which she employs them to mount a radical critique of traditional "gender-structured" families in her 1989 book *Justice, Gender and the Family*. (By "gender-structured families" she means the traditional family pattern in which men are the main breadwinners and women are expected to bear most of the responsibility for child care and home-making.) Finally, I will argue that her attempt to enlist Rawls's theory of justice in support of her program to discourage gender-structured families is unsuccessful.

In part II, I briefly discuss her own positive position, showing how her position on gender issues has hardened in her most recent writings. Part III provides a brief critique and conclusion.

I. OKIN'S FEMINIST APPROPRIATION OF RAWLS'S *THEORY OF JUSTICE*

Rawls on the Family

The principles of justice, Rawls argues, are those that would be agreed upon by rational, self-interested agents, who had to decide what sort of institutions to adopt under what he calls a "veil of ignorance." Specifically the contractors in the original position would be ignorant of their own place in society, their physical characteristics, their intellectual abilities, and their own moral and religious convictions (they would not know, for example, whether they are atheists or religious believers). One of the principles he thinks they would agree about is that social and economic inequalities are justifiable only if they are attached to offices and positions open to all under the conditions of fair equality of opportunity and to the greatest benefit of the least advantaged. The principles thus derived, then, are used to evaluate various ways in which the basic institutions of society could be designed. Rawls concedes that the basic institutions of society include the family. He says, "the basic structure of a well-ordered society includes the family in some form"(TJ 463), [2] and lists "the monogamous family" as one of the major institutions of society (TJ 7). But he refrains from subjecting the family to the sort of scrutiny he gives to other social institutions. By taking the contractors in the original position to be "heads of households" or representatives of families, he effectively puts the internal structure of the family outside the scope of his theory of justice.

One reason for taking the contractors in the original position to be the heads or representatives of families is in order to insure that they have some link with future generations. This is necessary for Rawls in order to derive his just savings principle. The contractors must be motivated to take an interest in the welfare of their descendants (or at least the nearest of these) so that the interests of the next generation will be looked after (TJ 128–29).

Leaving aside, for the moment, the question of the internal structure of the family, the very existence of the family is already in some tension with Rawls's goal of providing fair equality of opportunity for all citizens. Rawls is aware of this problem, noting that "the principle of fair opportunity can be only imperfectly carried out, at least as long as the institution of the family exists. The extent to which natural capacities develop and reach fruition is affected by all kinds of social conditions and class attitudes. Even the willingness to make an effort, to try, and so to be deserving in the ordinary sense is itself dependent upon happy family and social circumstances" (TJ 74). In other words, children with equal native endowments will not have equal chances of success so long as they are raised by their natural families. The family, thus, perpetuates inequality. Rawls, however, does not go so far as to recommend the abolition of the family. He says that "[t]aken by itself and given a certain primacy, the idea of equal opportunity inclines in this direction [the abolition of the family]. But within the context of the theory of justice as a whole, there is much less urgency to take this course" (TJ 511–12).

A rather more positive picture of the family is painted in the section of the *Theory of Justice* in which Rawls discusses families as one of the earliest institutions through which the moral education of children takes place. The first stage of moral development, the "morality of authority," is learned within the family. Ultimately, of course, the child must grow up to have a sense of justice as fairness, but the earliest stage of moral development occurs before the child is capable of understanding abstract principles. Acquiring this morality of authority requires that:

> First, the parents must love the child and be worthy objects of his admiration. In this way they arouse in him a sense of his own value and a desire to become the sort of person that they are. Secondly, they must enunciate clear and intelligible (and of course justifiable) rules adapted to the child's level of comprehension. In addition they should set out the reasons for these injunctions so far as these can be understood, and they must also follow these precepts insofar as they apply to them as well. The parents should exemplify the morality which they enjoin. (TJ 465–66)

The next stage of moral development also involves the family, in that it is the morality of association, and the family is a small association, "normally characterized by a definite hierarchy, in which each member has certain rights and duties. . . . The virtues of a good son or a good daughter are explained" (TJ 467). And then there are the larger associations to which the child belongs, such as the school or neighborhood. When he discusses the principles of moral psychology he also mentions the family, but he does not raise questions of justice internal to the family, but says, rather, "given that family institutions are just, and that the parents love the child . . . the child . . . comes to love them" (TJ 490) and then goes on to elaborate on how the child's sense of justice evolves.

Okin's Critique of Rawls

Okin takes exception to the way in which Rawls treats the family at a number of different points. She begins by arguing (persuasively, I think) that the family itself should be evaluated in terms of justice. The family is part of the basic structure of society, and different family structures and different distributions of rights and duties within families affect very deeply the life prospects of children—what they can expect to be and how well they can hope to do (JGF 93). Thus the internal structure of the family cannot be placed beyond moral scrutiny. Justice is not the only, or, as I shall argue later, even the most important virtue of families, but nonetheless, family structures ought to be evaluated in terms of something like justice. (It may be, of course, that the principles of "justice" that apply to the family are different in some ways from those that apply in the political or economic spheres.) For example, to structure the family in such a way that the youngest child is required to forgo marriage or career and serve as an unpaid slave to his or her parents until they die is, I think, unjust.

Rawls's emphasis on the role of the family in the moral development of the child is something that Okin notes with approval. And his emphasis on the development of fellow feeling, friendship, and trust within the family make his theory much more attractive, she thinks, than the arid rationalism of Kant.[3] She objects, however, to the fact that he simply assumes that the family is just rather than examining whether it really is just. For if the family is not just, how can it serve as a place in which future citizens can develop a proper sense of justice? Since he does not submit family structures to scrutiny in light of the principles of justice derived under the veil of ignorance, Okin notes, "they must become just in some different way (unspecified by him) from other institution" (JGF 94). But how?

This question raises a very real difficulty for Rawls's theory. For, since he does not analyze the family in terms of his two principles of justice, but nonetheless talks about the family as being just, it is incumbent upon him to give some explanation of what type of justice is appropriate to family contexts. But he fails to do so.[4] This being the case, Okin proposes to apply the same principles governing the assignment of rights and duties and the distribution of social and economic advantages developed by Rawls in the political context to the intimate association of the family. Her central claim is that when we do this, it becomes apparent that the "gender-structured" family as such is an unjust institution. Rawls would resist this sort of move because of his commitment to the private/public distinction, but since he provides no explanation of how families might be just or unjust (in any sense of "just"), it is an interesting thought experiment, at least, to try to imagine what sort of family structure would be devised by contractors behind a veil of ignorance about whether they are male or female.

What most attracts Okin to Rawls's use of the original position and the veil of ignorance is that it appears to allow for a clean sweep of previous traditions, which in her view are irredeemably sexist and elitist. The contextually based theories of people like MacIntyre and Walzer build on the prevailing ideologies of male elites, and therefore, in Okin's words, "lack moral force because their neglect of domination leaves the rest of us deprived of a voice in the construction of morality" (JGF 72). Since Rawls imagines the contractors in the original position to be heads of households, she believes that this implies that the interests of those members of the family who are not heads of households go unrepresented. But if we imagine that all adult members of society participate equally in drawing up the social contract, then the potential of Rawls's theory for providing a radical critique of our current gender system can be brought out.

Assuming, as Rawls intends, that it is possible to hypothesize the moral thinking of representative human beings as ignorant of their sex (an assumption she later calls into question), those in the original position will, she thinks, take special account of the perspective of women. And since their knowledge of the general facts about human society "must include the knowledge that women have been and continue to be the less advantaged sex in a great number of respects"(JGF 102), they will be likely to take a special interest in family structure. Rawls's second principle requires that inequalities be both to the greatest benefit of the least advantaged and attached to offices and positions open to all. She then argues that:

> if any roles or positions analogous to our current sex roles—including those of husband and wife, mother and father—were to survive the demands of the first requirement, the second requirement would prohibit any linkage between these roles and sex. Gender, with its ascriptive designation of positions and expectations of behavior in accordance with the inborn characteristic of sex, could no longer form a legitimate part of the social structure, whether inside or outside the family. (JGF 103)

Okin then offers three illustrations intended to link this conclusion with broader features of Rawls's requirements of a just society. First, "free choice of occupation" is an important form of liberty for Rawls, and customary assignment of certain sorts of work to women compromises their liberty, not only in the straightforward sense that they are not as free as men to choose not to do unpaid domestic work but also in the sense that their career choices over the course of a lifetime are more restricted than those of men. Rawls does not want anyone to be "servilely dependent on others and made to choose between monotonous and routine occupations which are deadening to human thought and sensibility" and wants work to be "meaningful for all" (JGF 103). Okin believes that these conditions are more likely to prevail in societies that do not assign family responsibilities in such a way that women are a marginal sector of the paid work force and economically dependent on men.

Second, she wants to extend Rawls's requirement that those who devote themselves to politics should be "drawn more or less equally from all sectors of society," to include not only class differences (as Rawls intended) but also sex differences, so that a just society would require equal political representation of women and men. This, she believes, cannot occur until there is "a revolution in shared responsibilities for the family" (JGF 104). And finally, she suggests that the primary good of self respect will be more equally distributed between the sexes if we protect either sex "from the need to pander to or servilely provide for the pleasures of the other. . . . In general, they [the contractors] would be unlikely to tolerate basic social institutions that asymmetrically either forced or gave strong incentives to members of one sex to serve as sex objects for the other" (JGF 105). Just what is meant by serving as a "sex object" is not clarified here. Presumably she means something more than finding a member of the opposite sex attractive and desiring sexual relations with him or her. She may mean what is sometimes called "lust", namely, disregarding the other's humanity for the sake of sexual gratification.

After making these three points, Okin concludes her chapter on Rawls by bringing into question her starting assumption that there is a standpoint that the original contractors can adopt independent of their sex. Citing Nancy Chowdorow's work, she argues that in a gender-structured society in which small children are primarily cared for by women, women and men develop different personality structures and follow different paths in terms of their moral development.[5] If this is in fact true, then thinking about justice under a veil of ignorance about one's sex would be impossible, and since men and women would reason differently about justice, they could not be expected to come to any agreement. Okin says:

> If principles of justice are to be adopted unanimously by representative human beings ignorant of their particular characteristics and positions in society, they must be persons whose psychological and moral development is in all essentials identical. This means that the social factors influencing the differences presently found between the sexes—from female parenting to all the manifestations of

female subordination and dependence—would have to be replaced by gender-less institutions and customs (JGF 107).

Taking seriously the standpoint of women would, Okin thinks, lead to a variety of changes in Rawls's theory. For example the primary goods might focus more on relationships, or on the importance of good early nurturing for a healthy sense of self-esteem.[6] Ultimately, though, she concludes that Rawls's theory of justice is only of mixed value from a feminist viewpoint. For one thing, he continues to cling to the private/public dichotomy and to regard the family as a private and nonpolitical association.

In the last chapter of *Justice, Gender and the Family,* she again employs the original position and the veil of ignorance to argue that the goals and policies she recommends would be acceptable to the contractors under a veil of ignorance about their sex *and* about whether they are feminist or traditionalist in their beliefs about gender and family structure.

She begins by ruling out certain extreme traditionalist positions:

> since they violate such fundamentals as basic liberty and self respect. We need not and should not admit for consideration views based on the notion that women are inherently inferior beings whose function is to fulfill the needs of men. Such a view is no more admissible in the construction of just institutions for a modern pluralist society than is the view, however deeply held, that some are naturally slaves and others naturally and justifiably their masters. We need not, therefore consider approaches to marriage that view it as an inherently and desirably hierarchical structure of dominance and subordination (JGF 174–75).

Building on her earlier argument, then, she says that the contractors would agree on a model of family that would minimize gender. But since they are not sure whether they might turn out to be believers in more traditional patterns of family life, they would want to adopt policies with built-in protections for those who wish to follow gender-structured modes of life.

She therefore suggests a variety of policies devised to discourage the gender-structured family (and indeed all customary gender role differences), but stops short of actually forbidding the traditional division of labor within the family. For example, she proposes that if a couple elects to have a traditional (gender-structured) family, then the wage earning spouse's paycheck will be cut in half, and half of it paid to the stay-at-home spouse.[7]

Critique of Okin's Feminist Appropriation of Rawls

Okin realizes she is parting ways with Rawls by applying the principles of political justice to intrafamilial relationships, insisting, as many feminists have, that "the personal is the political" and that what happens in the private sphere is of enormous importance for the position of women in the economic and political spheres. Assuming, then, as she does, that "justice" is a property that can be univocally applied to political institutions *and* the family, would the contractors choose what she says they would? There are some very serious difficulties with Okin's attempted appropriation of the original position that lie quite close to the surface.

First, she completely omits the interests of children, except occasionally as a sort of makeweight. Rawls does not include them either, of course, but that is because he thinks of the "head of household" as in fact representing the interests of all members of the household and not just his own. But since Okin is treating family members as individuals, the interests of children should be directly represented, instead of just being included along with their mothers when she worries about the poverty of female-headed families (consider, for example, their interest in having their fathers present in the home).

Second, the general knowledge about society that she allows the contractors to have includes the fact that women are generally less advantaged, but she omits various other facts that, if included, would lead to quite different results. Consider, for example, the fact that primary care of small children is a task that women will, in fact, tend to gravitate to far more often than men will, and that therefore most couples, given a genuine choice, will choose to arrange their domestic life in accord with the traditional pattern. This problem is not one specific to Okin but rather a general problem with using the veil of ignorance. The procedure resembles that of the magician who produces rabbits from a hat: he finds only the rabbits previously hidden there.

Her use of the original position is further vitiated by the fact that after assuming, as Rawls does, that it is possible to reason about justice under a veil of ignorance about one's own sex, she then undercuts this assumption by suggesting that women and men will reason about justice in such deeply different ways that they would be unable to attain unanimous agreement about the principles of justice. Such agreement would be possible only if they had identical psychological and moral development, and this in turn could occur only if the contractors had grown up in a genderless society. But if she is right that our sex is something we cannot shed under a veil of ignorance, then no conclusions at all can be derived about social institutions under a veil of ignorance about one's sex. We are simply at an impasse.[8]

Another problem with her attempt to justify her policies on Rawlsian principles is that her claim in the last chapter that her goals and policies would be acceptable to the contractors under a veil of ignorance *both* about their sex and about their own views on gender relations (i.e., whether they are feminists or believers in the traditional family) is argued for in a way that is internally inconsistent and that shows a serious misunderstanding of the whole point of the veil of ignorance. To make the second point first, the veil of ignorance is used to derive the principles of justice and to reason about basic institutions. It is not used to reflect on which policies would be most expedient to adopt as means to achieve our goals.

The inconsistencies are of two sorts. First, she says the contractors can suppose themselves ignorant of their own views about what the proper structure of the family should be, but yet agree to policies designed to move us in the direction of eliminating the "gender-structured" family. This makes no sense. Second, if we can suppose that the traditional family is something that we might be committed to once the veil of ignorance is lifted, then in some minimal sense at least, the traditional family must be just.[9]

Okin has not even succeeded in showing that Rawls's principles require us to rule out strong forms of the traditional family in which the father is accorded special authority as head of the family. Not all hierarchy or authority necessarily involves the sort of exploitation and dominance she seems to assume it does, and in any case, Rawls's theory clearly does allow for even significant inequalities provided they are to the benefit of the worst off. One could argue, for example, that a certain amount of hierarchy and division of labor makes for greater efficiency and stability and that all members of the family benefit from this. Okin realizes this, for she says that even if gender roles passed the first of Rawls's criteria (being to the advantage of the worst off) they would be rejected because Rawls says that offices and positions that carry with them significant political or economic benefits must be open to all under conditions of fair equality of opportunity. She says that any "roles or positions analogous to our current sex roles—including those of husband and wife, mother and father" could not pass this second test, and that they would therefore be rejected under a veil of ignorance about one's sex. In fact she says that gender itself, "with its ascriptive designation of positions and expectations of behavior in accordance with the inborn characteristic of sex," would be rejected as unjust (JGF 103).

In stipulating that inequalities be both to the greatest benefit of the least advantaged and "attached to offices and positions open to all," Rawls was clearly thinking about positions of power and authority in business or politics. It makes very little sense to apply Rawls's principles to roles like "mother" and "father" or "husband" or "wife," or worse yet to the whole gender system itself. Terms like "father" and "mother" are conceptually tied to biological sex. While women can perform many of the tasks traditionally performed by fathers, this does not make them "fathers." One may jokingly call a man who regularly performs most of the childcare duties in a family "Mr. Mom," but this does not *make* him a mother.

Finally, her argument that children can grow up to be citizens with a healthy sense of justice only if their families teach them about justice by precept and example has a certain merit. But to argue that this requires us to eliminate sex role differentiation between the parents begs all the important questions.

II. RECENT DEVELOPMENTS IN OKIN'S THOUGHT

Okin's most recent word on gender and family issues is in *Is Multiculturalism Bad for Women?*[10] One issue that comes to center stage in this volume is the freedom of traditional religious groups to educate their children in their own tradition. Making decisions about the education of children has always been the Achilles' heel of liberals of all stripes. Children are not yet autonomous, and it is impossible for parents to avoid shaping them in one way or another. The problem is particularly difficult for Rawlsian liberals, since the contractors could not reason about how children should be raised under a veil of ignorance about their own most deeply held beliefs. Persons ignorant of their own view of the good life could have no basis for deciding between alternative family structures, since family structures have an important role in shaping what the next generation of human beings will be like. Teaching children to place the highest possible value on autonomy and tolerance of alternative ways of life shapes them just as much as teaching them that fidelity to one's own commitments and/or to the moral teachings of their own religious tradition are of highest importance. Ultimately Okin's position is one that would justify almost limitless governmental interference in the internal workings of families and religious communities in order to safeguard the autonomy of the children being educated in them.

Okin comes down strongly against group rights, noting that a very high proportion of the cultural practices seeking to be respected are ones involving male-female relationships, sex and family; and that these all involve male control of women's sexuality. She begins with horrifying cases of crimes committed against immigrant women or children in the United States or in European countries, in which the perpetrator tried to excuse himself or herself by pleading that these practices were part of his or her culture. Having gained a rhetorical advantage by getting the reader incensed over clitorectomy on infants, polygamy, or forced child marriages, she includes in her condemnation practices that are apparently benign. Veiling of women may or may not be a good thing, but it is not on a level with clitorectomy. She seems to regard it as an indication of their "sexual servitude" that women are valued highly for their virginity before marriage and fidelity within it (*Multiculturalism* 19) (although to be fair, the view she is criticizing is that these are women's "pre-eminent virtues"). She would not grant group rights to any group that "discriminates among [its members] on grounds of sex, race, or sexual preference." Limiting the priesthood to men and teaching children that homosexuality is a practice forbidden by God in the Bible would be very likely to put a group beyond the range of tolerance for her. She wants to address "very private and culturally reinforced kinds of discrimination" and interprets this very widely to prohibit virtually any differing roles for men and women at all. When considering according group rights to a group, she is prepared to dismiss the preferences of older women in that group on the grounds that they are "often co-opted into reinforcing gender inequality" (*Multiculturalism* 24).

In response, Azizah Y. al-Hibri, a Muslim woman who used to be a member of the Society of Women in Philosophy, criticizes Okin for her high-handed tone (she accuses her of being "patriarchal") and for falling under her own definition of fundamentalism (i.e., for thinking that "the best community is one in which all but their preferred . . . [gender] practices are outlawed" (45 in Okin essay, quoted from Kymlicka). There are also essays by Jews responding to Okin's critique of their religion, but the volume is notable for the absence of any self-professed Christian respondents, even though Christianity is certainly one of her main targets.

Martha Nussbaum (not usually considered a friend of traditional religion), comes to the defense of the positive role that religion plays in people's lives and argues that preserving religious freedom should be a high priority for liberals. Nussbaum says:

> Okin evinces contempt for religion in the very manner in which she discusses it offhandedly, via articles in the *New York Times* (hardly a source she would regard as decisive if she were investigating women's dignity!)[11] and via popular accounts of "founding myths" that religious people will surely find disrespectful in their casualness.[12]

Nussbaum distinguishes between what she calls "comprehensive liberalism" (roughly what I call "hegemonic" liberalism)[13] and "political liberalism," suggesting the Okin espouses the former, and aligning herself with the latter. Political liberals acknowledge that religious conceptions of the good are "prominent among those reasonable conceptions that citizens may legitimately pursue." (Nussbaum 107) It is hard, she notes, to see how we can "respect the bearers of such [religious] convictions and yet not respect the choices that they make to lead traditional religious lives" (Nussbaum 108).

In her reply, Okin makes some attempts to backpedal, but sticks to her guns about the oppressive and patriarchal nature of the major Western religions. Her dismissive attitude toward female adherents of traditional religions becomes, if anything, more marked. She simply cannot or will not acknowledge that many things self-evident to her would be regarded by women from other cultures (or even by some women in our own) as every bit as crazy and incomprehensible as their practices appear to her.

On the question of whether she is a comprehensive liberal or a political liberal, Okin claims she is in between, and no doubt the issues are complicated (far more complicated than her cursory discussion acknowledges), but the sort of religious education that she is willing to admit would clearly fall short of what even many relatively moderate believers would want for their children. She expresses concern that people are free to send their children to private school that teach one religion as the only truth, or to home-school them in such beliefs. Although adults may be allowed to choose a certain degree of nonautonomy, this should not be thrust on children by parents or peers "through indoctrination—including sexist socialization—and lack of exposure to alternatives" (*Multiculturalism* 129–30). Thus religious education may not be confined to any single religion, and must not be sex discriminatory in any way.

In short, she is so convinced of the value of autonomy that she is prepared to restrain parents from seriously raising their children to believe that their own religion is true. Her willingness to forbid sexist socialization would most likely lead her to not permit members of a traditional culture to raise their children with any sort of differing sex roles, or to engage in religious practices (such as separate sections for women in Orthodox Jewish synagogues) that Okin would regard as sexist.

Her 1997 essay in a volume edited by Nussbaum and David Eastlund[14] sheds some light on just what Okin's ideal, nonsexist society would look like.

> The gender-free society . . . would result from the diminution and eventual disappearance of sex roles, of expectations that persons of different sexes think, act, dress, and adorn themselves, feel or react in ways supposedly representative of or proper to their sex. In such a society, no assumptions would be made about "male" and "female" roles, and men and women would participate in more or less equal numbers in every sphere of life, from infant care to different kinds of paid work to high-level politics. . . . [The society] that I envision would not be boring; rather it would be filled with diversity. Its people would vary in innumerable respects, including those we now associate with masculinity and femininity. The difference between it and our present society is that the different personal characteristics, appearances, capacities would not be distributed—or be expected to be distributed—along the lines of sex.

In a gender-free society, homosexuality would not be stigmatized as it is now. She says:

> If a person's sex were of almost no social or legal significance, then the sex of whomever a person was sexually attracted to would be ipso facto, similarly lacking in social salience. If a person's sex were of greatly diminished social and

legal significance, then it would also be seen as of little matter whether a child who had two parents had two parents of the same sex or different sexes.[15]

This is a far cry from her approval of Chowdorow's theory about the importance of children receiving their early nurturing equally from males and females (JGF 107), and a large step in the direction of one particular version of feminism, sometimes (rather pejoratively) referred to as "gender blending."[16]

In Okin's case the root motivation for eliminating gender seems to be a notion of autonomy that allows everyone to choose who he or she will be with no influence from either biology or culture.[17] The limits upon one's autonomy that stem from a religious understanding of the world and our place in it are particularly offensive to her. The major monotheistic religions, for example, all believe in a God who stands in judgment of us—who enjoins certain behaviors and forbids others—and that therefore *we* are not sole arbiters of what is good and evil. Even apart from religion, our freedom is already limited by numerous factors beyond our control, including our parents and being born in a male body or in a female body, but those feminists who advocate the abolition of gender can at least try to minimize the constraints that such differences impose on people. If, however, there is a God who created people male and female or who enjoins different ritual duties for women and men, then this would pose a serious obstacle to those whose goal is to eliminate gender as a socially important category.

Rather ironically, then, Okin is prepared, in the name of autonomy, to prevent other people from carrying out what they regard as their most important parental obligations, if the traditional practices they value are ones that she regards as "sexist." But not allowing other women to pass on cultural and religious practices that *she* regards as sexist is, among other things, an attempt by Okin and other elite women to control less powerful women who prefer traditional patterns, many (but by no means all) of whom are less educated, articulate, and well-placed to make their views heard in the public arena. Such women might well perceive Okin's policies as designed to liberate women from male control in order to subject them to control by feminists who claim to know what is best for them better than they do.

III. CRITIQUE AND CONCLUSION

Okin's primary allegiance is to feminism, and she takes her ideal of the genderless society from feminist theorists. As a result, she takes certain assumptions for granted that need to be examined if she is to make her views plausible to those outside the feminist camp. One of these is the analogy between sex and race.

Feminism in the United States arose out of the civil rights movement,[18] whose goal was a society in which one's skin color was of no social importance. This is sometimes called a "color-blind" society. The term "sexism" was chosen by feminists in order to emphasize the similarity between sexual and racial discrimination, and the corresponding ideal in the case of women, then, is a society in which one's sex is of no more importance socially than the color of one's eyes is in ours. But while a color-blind society is both thinkable and desirable as a social goal, a sex-blind society is arguably neither.

A related assumption is that proportional representation of various groups in all the professions is a requirement of justice. As the black civil rights movement began to move more in the direction of demanding proportional representation rather than just nondiscrimination, feminists also began to call for proportional representation of women at all levels in all the various professions, and Okin takes it as axiomatic that this is a goal we should aim at. Serious objections can be raised against pursuing proportional representation in the more plausible cases of race or ethnic origin. But in the case of women, there is even less justification for pursuing this as an ideal.[19] Women's own choices about balancing family and career are bound to affect the statistics, and one ought to respect people's preferences absent some really overriding matter of grave danger to the common good. Besides, the widely cherished hope that by achieving proportional representation in politics women will have more say about policies directly affecting them is based on the erroneous assumption that women are in agreement about such issues. In fact, women disagree every bit as much as men over virtually all the controversial issues. There simply *is* no such thing as "the woman's perspective" to represent.

Although Okin has been influenced by liberal feminism, she is closer to the radical feminists than is sometimes acknowledged. Liberal feminism focused on obtaining fairness for women, and therefore had a wide appeal to men as well as women. Radical feminists, however, think in terms of power rather than fairness, and see their main task to be exposed the ways in which domination of women by men has pervaded all cultures and to try to empower women. Thus, Okin analyzes every culture, institution, or religion solely in terms of the way it distributes power, which distorts her understanding of both culture and religion. Moreover, she has a very narrow and inadequate understanding of what power is, focusing only on political power, especially that conferred by money, political office, wearing a badge, or carrying a gun.[20] The power mothers have to shape the next generation of human beings, for example, does not count. If power involves being able to get what you want, many people who appear to be in a subordinate role may turn out upon careful examination to have the upper hand in a relationship.

Okin's relationship to Rawlsian liberalism is a complicated one. I have argued above that she has failed to demonstrate that his principles of justice mandate the abolition of gender. Yet her thinking has been deeply influenced by Rawlsian liberalism, and, to the extent that the assumptions she takes over from Rawls are themselves problematic, this vitiates her own theory.

The first such assumption is an atomistic conception of social life, and a picture of society as like a race. Thinking about social justice in terms of distributive justice directs our attention to things that can be distributed among and possessed by individuals, and the basic goods recognized by Rawls's theory include wealth and income but not friendship. Not only are citizens thought of as disconnected atoms but they are also thought of as competing against each other in a race to attain positions of wealth and power. Both of these features of Rawls's theory are open to serious criticism, and they have been ably criticized by communitarians of various stripes.[21] Women have characteristically tended to find fulfillment more within the communal realm of family and neighborhood than in business or politics. Hence, many women would oppose an invasion of the private and communal sphere by political principles of justice that would bring the sort of anomic social atomism that prevails in the business world into the heart of the family.[22]

Rawlsian liberals (and Okin along with them) have generally been blind to the distinctive types of virtues obtainable within families. While emphasizing justice and autonomy, they tend to neglect virtues such as loyalty, gratefulness, respect for people that is not contingent upon their ability to perform particular functions efficiently, cooperation for shared ends instead of competition, concern for the needs of particular others and willingness to make sacrifices for them when necessary, and faithfulness to one's commitments — virtues people learn primarily from their families.

Another problem that arises for her theory as a result of assumptions she takes over from Rawlsian liberals concerns the notion of self-respect. Rawls had originally spoken about fair distribution of "self-respect" (tending to conflate it with self-esteem). But when it was pointed out to him that this was not the sort of thing that could be distributed, he retreated to speaking of "the social bases of self-respect." In practice, these tended to get collapsed into more measurable things like wealth or income. Okin goes along with this narrow materialistic reading of self-respect. The key component of self-esteem for her seems to be having your own paycheck (and the larger the better). But the range of things people can base their self-respect or self-esteem on is extremely broad, and not having her own paycheck need not condemn a woman to a lack of self-esteem. To suppose that it would is to succumb to the most crude sort of capitalist ideology by conflating everyone's worth with his or her price.

Although I have been quite critical of Okin in this chapter, I believe that her work may have a certain salutary effect. Although she ultimately goes too far in the direction of hegemonic liberalism, she does pose a challenge to liberals that should not be ignored. The private realm and the public realm cannot be hermetically sealed off from each other. What happens in the public realm affects the private realm (affirmative action for women, for example, affects family structures) and what happens in the private realm affects the public realm (if women perform most of the homemaking and childcare duties in addition to their paid work in the labor force, this will make it harder for them to devote time to their careers). So far what has occurred has been a series of ad hoc accommodations: clitorectomy on infants cannot be tolerated, while evangelical Christians who accord fathers special authority in familial decision making are accepted (so long as none of their decisions will produce permanent physical injury to their children).

Real thought, then, needs to be given to articulating some principles for determining the limits to toleration of various types of family structures. Christina Sommers's groundbreaking essay "Filial Morality"[23] made a serious attempt at an answer, but she unfortunately has not developed her line of thought further, and more work needs to be done defending the theory and responding to objections.

Finally, reflection on the family cannot be separated from a discussion of the appropriate shape of other institutions, such as the polity and the workplace. In an early work, Okin acknowledged this point, writing that

> If, as seems likely, the assumed love and altruism of the family, founded as it is on the radical inequality of women, has served to soften the full impact of a world of self-interested individuals, maybe one of the results of treating women as beings with their own personalities and interests will be to expose the full implications of a theory in which self-interest is assumed to be the norm for political and economic life. Without the total selflessness that was supposed to exist within families, the total self-interestedness that liberalism assumes exists outside of them may seem to be more in need of reconsideration.[24]

Unfortunately, rather than pursuing this insight, Okin has chosen to import "liberal" conceptions of the primacy of self-interest into the family, and to attempt to remove, by coercion if necessary, whatever obstacles religion or traditional culture may put in the way of this transformation.

NOTES

1. Susan Moller Okin, *Justice, Gender and the Family* (New York: Basic Books, 1989) [cited in the text hereinafter as JGF].

2. John Rawls, *A Theory of Justice* (Cambridge, Mass.: Harvard University Press, 1971) [cited in the text hereinafter as TJ].

3. For a discussion of this issue, see Okin's 1989 article, "Reason and Feeling in Thinking about Justice," *Ethics,* January 1989, 229–49.

4. He does attempt to respond to feminist critics in "The Idea of Public Reason Revisited," *University of Chicago Law Review* 64 (1997): 765–807, but fails to clarify what sort of standards of justice might be relevant to intrafamily relationships or to really grapple with the arguments made by Okin and others. For further discussion of this article, see my article, "Rawlsian and Feminist Critiques of the Traditional Family," in *The Family, Civil Society and the State*, ed. Christopher Wolfe (Lanham, Md.: Rowman & Littlefield, 1998).

5. These differences are the sort of thing Carol Gilligan built on in her seminal book on moral development, *In a Different Voice* (Cambridge, Mass.: Harvard University Press, 1982).

6. Janna Thompson, in her very interesting article "What Do Women Want? Rewriting the Social Contract," *International Journal of Moral and Social Studies* 8, no. 3 (autumn 1993), tries seriously to think through what the social contract might look like if all the original contractors were female and reasoned about social structures in terms of the sort of "feminine voice" virtues lauded by Gilligan.

7. For an extended discussion and critique of her policy recommendations, see my article, "Rawlsian and Feminist Critiques of the Traditional Family," in *The Family, Civil Society and the State* (above, n. 4).

8. Scott Sehon, in "Okin on Feminism and Rawls," *The Philosophical Forum* 27, no. 4 (summer 1996): 321–32, exposes clearly some of Okin's deep confusions about the issue of whether or not it is possible to reason about justice under a veil of ignorance about one's sex, and argues that much of her argument makes no sense within the framework of Rawls's theory. Also of interest on this point is J. S. Russell's article "Okin's Rawlsian Feminism?" *Social Theory and Practice* 21, no. 3 (fall 1995): 397–426.

9. I am partly indebted on this point to J. S. Russell (above, n. 8), 405.

10. Joshua Cohen, Matthew Howard, and Martha C. Nussbaum, eds. *Is Multiculturalism Bad for Women?: Susan Moller Okin with Respondents* (Princeton, N.J.: Princeton University Press, 1999).

11. A reference to the fact that Okin condemns John Paul II's recent apostolic letter entitled "On the Dignity of Women" on the basis of a two-page article in the *New York Times* (taking violent exception to the suggestion that they have a special capacity to care for others, and that they ought to be either celibate or mothers).

12. Martha Nussbaum, "A Plea for Difficulty," in *Is Multiculturalism Bad for Women?*

13. Nussbaum's definition of "comprehensive liberalism" is that it is a vision in which "liberal values of autonomy and dignity pervade the fabric of the body politic, determining not only the core of the political conception but many noncore social and political matters as well."

14. Okin, "Sexual Orientation and Gender: Dichotomizing Differences," in *Sex, Preference, and Family,* ed. David Estlund and Martha Nussbaum (New York: Oxford University Press, 1997).

15. Okin, "Sexual Orientation and Gender," 45–46.

16. Okin could avoid this problem by recognizing the present importance of being raised by parents of both sexes, while arguing that eventually the gender of one's parents will cease to be important (like all other gender differences). But she owes us some argument that such a result is likely or even possible.

17. In this regard her ideal is very much like what Richard Wasserstrom, in *Philosophy and Social Issues* (South Bend, Ind.: University of Notre Dame Press, 1980), calls a society that is assimilationist in regard to sex.

18. This accounts for the fact that feminism in this country has taken a very different form from feminism in Europe. For a contrast between American and European feminism, see Sylvia Ann Hewlett's book *A Lesser Life: The Myth of Women's Liberation in America* (New York: W. Morrow, 1986).

19. See, on this point, Wolf-Devine, "Proportional Representation of Women and Minorities," in *Affirmative Action and the University,* ed. Steven Cahn (Philadelphia: Temple University Press, 1993), and *Diversity and Community in the Academy: Affirmative Action in Faculty Appointments* (Lanham, Md.: Rowman & Littlefield, 1997), 18–20, 129–35, 160–62.

20. Jean Bethke Elshtain's book *Power Trips and Other Journeys: Essays in Feminism as Civic Discourse* (Madison: University of Wisconsin Press, 1990) provides an astute analysis of this sort of distorted notion of power, particularly in the chapter entitled "The Power and Powerlessness of Women."

21. See, for example, the writings of Alasdair MacIntyre, Mary Ann Glendon, Charles Taylor, and Michael Sandel. See, also, my *Diversity and Community* (above, n. 19), 166–72.

22. Jean Bethke Elshtain has made this sort of point in "Feminists against the Family," *The Nation* 229 (1979). Reprinted in *Sex and Gender: A Spectrum of Views,* ed. Philip Devine and Celia Wolf-Devine (Belmont, Calif.: Wadsworth, 2002).

23. Christina Hoff Sommers, "Filial Morality," *Journal of Philosophy* 83, no. 8 (1986): 439–56.

24. Okin, *Women in Western Political Thought* (Princeton, N.J.: Princeton University Press, 1979), 286–87.

4

Robert Nozick and the Foundations of Political Individualism

R. George Wright

Robert Nozick's *Anarchy, State, and Utopia,*[1] published in 1974, stands as the most philosophically sophisticated defense in many years of the minimal or "night watchman" state. Reaction to many of the book's most important substantive theses, however, has deservedly been generally critical.[2] Nozick himself eventually retreated from some of the book's principal conclusions (as I shall describe briefly below).

There remain, however, two reasons to take Nozick's early, and still much better known, views seriously. First, is the profit to be derived from engaging with Nozick's formidable intellectual and forensic abilities. Second, and not unrelatedly, certain deficiencies in Nozick's early work exemplify clearly, in hypertrophied form, maladies that afflict a broad range of contemporary political thought.

In particular, it is vitally important to notice what *Anarchy, State, and Utopia* takes largely for granted, or at least does not, for whatever reason, attempt to justify at any length. Nozick begins with the controversial premise that individuals have a generally, if not absolutely,[3] inviolable moral right to be free, in their person and property, from theft, force, fraud, and, on some understandings of the term, from coercion,[4] and that individuals have no other general moral rights.

From this and other premises, Nozick infers the initial legitimacy of an individualistic, reasonably benign anarchistic society that is legitimately superseded by a minimal state, as a perhaps unintended result of a series of morally unobjectionable transition stages.[5] It is this argument that is philosophically ambitious.

Nozick then goes on to conclude that no state more elaborate, redistributionist, paternalistic, or welfare-oriented than the minimal state can be justified. This conclusion is of far greater practical import than any derivation of the minimal state. But Nozick's argument against a more-than-minimal state is quite limited. Nozick's rejection of any greater-than-minimal state proceeds largely through the uninteresting deployment of his controversial individual rights premise formulated above. From that premise, there are only modest obstacles to Nozick's inference that, complications aside, no one may be deprived of any legitimately and harmlessly acquired property through fraud or force, including governmental force or taxation. This result obtains despite any competing moral claims of need, desert, equality, merit, virtue, utility, happiness, perfectionism, community or solidarity, or social progress. Each of the latter considerations is trumped by strong rights claims.

Nozick's crucial conclusion, then, largely follows uninterestingly from his starting point. This state of affairs dramatically emphasizes the importance of Nozick's premises, and in particular his controversial understanding of the existence, nature, and scope of moral rights. Of course, Nozick must start somewhere, or accept some most general moral belief.[6] It would be unfair for any critic to press Nozick's argument back beyond a certain point. But the degree of explanation, elaboration, or accounting for a basic premise—presumably, strict argument for a basic premise would be self-contradictory—should be proportionate to the controversiality of that basic premise, or of the conclusion derived therefrom, as well as to the "sensitivity" of the conclusion; that is, the likelihood that the conclusion will be altered significantly if the basic premise is even slightly modified.

At this crucial point, Nozick essentially admits that he presents no elaborated accounting for his view of individual moral rights.[7] In large measure, the reader is left to assess Nozick's premises based on the degree of attractiveness of the conclusions to which the premises lead. To many, Nozick's conclusions are unattractive indeed, as they conjure up the London of Charles Dickens or the Manchester of Karl Marx and Friedrich Engels.

Nozick argues, however, that the minimal state is not merely coldly just, but genuinely inspiring[8] (ASU 310). At least in principle, Nozick argues, the minimal state allows for great diversity of practice and ethos among the many potentially viable voluntary associations constituting that society. Each group may, for itself, choose to live by stringently egalitarian, perfectionist, hedonistic, antimaterialist, aesthetic, bucolic, profoundly religious, ascetic, or intensely competitive lifestyles. Although no such lifestyle can be guaranteed to be practically available, this may be the price paid for the society's inherent dynamism. Of course, some sorts of universally applicable rules about the common inculcation of the basic structural libertarian principles governing the overall society would have to be worked out, along with rules governing exit from viable or defunct communities. Some sorts of communities, presumably including groups practicing massive wealth redistribution internally, or highly traditionalist groups, may not be viable beyond a certain scale unless exit is restricted or membership compulsory.

It is important to note that Nozick's view of the inspiring society—let a hundred flowers bloom or wilt—is hardly idiosyncratic or distinctively right-wing. Readers who are familiar, for example, with the work of Bruce Ackerman will detect in Nozick and Ackerman a common general, if not exceptionless, official indifference to personal conceptions of the nature of the good, or of the good life. More generally, there are important dimensions, such as the coherence and desirability of a more or less thorough public neutrality toward private conceptions of the good life, along which writers such as Ackerman, Charles Larmore, and many others are closer to Nozick than to, say, William Galston or Stephen Macedo.[9] Again, however, anyone seeking a deep justification of public indifference to private conceptions of the good must look elsewhere than to Nozick's book.

As we have seen, Nozick can enhance the attractiveness of his basic premises by arguing that those premises lead to inspiring conclusions. It is also possible for Nozick to seek to strengthen the appeal of his premises by arguing, for example, that those premises take rights seriously, or that they enhance liberty or autonomy, or even that they bespeak a Kantian respect for persons.

It is Nozick's view, for example, that at least short of a moral catastrophe,[10] rights must not be violated for the sake of some desired goal, such as happiness, and that they must not be violated even to maximize overall respect for rights in that society. We must not only not sacrifice a person's rights for the sake of a great utility windfall, we must not violate a right even to prevent a tyrant's violating the most basic rights of many other people. Again, however, whether we find this view attractive or not, it is hardly unique to Nozick or his ideological confreres. The rejection of an overall maximization of respect for rights is held as well by some, across the political spectrum, who hold little else in common with Nozick.[11]

It might be argued, however, that although Nozick does not establish the pursuit of liberty, autonomy, or Kantian respect as explicit aims or premises, his premises incidentally generate principles or rules uniquely promotive of these laudable notions. Perhaps the central difficulty with this argument is that the concepts of liberty, autonomy, and Kantian respect are by now intractably ambiguous and equivocal, if not essentially contested. Let us grant for the moment that there is some sense of these terms in which the minimal state optimally promotes liberty, autonomy, and Kantian respect. It remains the case, however, that there are well-pedigreed, authentic, no less important senses of these same terms in which the minimal state leaves much to be desired.

Liberty, for example, notoriously may mean the "negative" liberty, or absence of social restraint, emphasized by Thomas Hobbes, John Locke, and John Stuart Mill, as well as the "positive" liberty, or rational moral development, emphasized by Jean-Jacques Rousseau, Immanuel Kant, and Georg Wilhelm Friedrich Hegel.[12] Nozick is presumably less interested in the latter understanding of liberty than in the former. But it is impossible to account Nozick a champion of liberty *simpliciter.*

More crucially, it has not been universally conceded that Nozick is an unequivocal champion of liberty even in its negative sense. One who, through the workings of inheritance laws, discrimination, the absence of public schooling, and the absence of a redistributive "safety net," is free to sleep under the bridges may be said not only to lack equality or high-valued liberty but to simply have less liberty in the negative sense of the absence of societal constriction of the range of his or her practical choices.[13] Whether this diminution of the negative liberty of the poor, or of those subject to invidious discrimination by the majority, can somehow be morally justified, perhaps as the necessary price for the liberty of the majority, is a separate issue. But in the meantime, we cannot simply assume that one who sleeps under the bridges is acting on the basis of negative political freedom.

Nozick also argues that his premises, and the minimal state, are particularly faithful to our sense of the separateness of persons, of the dignity of the individual, and to the Kantian injunction to always treat persons not merely as means but also as ends in themselves.[14] Nozick effectively argues that our belief that we do not morally deserve the genetic equipment with which we are born does not, without more, imply that those with binocular vision must consider their second eye merely an element of a common resource pool of eyes to be available for mandatory reallocation to those less favored by nature.

But not all redistribution of wealth is brutally intrusive. A government might refuse to view each person as an island and insist upon a measure of wealth redistribution in appropriate cases, on the understanding that personal identity is socially constituted, that fellow citizens are inherently related, and in some sense, responsible to and for one another. Certainly not all redistributive schemes need be paternalistic or degrading. They may, in the best cases, rescue the beneficiary from degradation and afford the beneficiary the material resources and opportunities necessary to actively infuse her life with meaning, with no corresponding loss of meaning on the part of her involuntary benefactors.[15]

One must ask, ultimately, whether the typical market transaction, in which persons A and B exchange objects Y and Z because A values Z more than Y, and B values Y more than Z, tends to promote each person's concern for the other as a moral end, rather than as merely a means to enhanced welfare. More vividly, do market actors necessarily tend to treat one another as more than animated vending machines? Of course, the existence of a market does not preclude generosity, altruism, or self-sacrifice. But the rise of the market does not usher in the Kingdom of Ends. The interesting cultural question is whether markets can be sustained in practice over the long term unless most persons adopt moral codes more demanding than the mere avoidance of force, fraud, and breach of contract.

As well, some may, with Nozick, refuse to acknowledge an enforceable moral duty to perform virtually riskless, costless rescues of strangers. But it is hardly clear that this view, however central to Nozick's overall view, and however generally well entrenched in the law, unequivocally advances the idea of each person as possessed of a dignity beyond price, and as a moral end.[16]

Thus there is no reason to suppose that the attractiveness of the notions of liberty, autonomy, or Kantian respect uniquely point in the direction of Nozick's otherwise largely unargued for principles of individual rights, or that Nozick's view best balances these several values. We turn, then, to a brief sketch of Nozick's more richly developed argument for the morally legitimate derivation of the minimal state from an initial condition of more or less benign individualist anarchy.

THE MINIMAL STATE

Nozick's ingenious and richly detailed argument deriving a legitimate minimal state assumes a preexisting condition of free individuals who may be passionate, selfish, or not fully impartial in defending their interests, but who are generally rational and well meaning. They are assumed to be persons who seek to improve their lot without intending to act immorally.[17] In seeking individually and contractually to protect their welfare, they may collectively "back in" to the minimal state without so intending. Thus the social evolutionary process generating the minimal state is neither an instance of might making right nor of any sort of traditional Hobbesian or Lockean social contract.[18]

No brief sketch of Nozick's derivation of the minimal state can do justice to its subtlety. Nevertheless, it may be said that the theory in some sense begins with the idea of individual self-help remedies for violations of the basic moral rights elaborated by Nozick and discussed above. The disadvantages of a scheme of purely individual prosecution of rights violations by the aggrieved party seem obvious enough. A second stage in the evolutionary process involves the victim's obtaining the assistance of the victim's relatives, friends, of those who may be grateful to the victim for some favor, of the public-spirited, and of the merely opportunistic.

This stage, too, has its unnecessary individual and social costs, and at a third stage is supplemented by the development of voluntary contractual mutual protective associations. Such associations presumably would tend over time to reflect the advantages of specialization and the division of labor. The associations tend over time to rely less on in-kind contributions of assistance by subscribers and instead become more "commercial." All may be better off, for example, if the infirm contribute capital, rather than physical protection in kind. Commercial protection agencies also tend, at least among their own actual and potential clients, to be more dispassionate and disinterested than the immediate parties to any conflict. This tendency is assumed to reflect basic principles of human psychology.

A fourth stage involves the tendency of competing mutual protective associations to merge, or at least loosely federate or cooperate. This tendency reflects obvious economies of scale, and perhaps a tendency in this particular kind of market toward natural monopoly. All else equal, we tend to prefer to be protected by an entity with greater, rather than lesser, resources at its command. Clearly, important gains are to be had from resolving conflicts between competing protective associations by contract or arbitration, rather than by battle.

At this point, we may assume that there are several independent persons who have not joined the dominant protective association, or the dominant federation of protective associations. An independent is any person who seeks to retain the unconstrained right to mete out just punishment for violations of her substantive moral rights. But, crucially, the dominant protective agency may compare its own generally dispassionate approach to justice with the presumably greater unpredictability, bias, potential selfishness, or emotionalism of those who wish to enforce their rights unilaterally, and deem the latter prospect to constitute an unnecessary and excessive risk of injustice for its own clients. To preclude this unnecessary risk of biased enforcement of rights claims against its clients, the dominant protective agency is led by market forces, client wishes, or a sense of obligation and fairness, to limit or control, if not prohibit, the exercise of private violence by independents against its clients.

Nozick argues that although the dominant protective agency is entitled to so act to protect its clients against an unnecessarily large risk of unjust treatment, it nevertheless owes compensation in some form to those former independents whose right of unilateral enforcement of their substantive moral rights has now been practically limited. Nozick concludes that the most natural, low-cost means of compensating former independents would be for the dominant protective association to offer former independents subsidized protection against violations of their own substantive rights, or at least as against those violations committed by the dominant protective association's own clients. Such a subsidy is thus merely compensatory, by analogy to the just compensation paid by the government in cases of eminent domain or condemnation of property for public use, rather than truly redistributive.

At this point, we thus have a dominant protective association asserting, as against all persons within its territorial domain, a right to limit or control their use of violence, and assuming with respect to each person some obligation of protection. For most practical purposes, this set of circumstances may be called the minimal or night watchman state.

Now, many readers will find individualistic state of nature theory to be incoherent or morally irrelevant. If we choose, however, to grant the meaningfulness of state of nature theory, and of Nozick's assumptions as to motivation and behavior in the state of nature, does Nozick's account work well on its own terms? Nozick's account does have a certain robustness.

Consider, for example, that the dominant protective agency provides a collective or public good, from the benefits of which it is not practical to exclude free riders. Any time the dominant protective agency incarcerates a dangerous person for attacking a client, nonclients are thereby inadvertently protected as well, whether they have paid for the protection or not. Protection is thus a positive externality. But we have seen that the dominant protective agency overcomes the free rider problem by claiming a monopoly on the right to set standards for the use of force, and compensating nonjoiners in kind.

It also might be supposed that, at an earlier stage, some persons will join one of the rudimentary protective associations with the intention of calling upon the association's membership for help if attacked, but of abandoning the protective association if some other member of the association needs help first, at least where such help could only be provided at substantial risk.[19] This sort of behavior might destabilize the rudimentary protective associations before they could develop or implement a division of labor. But there are several reasons to conclude that this problem would be of limited import. Abandoning the rudimentary protective association would presumably run counter to whatever sense of fairness Nozick builds into persons in the state of nature, and may well, at this early stage, involve abandoning one's relatives and friends. Some costs are unavoidably associated with unfairly abandoning any organization, including effects on one's reputation for trustworthiness. As well, it is also possible that reneging on one's commitment to respond to aggression today may simply enhance the personal danger one faces from a strengthened aggressor tomorrow.

It might also be objected, though, that at a later stage in the process, a truly dominant protective agency might take advantage of its natural monopoly by unjustly exploiting its own clients. But, again, whatever sense of fairness Nozick builds into the relevant actors will inhibit this inclination. It is also useful to recall that the dominant protective association might well consist of only a loose confederation of a variety of groups with diverse histories, membership characteristics, sizes, interests, and priorities. There may be too much room for internal fracturing, dissent, and exit for an exploitive monopoly to be both widespread and stable over the long term. The less exploitive factions may be able to quickly recruit disgruntled clients of the more exploitive factions.

Thus on its own terms, there is a certain robustness to Nozick's argument. This does not mean, however, that Nozick's account of the rise of the minimal state is motivationally or morally unproblematic. For example, to be a minimal state, the dominant protective agency must in some sense be universal in its reach. But why is the dominant protective agency morally entitled to presume, apparently irrebutably, that an independent such as Mother Teresa poses a grave threat of irreparable or incompensable injury to its clients, in light of her presumed selfish bias and emotionalism in defending her rights, as to justify the agency in coercively limiting and controlling Mother Teresa in the defense of her rights? Must the dominant protective agency limit the enforcement rights of independents only on a costly, case-by-case basis?

Nor is it entirely clear, despite Nozick's recognition of the issue, why an independent is owed any compensation for the limitation of her defense rights. After all, what the dominant protective agency is depriving her of, presumably, is merely the opportunity to abuse the right of punishment irresponsibly, and not the right of fully legitimate punishment or self-defense itself. Note that in law, the government offers compensation in eminent domain cases, but not when it abates risks akin to a public nuisance.

On the other hand, if compensation of independents is both required and sufficient to justify the restrictions imposed on independents, why is compensation in the precise form of subsidized protection morally adequate? Of course, unless the dominant protective association offers universal protection, it may not technically rise to the level of a minimal state. But this does not establish that offers of subsidized protection are fair compensation for the restrictions imposed by the dominant protective agency upon independents. Apart from Mother Teresa, many independents choose to be independents, presumably because they highly value self-reliance, autonomy, and the opportunity to develop and exercise their powers of judgment. It is thus not obvious why a typical independent would see more value than disvalue in an offer of subsidized protection. A monumental problem of commensurability seems to lurk in an offer of protection to the independent-minded. How much subsidized protection, about which the independent is at best ambivalent, suffices to make up for losses of the autonomy and self-reliance that the independent may value most highly?[20]

Nozick's assumption that groups will be less biased or unfair in imposing punishments than the aggrieved individuals will doubtless generally be sound, but there may be interesting exceptions. It is possible that the majority influence on a dominant protective association may lead, for example, to a uniform, exceptionless association bias against racial minority defendants, or against those accused of aggression against racial majority group members, even in cases in which the actual individual victim of aggression is racially biased. In such cases, the accused would, all else being equal, be more likely to receive justice through more personal rights enforcement by the victim or those immediately controlled by her than at the hands of the dominant protective agency. Of course, Nozick may rule racial bias out of his scheme by assumption, but he does rely on the idea of different degrees of general bias or partiality.

Nozick is, finally, keenly aware that it is not clear precisely what his ingenious, detailed exposition of the transition from individualistic anarchy to the minimal state is supposed to accomplish. As Nozick recognizes, it is difficult to legitimize any actual minimal state, if that is Nozick's purpose, based on a succession of morally legitimate, but hypothetical, events. It hardly legitimizes the theft at gunpoint of a wallet which, under other circumstances, the victim might have freely given to the thief.[21]

LIMITS ON PROPERTY IN THE MINIMAL STATE

Nozick recognizes that even in a minimal state, there should be enforceable limits upon the acquisition and transfer of property beyond the mere prohibition of force and fraud. Building upon the work of John Locke, Nozick concludes that it may be unjust for anyone to seek to acquire an exclusive property right in such circumstances as to leave another person in a relevantly worse position than that other person was in before the property was claimed, or than that person would have occupied in some appropriately described state of nature. Nozick concludes from this rather hazy proviso that, for example, claiming and fencing off the sole source of water for hundreds of miles may be morally illegitimate. In contrast, winding up with the only source of water because of one's inventiveness or foresight in developing and preserving that source may vest one with enforceable property rights. Extracting whatever price one can for such water from the desperately thirsty may well amount to an enforceable transaction.

Another potential constraint on the use and transfer of property in the minimal state is, Nozick argues, the possibility of legitimate claims for rectification, or reparations, for injuries to oneself or one's ancestors in the form of dispossession, enslavement, or other historical exercise of force or fraud. It is hardly clear, for example, that some moral statute of limitations has expired regarding claims for compensation from the identifiable descendants of Native Americans or enslaved persons, or that any credit for public benefits supererogatorily conferred distinctively on such persons has wiped out all moral debts incurred. Nozick raises and discusses such matters in a nuanced way, but obviously he cannot treat all of the interesting issues raised in the available space.

A third possible constraint on the use and transfer of property in the minimal state might be thought to involve unintended aggregate effects of numerous uncoordinated individual decisions. Nozick in effect denies the legitimacy of any such constraint in his famous "Wilt Chamberlain" example, in which a famous basketball player is able, in by now strikingly outdated terms, to agree to a contract worth $250,000 per year, based essentially on the willingness of many spectators individually to pay to watch him play.[22]

The primary problem with this example is not its atypicality, or even its taking the justness of the preexisting distribution of wealth for granted. Instead, the Wilt Chamberlain example does not adequately refute the claim that our individual preferences concerning aggregate or macro-level effects of many individual choices, or patterns, may be as legitimate and as morally important as our preferences concerning our own individual contributions to an overall distribution of income and wealth. Let us consider another, equally benign example. I may choose to allocate all of my charitable contributions this year to a particularly worthy charity, such as the March of Dimes or Amnesty International. But I could quite consistently view it as a pragmatic, if not a moral, disaster if, unexpectedly, nearly everyone chose to follow my lead and contribute only to my own chosen charity. That I would be dismayed by this aggregate outcome hardly shows that my original choice was somehow morally defective. Similarly, I may be willing to pay a particular price to watch a basketball player, or compensate a corporate chief executive officer, while consistently believing that regardless of the player's popularity in the market, total overall payments to such persons should somehow be limited, or at least that their income should be taxed for redistributive purposes. Each individual patron may reason in parallel.

There is of course much more to say about Nozick's *Anarchy, State, and Utopia*. There is much that is provocative in the work. Perhaps the most serious criticism that can be leveled is that in building an exceedingly top-heavy structure of strong rights claims on extremely sketchily defended premises, Nozick mirrors and in some measure abets an unfortunate contemporary trend toward basing stringent, if selective, moral or political platforms on remarkably attenuated and ultimately inadequate normative or metaethical premises. This trend contributes to the sense that much contemporary moral debate has a vaguely emotivist, pathologically interminable character. If we cannot offer a sound, convincing account of why our society ought to adopt one set of principles rather than another, whether libertarian or not, we should not be surprised if society's adherence to any set of principles proves unstable.[23]

THE LATER NOZICK

Nozick recognized the absence of any sort of "foundational" argument for his theory of rights in a later work,[24] *Philosophical Explanations*, but he did not therein remedy the deficiency. In another book,[25] *The Examined Life: Philosophical Meditations* (New York: Touchstone: 1989), Nozick repudiated to an indeterminate extent the atomistic property rights-based libertarianism of *Anarchy, State, and Utopia*, countenancing a broader scope for legitimate governmental activity and commending in particular both symbolic and substantive governmental activity recognizing the central importance of human solidarity, of the inescapability of social relatedness, of the imperative of broadly nondiscriminatory behavior, and of the shifting mix or balance of a range of partially competing joint or common goals.[26]

Nozick recognized that this range of governmental action may involve the coercion or cooptation of some dissenting citizens. But he noted that an official expression of principle or of concern by a society, as an authoritative public act, transcends and cannot be engaged in or adequately substituted for by even a large and wealthy group of private individuals.[27] This is more a matter of the qualitatively different meaning of an official public act than of the relative efficacy of public versus private action.

Nozick in *Anarchy, State, and Utopia* might well have been inclined to deny government the authority to "speak" or act where it can do so only through coercing or misrepresenting the views of some of its citizens. But for the later Nozick, whatever our government does, or consciously or unconsciously fails to do, is a potential source of great pride or great shame for us all. Each of us tends, rightly and inevitably, to identify with our society, and we tend to identify, negatively or positively, with our collective, public acts, including our public silences. To ask substantial majorities to refrain from public expression of solidaristic values because such values, or particular conceptions of them, are not universally shared is, in Nozick's later view, to ask too much.

Rather than see our collective life reduced to vast, sporadically interrupted expanses of public silence, where such silences cannot really be neutral in their meaning and effect, including their effect on our self-conception or personal identity, Nozick later sought some mechanism, based in the tax system for allowing for, without encouraging, a range of genuinely conscientious opting out by persons who wish to dissociate themselves from any particular public "message."

Nozick's discussion was, at this point, suggestive rather than thorough. He did not, for example, address the obvious trade-off problem: the greater the scope of "opt out" rights actually exercised, the greater the demonstrated falsity of any government claim to speak in the name of the whole. I shall have no more to say about Nozick's later views in this chapter. Although they are no doubt substantively much more palatable to most of us, they are neither distinctive in themselves nor argued for strikingly or at any length. Ironically, it was only Nozick's prior, generally less attractive, views that were elaborated with energy, acuity, and imagination.

A NOTE ON THE "PHILOSOPHERS' BRIEF"

Interest in the substantial redistribution of wealth in favor of the poor has perhaps waned in the years since the publication of *Anarchy, State and Utopia*. In contrast, a sort of ultimately ungrounded, generally nonauthoritatively redistributive libertarianism informs the brief amicus curiae filed by Nozick along with several other leading philosophers in the assisted-suicide cases of *Washington v Glucksberg* and *Vacco v Quill*.[28]

The amicus brief does not really argue that government can and should be neutral as among all conceptions of the good life for competent adults, and in particular as to the various ways of bringing one's life to its conclusion. The brief, of course, need not aspire to philosophy, as distinct from cogent constitutional argument.

The real thrust of the amicus brief is instead that a competent choice of assisted suicide, at least under limited circumstances, is typically so intimate, personal, and basically self-defining as to deserve inclusion within the range of autonomy or liberty rights already recognized and protected by the court, generally under its substantive due process rubric. The constitutional right of autonomous life-shaping, at least in crucial respects and within appropriate limits, is contrasted, interestingly, not merely with government restriction motivated by religion but by any sort of potentially unshared, perhaps entirely secular moral goal or motivation as well.

Again, amici curiae briefs are intended to operate at the constitutional or other legal doctrinal level, and not as independent, self-standing philosophy. There is, nonetheless, a sort of odd continuity running between *Anarchy, State, and Utopia* and the philosophers' amicus brief in the assisted-suicide case.

In particular, there is a combination of apparent moral certitude in the substantive or political result—that persons have certain specified, more or less inviolable rights—along with the underdeveloped interest in any convincing explanation of why the specified rights, and not others, follow from the premises invoked, or, more crucially, why those underlying premises themselves have been adopted.

At the constitutional level, one could, if one wishes, and as the Supreme Court itself did, choose to doubt that the precedential ground for a right to assisted suicide was as well furrowed as the philosophers' amicus brief argued it to be. At a deeper, more philosophical level, one might express unsatisfied curiosity as to the basic methodology by which dignity, individual autonomy, or conduct libertarianism are derived or defined, characterized, fundamentally linked to the world, defended as ultimately coherent, and assigned their moral status and priority.

Despite recent work by Nozick and, among others, his colleagues on the joint amicus brief, it would seem that a satisfactory understanding of the very definition, nature, origin, and moral status of dignity and of individual autonomy and conduct libertarianism is as far away as ever.

NOTES

1. Robert Nozick, *Anarchy, State, and Utopia* (New York: Basic Books, 1974) (hereinafter cited in the text as ASU).

2. See, for example, the essays by Thomas Nagel, Onora O'Neill, Cheyney Ryan, T. M. Scanlon, Peter Singer, Hillel Steiner, and Bernard Williams in *Reading Nozick*, ed. Jeffrey Paul (Totowa, N.J.: Rowman & Littlefield, 1982). Among the vast relevant literature, particularly notable is a recent full-length treatment, Jonathan Wolff, *Robert Nozick: Property, Justice and the Minimal State* (Stanford, Calif.: Stanford University Press, 1991). See also Ian Shapiro, *The Evolution of Rights in Liberal Theory* (Cambridge: Cambridge University Press, 1986); Michael A. Lamson, ed., "Robert Nozick's Anarchy, State, and Utopia," *Arizona Law Review* 19 (1977): 2–283. Symposium, *Ethics* 87 (1977):97–152; Ronald Dworkin, "What Is Equality? Part 2: Equality of Resources," *Philosophy & Public Affairs* 10 (1981): 283, 336–38, 345; Virginia Held, "John Locke on Robert Nozick," *Social Research* 43 (1976):169–95. The present author briefly reacted to Nozick's work in R. George Wright, "The Paradox of External Criticism," *Western Political Quarterly* 29 (1976):193–94.

3. Nozick considers, and at least does not dismiss, the possibility of a "moral catastrophe" avoidance limitation on the assertion of moral rights in *Anarchy, State, and Utopia*, 29–30. See also Judith Jarvis Thomson, *Rights, Restitution, & Risk*, ed. William Parent (Cambridge, Mass.: Harvard University Press, 1986), 56.

4. For Nozick's controversially narrow understanding of the concept of coercion, see Robert Nozick, "Coercion," in *Philosophy, Science, and Method,* ed. S. Morgenbesser, P. Suppes, and M. White (New York: St. Martin's Press, 1969), 440–72, reprinted in *Philosophy, Politics and Society,* ed. P. Laslett, W. G. Runciman, and Q. Skinner (New York: Barnes & Noble, 1972), 101–35.

5. On Nozick's account, it is not entirely clear whether the transition from anarchy to the minimal state is morally obligatory (see *Anarchy,* 52, 232) or practically inevitable (see p. 5), or both.

6. Our discussion of Nozick will seek to remain neutral as between what has been called ethical foundationalism and ethical coherentism. For discussion, see, for example, Robert Audi, "Axiological Foundationalism," *Canadian Journal of Philosophy* 12 (1982):163–83; Norman Daniels, "Reflective Equilibrium and Archimedean Points," *Canadian Journal of Philosophy* 10 (1980):83–103; R. George Wright, "Two Models of Constitutional Adjudication," *American University Law Review* 40 (1991):1357–88.

7. Nozick, *Anarchy,* 150.

8. Nozick, *Anarchy,* 310.

9. Compare mutually Bruce Ackerman, *Social Justice in the Liberal State* (New Haven: Yale University Press, 1980); Charles Larmore, "Political Liberalism," *Political Theory* 18 (1990): 339–60; William Galston, *Liberal Purposes* (Cambridge: Cambridge University Press, 1991); Stephen Macedo, *Liberal Virtues* (Oxford: Oxford University Press, 1990).

10. Nozick, *Anarchy,* 30.

11. While they do not argue in terms of rights or rights violation, it is not unreasonable to cite here John Finnis, Joseph Boyle, and Germain Grisez, *Nuclear Deterrence, Morality and Realism* (Oxford: Clarendon Press, 1987): "The norm . . . which forbids hanging one innocent person to satisfy a mob and protect any number of others is an absolute" (293).

12. For background, see Isaiah Berlin, "Two Concepts of Liberty," in *Four Essays on Liberty* (London: Oxford University Press, 1969), 118–72. A parallel discussion of the equivocal meaning of "autonomy" could also be readily developed.

13. For some doubts as to whether capitalism unequivocally maximizes the negative liberty of all those involved, see C. B. Macpherson, "Elegant Tombstones: A Note on Friedman's Freedom," in *Democratic Theory: Essays in Retrieval* (Oxford: Oxford University Press, 1973), 143–56.

14. Nozick, *Anarchy,* 31.

15. For discussion, see Joseph Raz, *The Morality of Freedom* (Oxford: Oxford University Press, 1986), 273–74.

16. For Nozick's understanding of the scope of the right to life, see *Anarchy, State, and Utopia,* 179. Again, this is not to suggest that Nozick rules out voluntary acts of individual or collective charity, or that he would not generally welcome the development of voluntary insurance markets to protect against all sorts of contingencies.

17. For an example of a less discretely atomistic approach to human nature, see Michael Sandel, *Liberalism and the Limits of Justice* (Cambridge: Cambridge University Press, 1982), 79–82.

18. Nozick, *Anarchy,* 132–33.

19. Nozick, *Anarchy,* 113.

20. It is possible that the dominant protective agency may want to issue clean bills of health to any local Mother Teresas, in the sense of disclaiming any current wish to impose substantive restrictions on their self-defense rights, contingent upon their providing continuing evidence of fitness for this distinction. But does imposing this condition itself require payment of any compensation?

21. Nozick, *Anarchy,* 151–52.

22. Nozick, *Anarchy,* 161.

23. To Nozick's credit, though, is his celebrated discussion (see *Anarchy,* 42–45) of our presumed disinclination to turn our lives over to what he imaginatively characterizes as an "experience machine," a "transformation machine," or a "result machine." It is worth asking contemporary pragmatists, and at least some of those who would adopt a thoroughgoing public indifference to the choice of private good, what would, over the long term, substantially discourage future generations from plugging into such machines on a permanent basis.

24. Robert Nozick, *Philosophical Explanations* (Cambridge, Mass.: Harvard University Press, 1981), 498–99.

25. Robert Nozick, *The Examined Life: Philosophical Meditations* (New York: Touchstone: 1989).

26. See Robert Nozick, *The Examined Life,* 286–96.

27. See Nozick, *The Examined Life,* 288–89.

28. *Washington v Glucksberg,* 521 U.S. 702 (1997) and *Vacco v Quill,* 521 U.S. 793 (1997). This amicus brief is available on Westlaw at 1996 WL 708956, and is reprinted in *Issues on Law and Medicine* 15 (1999): 183.

5

Richard Posner: Pragmatist, Classical Liberal, and Legal Anti-Positivist

Jack Wade Nowlin

Richard Posner is chief judge of the U.S. Court of Appeals for the Seventh Circuit, where he has served since 1981, and a senior lecturer at the University of Chicago Law School. He is also the author of more than thirty books, three hundred articles, and fifteen hundred judicial opinions, and he is undeniably one of the most prolific, influential, and frequently cited legal writers in the United States today. Posner has degrees in literature and law and served as a law clerk to Judge Henry Friendly and Justice William Brennan. He has written on a wide range of topics, including law and economics, law and literature, sexuality, aging, jurisprudence, moral and legal theory, legal reputation, and the impeachment of President Clinton.

POSNER'S "PRAGMATISM"

Posner's general philosophical and theoretical orientation is toward a form of what he calls "pragmatism." Indeed, Posner understands, defends, and justifies both his classical liberalism and his legal anti-positivism in fundamentally "pragmatic" terms. What, then, more precisely, does Posner *mean* by pragmatism, a term which he recognizes "has no canonical concept" and which is thus open to a "wide range of potential definitions."[1] For Posner, the term pragmatism suggests not a "distinct philosophical movement," but rather "an umbrella term for diverse tendencies in philosophical thought."[2] Pragmatism signals, in Posner's view, an "orientation," a "method, approach, or attitude," and *not* "a moral, legal, or political algorithm," that one can expect to "resolve any moral or legal disagreement."[3]

What, more concretely, is the nature of this "orientation," "approach," or "attitude"? Posner writes that "pragmatism" in his particular sense of the term:

> means looking at problems concretely, experimentally, without illusions, with full awareness of the limitations of human reason, with a sense of the 'localness' of human knowledge, the difficulty of translations between cultures, the unattainability of 'truth,' the consequent importance of keeping diverse paths of inquiry open, the dependence of inquiry on culture and social institutions, and above all the insistence that social thought and action be evaluated as instruments to valued human goals rather than ends in themselves.[4]

Posner has also defined pragmatism in his sense, even more narrowly and precisely, "as a disposition to ground policy judgments on facts and consequences rather than on conceptualisms and generalities."[5] It is in fact this focus on *empiricism* and *instrumentalism,* on "facts" and "consequences" as they relate to valued "social goals," that provides us with the sparest and sharpest definition of Posner's pragmatism.

Though Posner has not always referred to himself as a "pragmatist," one can see the genesis of this empirical and instrumental approach to law in his early work as one of the founders of the "law and economics" movement, which involved the application of an essentially "pragmatic" economic analysis to law and legal policy.[6] Indeed, as Posner has written from a later and self-consciously pragmatic standpoint, the law and economics approach is simply *one* form of legal pragmatism because it "epitomizes the operation in law of the ethic of scientific inquiry, *pragmatically* understood."[7] The social science of economics, Posner maintains, is in fact "the *instrumental* science par excellence" and one that has a fundamentally empirical, results-oriented, social scientific orientation.[8] Its chief project is one crucial to the question of formulating public policy: "to construct and test models of human behavior for the purpose of predicting and (where appropriate) controlling that behavior."[9] The pragmatist, then, must turn to economics—as well as "related disciplines," such as sociology, psychology, and even evolutionary biology—in the formulation of public policy.[10] It should be clear, then, that Posner's self-described "pragmatic" approach to questions of law, justice, sexuality, aging, and other (overlapping) social matters is most fundamentally an empirically-oriented, instrumental, and interdisciplinary (if heavily economic) social science approach.

Posner is thus a critic of "non-pragmatic"—that is, noninstrumental and non-empirical approaches—to questions of law and social policy. In particular, Posner is highly critical of the theoretical enterprise he describes pejoratively as "academic moralism," which includes reasoning about the requirements of a "moral order accessible to human intelligence and neither time-bound nor local, an or-

der that furnishes objective criteria for praising or condemning beliefs and behavior of individuals and the design and operation of legal institutions."[11] Indeed, Posner's reserves his harshest criticism for this approach in its most sophisticated and elaborate forms, such as one finds in the work of serious
academic moral theorists, including, in particular, John Rawls, Ronald Dworkin,
and John Finnis.[12]

Posner's rejection of "academic moralism" is itself justified in purely pragmatic terms, at a number of levels, founded on the judgment that "academic
moralism" is simply not (sufficiently) *useful* to be worth the effort it involves.
First, precisely because noninstrumental, nonempirical approaches do not pay
(sufficient) attention to the arena of "facts and consequences" they may tend
to generate (perhaps unintentionally) "un-pragmatic" results. In short, policy
debates that center around abstract moral ideals such as "equality" or "due
process," rather than empirical analysis of the likely consequences of policy
choices, are simply much more likely—given their lack of "consequentialist"
analysis—to produce choices the *ultimate costs* of which are prohibitively
high, perhaps even self-defeating, in light of their goals and benefits. In short,
Posner asserts that a debate centered "pragmatically" on the "facts" and "consequences" of a particular policy is likely to result in *better policy* in terms of
achieving one's own ultimate social goals than is an "abstract" moral debate.
Posner suggests, for example, that the Warren Court's "adventurous" rulings
in criminal procedure may in fact have been *self-defeating* from the perspective of achieving "the very goals most plausibly ascribed to it, of making the
nation more peaceable, secure, and civilized."[13] This is so because decisions
enlarging the rights of criminal defendants in light of abstract legal concepts
such as "due process" may have also *impaired* basic rights by "undermining
the protection of property and personal safety, which are endangered by
crime," by "stimulating a legislative backlash" against the rights of defendants, and by raising the costs of the administration of justice and thus increasing the tax burden on "property and hence property rights" directly and
indirectly.[14] At the very least, Posner concludes, policy-makers (including
judges) should carefully consider, from a sophisticated social science perspective, the various "real world" consequences of a particular policy, its
costs and benefits, and in particular, whether it is self-defeating in terms of its
own presumptive goals, before deciding to embrace it.

Second, Posner argues that our debates about contentious issues such as affirmative action or the rights of the accused are simply *unproductive* when
they concern the moral requirements of an abstract ideal such as "racial
equality" or "due process."[15] This conclusion is rooted in what Posner sees as
the fundamental *epistemic* limitations of "academic" moral reasoning. In Posner's view, academic moral argument, however elaborate and sophisticated it

may happen to be, is simply *too weak* to overcome the pull of either our strongly held moral intuitions or our basic self-interestedness. In fact, Posner maintains that our contemporary moral divisions more often reflect "*unbridgeable* differences in values that have their origin in temperament, upbringing, and life experiences rather than reasoning to divergent conclusions from shared premises."[16] Posner holds, then, that "most of our firmly grounded beliefs, moral as well as epistemological, are products of *intuition* rather than reasoning."[17] One is not "reasoned" into these basic moral beliefs and one cannot be "reasoned" out of them. In fact, the only sort of moral argument not rooted in shared premises that has "pragmatic" value is *rhetorical* in nature rather than analytic and is the province *not* of the academic moralist but rather of those whom Posner calls the "moral entrepreneurs," the "charismatic moral innovators" who employ "techniques of nonrational persuasion" such as appeals to emotion and self-interest.[18] Therefore, academic moral argumentation, however serious and rigorous, is simply not capable of aiding the resolution of core intuition-based differences in moral outlook.

Posner observes, for instance, that an "academic moralist" such as Ronald Dworkin "no doubt believes that he has won his duels with his [morally conservative] academic opponents over abortion and euthanasia and the like," and the very same can be said as well for Dworkin's opponents, who no doubt believe *they* have won these debates, but Posner maintains that those "who do not have strong views on these questions rates these duels as *ties*" rather than as victories for either side.[19] Posner, then, concludes that the "fine-spun arguments" of academic moralists are "gossamer that cannot budge the rock of moral intuition"[20] and therefore our unreasoned and "unbridgeable" differences in basic moral values simply generate a degree of interminable moral division on disputed questions that "academic moralism" cannot hope to resolve. Such arguments, then, cannot change our minds or "make us morally better people in either our private or public roles."[21] Therefore, Posner concludes that academic moral theorizing simply "does not provide a *usable* basis for moral judgments," given its tendency to produce "un-pragmatic" results and in light of the tenacity of our deeply-held rival moral visions.[22]

Posner's pragmatism is, then, fundamentally rooted in a rejection of what we may call the moral realist-rationalist project of attempting to discern through reasoned argument the requirements of an "objective" morality, including, apparently, a wholesale rejection of reasoning about the *ultimate moral-political ends* to which even "pragmatic" policies are directed. What Posner's pragmatism is marked by, then, in the final analysis, is its interdisciplinary, social scientific, empirical focus; its instrumentalism, consequentialism, and functionalism; and its skepticism, antifoundationalism, and antidogmatism, including a sweeping rejection of the value of reasoning about moral questions except in very narrowly empirical and instrumental terms as they relate to "unreasoned" social values and goals.

POSNER'S CLASSICAL LIBERALISM

Posner regularly describes himself as a "classical" or "Millian" liberal, terms meant to invoke his libertarian support for both the free market and for legal recognition of a very broad sphere of personal autonomy. Posner has neatly summarized his basic political position, noting that he:

> take[s] [his] stand with the John Stuart Mill of *On Liberty* (1859), the classic statement of classical liberalism. *On Liberty* argues that every person is entitled to the maximum liberty—both personal and economic—consistent with the liberty of every other person in society. Neither government nor public opinion should seek to repress "self-regarding" behavior, that is, behavior that does not *palpably* harm other people.[23]

Posner, then, in the vernacular of contemporary politics, tends to be a "libertarian": economically conservative and socially liberal.

Posner, however, is a *pragmatist* rather than nonpragmatist classical liberal. He maintains, then, that the case for classical liberalism is pragmatic as it is with any moral, political, or economic viewpoint.[24] The political justification, then, for classical liberalism remains in Posner's view pragmatic, rather than moralistic, and is thus rooted in an empirical and consequentialist analysis of the "facts" and "consequences" of liberalism in relation to the ultimate "unreasoned" moral preferences, preferences that are themselves heavily the product of temperament, upbringing, and life experiences. Consequently, Posner notes that though when he makes "recommendations about policy, including legal policy, [he is] guided by the kind of vague utilitarianism, or 'soft core' classical liberalism," associated with J. S. Mill,[25] he must also readily concede, quite consistent with his broad rejection of "academic moralism," that "Mill's moral or political philosophy cannot be shown to be *correct* any more than any other moral or political philosophy can be."[26]

Still, Posner notes that pragmatism and classical liberalism do share certain clear affinities. He observes, for instance, that both philosophical stances involve the rejection of the "the idea of using some comprehensive doctrine (whether Aquinas's, or Mohammed's, or Calvin's, or Kant's, or Marx's) to supply the answers to questions about either reality or personal conduct." Indeed, pragmatism rejects such a reliance on comprehensive doctrines "at the level of general philosophy" and liberalism "at the level of political philosophy."[27] Posner concludes, then, that liberalism and pragmatism do "fit well with each other."[28]

Posner, then, recognizes that those who reject Milllian liberalism on purely *nonpragmatic* grounds, such as their belief in the commandments of a divinity or in the deontological requirements of some form of objective morality, will simply disagree with him and other proponents of pragmatism, claiming they have missed the point of moral inquiry entirely. In fact, even a fellow pragmatist who was committed to a different set or ordering of ultimate ends, as "unreasoned" moral preferences, would very likely disagree with Posner's policy prescriptions because Posner's would be directed "pragmatically" to a different value scheme. These differences in fundamental moral sensibility are not the product of reason, but rather of what we may broadly call psychological and sociological forces.

Why, then, bother to *defend* classical liberalism, even pragmatically, if non-Millians cannot be converted to one's cause? Posner explains, quite pragmatically, that Millian liberalism does happen to "sketch [ ] a form of life that when properly understood is *attractive* to many people in the United States and similar wealthy modern societies, and not just to me. That is a ground enough for me to indicate how I would resolve particular issues."[29] Posner recognizes, therefore, that if Millian liberalism, "properly understood," sketches a form of life one finds *un*attractive, even, perhaps repugnant, whether because of one's views on religion, objective morality, or simply one's other politicocultural preferences, there is really very little to be said on the matter by way of rational argument. Still, the simple fact that many people *do* find it attractive is for Posner a solid enough basis for looking into the matter more deeply.

Moreover, Posner does not quite dismiss *all* "moral" argument as worthless, simply those "academic" moral arguments *not* rooted in a "pragmatic" discussion of facts and consequences. He does maintain, then, that "moral claims can be profitably discussed *if* they depend on factual claims"[30] at least, presumably, as those factual claims relate to *shared ultimate ends,* and thus he endeavors, as a pragmatic classical liberal, "to show that liberal individualism can be defended pragmatically by comparing its consequences with those likely to be produced by such alternatives as social democracy and moral conservatism."[31] Therefore an empirical, instrumental argument about the consequences of differing moral outlooks with respect to widely accepted "human goals" is a worthwhile line of inquiry.

Posner, for instance, takes pains to distinguish his putatively "conservative" classical liberalism from "true" social conservatism and also to assert the *superiority* of Millian liberalism to its traditionalist rival in "pragmatic terms." Posner thus notes that "we modern Millians are apt to be classified as conservatives rather than as liberals,"[32] but that "real conservatives," like James Fitzjames Stephen, "believe with Plato and Leo Strauss" that the state "should inculcate virtue, promote piety, punish immorality, discourage hedonism."[33] As we have seen, Posner takes an antiperfectionist, libertarian stand with John Stuart Mill, endorsing what he sees as a "common-sense" version of the "harm" principle.[34]

POSNER ON SEX AND PUBLIC POLICY

One may also shed some light on Posner's liberalism by turning to his "pragmatic" liberal views on questions of sexual morality and public policy. Posner is decidedly a Millian, social liberal, or libertarian in his views on sexual morality and public policy, but he is, again, clearly *not* a nonconsequentialist Millian. He is rather an emphatically *pragmatist* Millian—"social scientific" in outlook and thus open to empirical evidence and instrumental analysis as it concerns the "facts" and "consequences" of social policy on questions involving sex, procreation, and child-rearing. Posner thus describes his general theory of sexuality as "libertarian" (rather than "libertine" or "modern liberal")[35] in its conclusions and "economic" (and thus "incompatible" with much more common "moral" approaches to sexuality) in its philosophic basis.[36]

Indeed, Posner avers that this "economic" theory's "uncompromising," "truly unassimilable rival" is a "heterogeneous cluster of *moral* theories," including those of liberals such as Kant, Joel Feinberg, and Ronald Dworkin.[37] Some of these theorists' conclusions may broadly track Posner's Millian social liberalism, but they, unlike him, hold that the "key to both understanding and judging sexual practices and norms" lies in "moral and religious beliefs that are irreducible to genuine social interests or practical incentives."[38] The "economic theory," by contrast, is marked by Posnerian pragmatism. "Functional, secular, instrumental, utilitarian," it "relies heavily on economic analysis"[39] where economics is understood as "the science of rational human behavior."[40] Economic analysis is an "acid bath," Posner avers, that can peel away "layers of ignorance, ideology, superstition, and prejudice."[41] Posner also notes the economic theory's potential broader appeal, claiming that "[a]n approximation to a scientific, nonmoral outlook on sexuality is highly influential today in northern Europe, especially Sweden, Denmark, and the Netherlands, as well as in Japan and other areas of East Asia."[42]

One can certainly see that Posner's economic approach to "judging and understanding" sexual practices and norms is based directly on key economic concepts such as rational choice, cost/benefit analyses, searching costs, signaling, and externalities.[43] This analysis, Posner maintains, has substantial *explanatory* power with respect to the question of cultural diversity on matters of sexual practice, which, Posner believes, are "adaptive" to differing socio-economic contexts. Posner's economic approach, then, suggests that the quite diverse sexual mores and behaviors found in different cultures at different times are often simply the result of "rational choices" flowing out of basic economic and technological conditions.

For instance, Posner maintains that such sexual practices as keeping concubines and sequestering wives can be explained as a "rational" choice flowing out of the social norm of "non-companionate marriage," a norm which itself is linked to the society's larger socioeconomic context. If economic and technological conditions are such that "non-companionate" marriage (rooted in an exchange of male economic support for female child-bearing) predominates over "companionate" marriage (rooted in emotional intimacy), there is likely to be relatively little emotional intimacy between spouses, thus adulterous intercourse becomes a more "satisfying" substitute for marital intercourse, and therefore the rate of adultery consequently increases. Non-companionate husbands, who are in a greater position of power, then, have strong incentives both to keep concubines for themselves and to sequester their wives to ensure spousal fidelity.[44] Moreover, whether "non-companionate" marriage or "companionate" marriage predominates in a given society will often depend upon the status of women in that society, and that in turn will often depend upon the society's economic structure and its degree of technological advancement. Posner contends that many sexual practices can be explained through this sort of "economic" analysis, noting, for instance, that various "marriage-related laws regulating sex have been on the whole efficient adaptions to social conditions"[45] related to variables such as technology, urbanization, income, the occupational profile of women, and female economic independence.[46]

Posner also maintains that the major, closely related, technological, economic, and social changes of recent decades have rendered policies associated with traditional morality difficult, if not impossible, to achieve in the United States—at least consistent with the preservation of basic freedoms. In particular, he notes that:

> The advent of safe and effective contraception and of household labor-saving devices, advances in reproductive technology, the reduction in infant mortality to near zero and the transformation of the economy into a service economy in which little work requires masculine strength—the interplay of these developments was bound to free (or, if you prefer, eject) women from their traditional role, and by doing so bring about a profound change in sexual behavior and family structure. Unless we want to go the way of Iran, we shall not be able to return to the era of premarital chastity, low divorce, stay-at-home moms, pornography-free media and the closeting of homosexuals and adulterers.[47]

In Posner's view, "economic" analysis can thus at least *suggest* certain policy prescriptions, and Posner tentatively believes these to be largely libertarian in nature, at least in the context of contemporary Western societies, "supporting a diminished role for government."[48] In sum, Posner finds "unpersuasive on the basis of present knowledge" the "pragmatic" case for "forbidding abortion in the early months of pregnancy," "for criminalizing homosexual acts between consenting adults," "for discouraging contraception and premarital sex," "for refusing to enforce contracts of surrogate motherhood," "for regulating adoption as strictly as we do," "for trying to stamp out prostitution," and "for banning pornography by recognized artists."[49]

POSNER'S "PRAGMATIST" VIEW OF LAW, ADJUDICATION, AND THE JUDICIAL ROLE

Posner's pragmatism extends beyond the moral-political sphere to the legal and constitutional sphere. As a "legal pragmatist," Posner is a critic of legal formalism, legal positivism, and ambitious legal theories that seek to inform legal reasoning by reference to "theory" or "academic moralism." In fact, Posner recognizes the existence of pragmatism *at different levels of analysis* and thus observes that "a pragmatist committed to judging a legal system by the results the system produced might think that the best results would be produced if the judges did *not* make pragmatic judgments but simply applied rules" as a legal formalist or positivist would.[50] Such a legal pragmatist would be a kind of pragmatic legal formalist and, as Posner notes, "by analogy to a rule utilitarian," "a 'rule pragmatist.'"[51] Moreover, Posner observes, even if one were to reject pure legal formalism, there might, for instance, be "pragmatic reasons why it would be good for judges to consider themselves morally bound to follow precedent rather than to make a judgment in each case whether to follow the precedent."[52]

Posner is himself what one might term a "quasi-rule pragmatist" and thus rejects the claim that judges should simply try to make *each* judicial decision "pragmatic" without regard to the broader *systemic* pragmatic value of certain rule-based decisional constraints on judging, such as the doctrine of stare decisis or the "common-sense" limits of textual interpretation. Posner, then, rejects *both* what we might call judicial "act pragmatism" and *pure* judicial formalism in favor of a more narrow kind of judicial "rule pragmatism" that substantially limits judges' "decisional freedom" to ignore traditional sources of law, given the broader systemic pragmatic weight of "precedent, statutes, and constitutional text as both potentially valuable information about the likely best result in the present case and as signposts that [one] must be careful not to obliterate or obscure gratuitously, because people may be relying on them."[53]

Posner concludes that a "pragmatic adjudication" of his sort—recognizing the necessity and legitimacy of granting judges some limited "decisional freedom" to inquire into social consequences of the legal recognition of a particular claim—is itself pragmatically justified by its broader social consequences. Indeed, Posner maintains that the one "decisive objection to trying to embed a [purely] formalist approach to judging within a pragmatic or for that matter any other philosophical framework is that in our legal system formalism is an *unworkable* response to difficult cases."[54] Therefore, the purely pragmatic objection to pure legal formalism, and thus to a pragmatic defense of legal formalism rooted in what we might call "pure rule pragmatism," is that judges in the American system are simply *compelled* by circumstances to exercise routinely a limited creative, rule-making function.

In fact, Posner's basic position on law and adjudication is, as an empirical, sociological matter, to "accept much of [Dworkin's] jurisprudence, in particular his rejection of legal positivism as either a description of or guide to decision making by American judges, while rejecting [Dworkin's] moralism."[55] Posner thinks, descriptively, that Anglo-American judges do *not* simply apply rules, but *make* them as well, and that the rule-making activity in the "open or legally uncharted area" is understood, and accepted as a matter of political and legal convention, as "small" in the English system and "large" in the American system.[56] This suggests, as well, that in addition to the purely rule-pragmatic value of adhering to clear legal rules where possible, there is an added "institutional legitimacy" limitation on purely act-pragmatic decision-making by judges in both the English and American systems, though to different degrees in each system. A judge who exercises more decisional freedom than his system allows is, Posner admits, acting "lawlessly" with respect to his society's legal conventions, however pragmatically.[57]

Posner, then, thinks that H.L.A. Hart is "descriptively, though not semantically, more accurate [than Dworkin] in his account of judicial activity in the open area where the rules run out" because the "cases in that area are frequently indeterminate, rather than merely difficult" as Dworkin contends.[58] Posner, however, thinks that Dworkin is *semantically* more accurate because "when judges do these things they are [not necessarily] stepping *outside* the law" since the degree of proper rule-making authority granted to judges as part of their legal function, their degree of "decisional freedom," depends on the conventions of the political system.[59] Dworkin is, Posner notes, therefore, quite right to maintain, in Posner's terminology, that "doing" law includes quite a substantial amount of discretionary rule-making in the American system.[60] Posner concludes that "Dworkin's demonstration that legal positivism is not a workable approach for American judges is a genuine contribution to knowledge," and is "best described as a contribution to philosophical sociology."[61] Posner, then, while a Reagan appointee and a kind of "judicial conservative," emphatically rejects the positivistic and formalistic "originalism" espoused by such conservative judges as Robert Bork, Antonin Scalia, and Clarence Thomas.

Where Dworkin chiefly errs, in Posner's view, is in "dividing the judicial function into applying rules and doing moral theory."[62] The proper division is rather between applying rules and *making* rules, and a judge engaging in proper rule-making should do so *pragmatically,* drawing on empirical social science to determine the consequences of different rules and evaluating those consequences in "common sense" terms, without recourse to the esoterica of academic moral theory.[63] As we have seen, Posner does not believe that "academic" moral arguments provide a "pragmatic" basis for decision-making or for resolving moral disagreement and therefore their limited utility counts against their use by judges as well as other policymakers. In particular, Posner notes that moral theorizing "is not something judges are or can be made comfortable with or good at; it is socially divisive; and it does not mesh with the legal cases."[64] It is doubly or trebly un-pragmatic.

Posner's position, then, is that American judges as a matter of legal convention have substantial "decisional freedom" to make rules in "hard" cases, those cases where the rules "run out," and that they should do so *pragmatically,* with respect to facts and consequences, rejecting legal positivism, legal formalism, and "natural law" or "academic" moral theories. As Posner puts it, pragmatists believe "that the judge or other legal decision-maker thrust into the open area where the conventional sources of guidance run out (such sources as previously decided cases and clear statutory or constitutional texts), can do no better than to rely on notions of policy, common sense, personal and professional values, and intuition and opinion, including informed or crystallized public opinion."[65] Such legal pragmatists would emphasize "the methods of social science and common sense" in their rule-making activities.[66] Of particular value, among the social sciences in this context, is economics, though Posner recognizes that "the economic approach cannot be the whole content of legal pragmatism," particularly because the economic "approach works well only when there is at least a moderate agreement on ends" and because its "libertarian character" makes it "unsuitable to govern areas in which redistributive values command" a political consensus.[67]

There is, then, in addition to the simple unworkability of legal formalism, a "higher" or "broader" pragmatic justification for Posner's legal "quasi-rule" pragmatism: the overall systemic pragmatic social benefits that will occur if judges use their limited rule-making authority in individual "hard cases" pragmatically to formulate "good" (that is, "pragmatic") public policy. In fact, Posner describes the broader uses of a pragmatic mind-set in law as both

(1) "knock[ing] ambitious legal theories" of whatever kind, such as Scalia's or Dworkin's; and (2) "provid[ing] help in changing the character of the legal enterprise by nudging academic law a little closer to social science, and the judicial game a little closer to the scientific game."[68] Posner, then, does at least share Bork's rejection of judicial moralizing in light of controversial liberal political theory—even as he rejects Borkian originalism.

Obviously, Posner's "legal pragmatism," holding that American judges quite properly make rules in "hard cases" and should do so pragmatically with an eye to "facts and consequences," has certain affinities to the "pragmatism" of the earlier legal realist movement and even to the contemporary critical legal studies movement. Posner recognizes these affinities,[69] but he is quick to emphasize his differences with these movements—which seem to cluster around what Posner sees as their political and methodological failures. Indeed, a "shortcoming" of the legal realist movement, Posner notes, was "its naive enthusiasm for government." Posner, as a classical liberal, certainly does *not* share this enthusiasm and observes that this strong preference for governmental action "marked legal realism as a [left-] 'liberal' movement" and as, perhaps, one more politically dogmatic than pragmatic.[70] Another failure of legal realism, in Posner's view, "was its lack of method." Posner observes that the legal realists "knew what to do—think things not words, trace the actual consequences of legal doctrines, balance competing policies—but not *how* to do any of these good things."[71] Still, Posner believes that the significant advances in social science methods since the early days of legal pragmatism have ameliorated this problem substantially. Posner concludes that "[a]ll that a pragmatic jurisprudence really connotes—and it connoted it in 1897 or 1921 as much as it does today—is a rejection of the idea that law is something grounded in permanent principles and realized in logical manipulations of those principles, and a determination to use law as an *instrument* for social ends." [72]

Posner's defense of "legal pragmatism" and his critique of nonpragmatic legal theories extends as well to the important realm of American constitutional law. Indeed, Posner is a particularly harsh critic of the academic moralist pursuit known as "constitutional theory." Posner defends the antiphilosophical nature of his stance, noting that "while in one sense pragmatism is indeed a theory and a constitutional theory when applied to constitutional law, in another and more illuminating sense it is an avowal of skepticism about various kinds of theorizing, including the kind I am calling constitutional theorizing."[73] Posner notes that "[c]onstitutional theory is unresponsive to, and indeed tends to obscure, the greatest need of constitutional adjudicators, which is for *empirical knowledge*."[74] Therefore, "[c]onstitutional scholars would be more helpful to courts and society as a whole if they examined constitutional cases and doctrines pragmatically in relation" to what Posner calls "their causes, their costs, and their consequences."[75]

Posner also takes a strong stand against activist judging, even given his own rejection of positivist legal formalism and originalism. The origins of Posner's support for restraint is to be found in a cluster of reasons broadly pragmatic in nature, related to his view of the practical limits of judicial policymaking, particularly as seen in light of both American legal conventions and the proper role for courts in a democratic society. First, Posner notes that, of course, a pragmatist "might have good [pragmatic] reasons for thinking that courts should maintain a low profile."[76] For instance, he maintains that "[u]ntil judges acquire a better knowledge base, the limitations of moral and constitutional theory provide a compelling argument for judicial self-restraint."[77] He therefore notes that proponents of judicial restraint will "consider [judicial] ignorance of the consequences" of challenged social policies "a compelling reason for staying the judicial hand" in the absence of "sure guidance" from traditional legal materials.[78] One might note here the important role played by Posner's general skepticism with respect to the self-image of elite theorists as morally "enlightened" purveyors of wisdom to the benighted masses. Indeed, Posner compares his own view of the judicial role to Holmes and Hand, who, Posner observes, "assigned a smaller role to courts, partly because they had a less confident sense of where, as judges, they wanted the nation to be heading" and thus, in spite of their strong personal views on many political issues, their decided "inclination" was to leave the "more" political branches "pretty much alone."[79]

Second, there is also the question of the proper role for courts in light of both the legal limits on judicial discretion and the value of a "democratic society" and majority opinion. As we have seen, Posner holds that a judge who is "being *too* political to conform to the reigning conception in the judge's society of the outer bounds of a judge's decisional freedom" is acting "lawlessly"[80] and therefore that widely and deeply held political norms with respect to the judicial role inevitably places some outer limits on the exercise of judicial power. Posner maintains as well that there are substantial democratic limits on judicial policymaking, asserting that judges must show considerable deference to the views of democratic majorities.[81] Although Posner is quick to criticize "naive" conceptions of democracy, he also observes that one is certainly "correct to sense that people who look to the courts for social reform do not take democracy completely seriously."[82] Indeed, he maintains that "Dworkin is closer in spirit to Plato than to Andrew Jackson."[83]

Posner's position seems to be that neither of these two related norms, the legal conventional and democratic, are themselves academic "moral" claims, but rather both are "social policy" claims rooted in a number of

related pragmatic concerns: the value of societal reliance on legal materials,[84] the importance of "preserv[ing] avenues of [political] change" for
purposes of consensus building and social experimentation, and the crucial
need to avoid "roil[ing] the political waters unnecessarily,"[85] the last including the necessity of maintaining some reasonable conformity between
public policy and public opinion. Posner, then, is principally a proponent
of judicial restraint because he recognizes the substantial overlapping
pragmatic, conventional, and democratic legal limitations on the broad exercise of discretionary judicial power. Posner has, for instance, written approvingly of the *Roe* dissents, noting that they are "consistent with a general, and it seems . . . *prudent,* policy for judges of not taking sides on
moral issues."[86] He also observes that "a telling criticism of *Roe v Wade* is
that the Supreme Court prematurely nationalized the issue of abortion
rights," preventing the states from "experiment[ing] with different approaches to the abortion question" and perhaps finding through trial and
error a "pragmatic" compromise acceptable to the nation.[87] Indeed, then,
one can easily see the connection between what Mary Ann Glendon has
called Posner's "pragmatic, neo-classical" view of the ideal judge and the
"classical" ideal associated with proponents of judicial restraint, whom
Posner admires, such as Holmes, Hand, and Cardozo.[88]

One can see all of these threads in Posner's discussion of whether the
Supreme Court should, as some theorists have suggested, create a radically
innovative constitutional right to homosexual "marriage." Posner notes that
such an argument can be plausibly constructed out of available legal materials, but strongly counsels an overlapping pragmatic, conventionalist, and
democratic caution in this area. "The judges will," Posner observes, "have to
consider the political, empirical, prudential, and institutional issues, including
the public acceptability of a decision recognizing the new right" and also the
"feasibility and desirability of allowing the matter to simmer for a while before the heavy artillery of constitutional-rights making is trundled out."[89] Posner implies that these factors count strongly against the recognition of such a
right and suggests, then, that we allow a state legislature or an *elected* state
court, institutions with solid democratic pedigrees, to experiment with homosexual "marriage" and let the rest of the country "learn from the results." His
overall view is that judges in a democratic society should generally accord
considerable respect to the deeply held beliefs and preferences of the democratic majority when making new laws. [90] In short, then, while Posner clearly
rejects the "originalist" legal-formalist interpretive approach of theorists such
as Robert Bork, he does share with Bork a decided suspicion of elite judicial
moralizing and a general rejection of an aggressive policy-making role for
courts in areas marked by serious societal disagreement.

A FEW OBSERVATIONS

Given that the foundation of Posner's views on both liberalism and law are justified in pragmatic terms, it may be most helpful to focus here on Posner's pragmatism. First, one must note the quite limited traction Posner can get against the "academic moralists" he criticizes on their own terms, given the wholly "pragmatic" nature of the criticism. It is, of course, of only very limited value to tell, say, a Neo-Kantian, who emphatically rejects any sort of consequentialism as a basis for judging actions, that his nonconsequentialist moral theory will have bad consequences—or least not have very good ones. Posner's criticism, then, *may* be justified from his own "pragmatic" perspective but not from that of his "nonpragmatist" opponents who may not think the "pragmatic" value of their theories is a proper basis for judging them.

Second, Posner's brief against the value of "academic moralism" bites back against his own work, and does so whether we imagine Posnerian pragmatism to be in some sense an academic moral theory or instead the antithesis of such theories. If Posner is right about the general "thinness" of controversial moral "theorizing," one is forced to conclude that Posner's *own* theory is also simply too epistemically thin to convert those persons whose moral intuitions or self-interest leads them in "nonpragmatic" directions. In short, if Dworkin will never convince Finnis to become a Dworkinian liberal individualist, Posner will never convince Dworkin or Finnis to become Posnerian pragmatists. What this suggests is that Posner's own intrinsically theoretical plea for pragmatism is simply "nonpragmatic" in effect, given its likely non-impact on its apparent intended audience. Moreover, Posner's theory not only bites back but also bites *deeper,* given that it is Posner—and not necessarily the "academic moralists" he criticizes—who suggests that the value of academic moralism must be found, if at all, in its "practical" capacity to convince others to change their minds.

Of course, it may be that such moral theorizing generally *does* have more impact on its readers than Posner cares to admit. One should note that Posner does allow, almost as an afterthought, that moral theorizing may serve the purpose of reinforcing beliefs or "rallying the faithful." As Posner writes:

> Most preaching *is* to the converted. It serves the important function of convincing people who think like you that they are not alone in their beliefs; that they have the backing of someone who is confident, competent, articulate, thoughtful; and that there is a language in which to express and, by expressing, solidify and vivify those beliefs. It forges a community of believers.[91]

Further, to the extent that Posner recognizes the value of reasoning from *shared premises,* he must recognize the potential of making "progress" in reasoning from those shared premises and thus at least some value in the project of moral reasoning within what can be called a "tradition of moral inquiry."[92] Both these points seem to be implicit in Posner's (somewhat defensive) explanations for *his own* bothering to write at all on law and policy questions in light of the limits of moral theory—that his basic pragmatic Millian moral sensibility is one also *attractive* to many others and thus (apparently) that Posner will both reinforce that attraction and help those individuals to understand some of the less obvious implications of their shared moral sensibility. We might imagine, then, that Posner significantly *overstates* his case against "academic moralism," but that to the extent that he *is* right on this point, his criticism applies with even greater force to his own work.

Third, one suspects that Posner's critique of academic moralism as a "wrong turn" in social policy, an otiose distraction from the more "scientific" business of looking into "facts" and "consequences," may unintentionally *exaggerate,* substantially, the degree to which a "scientific, empirical, consequentialist approach to policy matters provides a sounder and less divisive basis for social action. In fact, empirical questions are often quite complex, the social sciences are notoriously "soft," and thus even "pragmatic" experts themselves often disagree quite dramatically and quite interminably about the "facts" and "consequences" surrounding various social policies. Economists, for instance, are not known either for their "scientific" agreements on matters of general economic policy or for the accuracy of their predictions about the effects of various social policies on the economy. Moreover, one can be sure that even where there *is* greater agreement on empirical matters, our "common-sense" moral judgments with respect to how one should weigh various moral values—and the balancing and trade-offs that must be made among them—will continue to diverge and therefore to divide us. In fact, it is precisely the unhappy presence of continuing social divisions with respect to how one should assess, weigh, and apply ultimate moral values that sparks the very sort of moral argument Posner finds so "unpragmatic."

It is also hard to imagine that *judges*—particularly given their general lack of training in the social sciences, their heavy case loads, and the limited fact-finding capabilities of the courts in which they sit—are in a very good position to evaluate the interminable battles that occur among "policy experts" about "facts" and "consequences," especially when the divisions may turn on quite abstruse questions of empirical methodology.[93] Therefore, it may be as true of "pragmatic" social science as it is of "academic" moral theory that it "is not something judges are or can be made comfortable with or good at; it is socially divisive; and it does not mesh with the legal cases."[94] The "pragmatic" case for judicial restraint may thus be even stronger than Posner allows.

What all this suggests ultimately is that while Posner may view his pragmatism and pragmatic moral, legal, and constitutional theories as the antithesis of "theorizing," it is unlikely that "nonpragmatists" will either share this view or find reasons to agree that Posner has managed to side-step the basic problems that afflict *all* legal and political decision making. Posner, no less than the "academic moralists" he condemns, must inevitably confront the problem of making public policy choices in the face of a high degree of interminable (and politically charged) disagreement among widely recognized "experts." Therefore Posner must also confront the obvious conclusion that either there are no "right" answers to these questions or, if there are "right" answers, then even the "experts," in light of their persistent divisions about what those "right" answers are, must be "wrong"a good deal of the time. If that state of affairs is indeed a "debacle," it is "pragmatism's" as surely as "theory's."[95]

NOTES

1. Richard A. Posner, *Overcoming Law* (Cambridge, Mass.: Harvard University Press, 1995), 4.

2. Posner, *Overcoming,* 388.

3. Richard A. Posner, *The Problematics of Moral and Legal Theory* (Cambridge, Mass.: Harvard University Press, 1999), xii.

4. Richard A. Posner, *The Problems of Jurisprudence* (Cambridge, Mass.: Harvard University Press, 1990), 465.

5. Posner, *Problematics,* 227.

6. See, e.g., Richard A. Posner, *Economic Analysis of Law* (Boston: Little, Brown, 1972).

7. Posner, *Overcoming,* 15–16 (emphasis added).

8. Posner, *Overcoming,* 15–16 (emphasis added).

9. Posner, *Overcoming,* 15–16.

10. Posner, *Problematics,* 211.

11. Posner, *Problematics,* 3.

12. See, e.g., Posner, *Problematics.*

13. Posner, *Problematics,* 60–61.

14. Posner, *Problematics,* 160–61.

15. "One can get nowhere discussing the morality of affirmative action." Posner, *Problematics,* 139.

16. Richard A. Posner, *An Affair of State: The Investigation, Impeachment, and Trial of President Clinton* (Cambridge, Mass.: Harvard University Press, 1999), 240.

17. Richard A. Posner, *Sex and Reason* (Cambridge, Mass.: Harvard University Press, 1992), 238 (italics added).

18. Posner, *Problematics,* 42.

19. Richard A. Posner, "Reply to Critics of 'The Problematics of Moral and Legal Theory,'" *Harvard Law Review* 111 (1998): 1796, 1802 (italics added).

20. Posner, *Problematics,* 80.

22. Posner, *Problematics,* 3.

22. Posner, *Problematics,* 3 (emphasis added).

23. Posner, *Overcoming,* 23–24 (footnotes omitted).

24. Posner, *Overcoming,* 25.

25. Posner, *Problematics,* xii.

26. Posner, *Problematics,* xiii (emphasis added).

27. Posner, *Overcoming,* 29.

28. Posner, *Overcoming,* 29.

29. Posner, *Problematics,* xiii (emphasis added).

30. Posner, *Problematics,* 66.

31. Posner, *Overcoming,* 29.

32. Posner, *Overcoming,* 264.

33. Posner, *Overcoming,* 264.

34. Posner, *Overcoming,* 264.

35. Posner, *Sex,* 3.

36. Posner, *Sex,* 3.

37. Posner, *Sex,* 3 (emphasis added).

38. Posner, *Sex,* 4.

39. Posner, Posner, Posner, *Sex,* 3.

40. Posner, *Sex,* 4.

41. Posner, *Sex,* 437.

42. Posner, *Sex,* 4.

43. Posner, *Sex,* 435.

44. Posner, *Sex,* 66.

45. Posner, *Sex,* 66.

46. Posner, *Sex,* 5.

47. Richard Posner, "The Moral Minority," review of Gertrude Himmelfarb, *One Nation, Two Cultures,* in *New York Times Book Review,* December 19, 1999.

48. Posner, *Sex,* 441.

49. Posner, *Sex,* 441.

50. Posner, *Problematics,* 241.

51. Posner, *Problematics,* 241.

52. Posner, *Overcoming,* 12.

53. Posner, *Problematics,* 242.

54. Posner, *Overcoming,* 12 (emphasis added).

55. Posner, *Problematics,* 5–6.

56. Posner, *Problematics,* 97.

57. Posner, *Problematics,* 96–97.

58. Posner, *Problematics,* 96.

59. Posner, *Problematics,* 96, 97 (emphasis added).

60. Posner, *Problematics,* 96.

61. Posner, *Problematics,* 13.

62. Posner, *Problematics,* 97.

63. Posner, *Problematics,* 97–98.

64. Posner, *Problematics,* 3 (note omitted).
65. Posner, *Problematics,* viii (footnote omitted).
66. Posner, *Problematics,* viii.
67. Posner, *Overcoming,* 404.
68. Posner, *Overcoming,* 395.
69. Posner, *Overcoming,* 13.
70. Posner, *Overcoming,* 393.
71. Posner, *Overcoming,* 393 (italics added).
72. Posner, *Overcoming,* 393.
73. Posner, *Problematics,* 154.
74. Posner, *Problematics,* 145 (emphasis added).
75. Posner, *Problematics,* x.
76. Posner, *Overcoming,* 5.
77. Posner, *Problematics,* x.
78. Posner, *Problematics,* 182.
79. Posner, *Problematics,* 154–55.
80. Posner, *Problematics,* 96–97.
81. Posner, *Problematics,* 251.
82. Posner, *Problematics,* 151.
83. Posner, *Problematics,* 151.
84. Posner, *Problematics,* 242.
85. Posner, *Overcoming,* 404.
86. Posner, *Problematics,* 135 (emphasis added).
87. Posner, *Problematics,* 254.
88. Mary Ann Glendon, *A Nation under Lawyers: How the Crisis in the Legal Profession Is Transforming American Society* (Cambridge, Mass.: Harvard University Press, 1992), 172.
89. Posner, *Problematics,* 250.
90. Posner, *Problematics,* 251.
91. Posner, *Problematics,* 90.
92. Cf. Alasdair MacIntyre, *Whose Justice? Which Rationality?* (South Bend, Ind.: University of Notre Dame Press, 1988).
93. Posner himself has been criticized for a faulty judicial evaluation of the "facts" and "consequences" surrounding the partial-birth abortion question by David Tell, who chides Posner for relying on "an imaginary 'consensus of medical opinion' that partial-birth abortions are a valuable life-and-health preserving technique." David Tell, For the Editors, "Partial Birth Abortion Revisited," *The Weekly Standard,* November 22, 1999.
94. Posner, *Problematics,* 3 (note omitted).
95. The phrase "theory's debacle" comes from Posner's discussion of the serious and predictably political and partisan divisions found among moral, political, and legal theorists on the various legal and political questions surrounding the impeachment of President Clinton, in *An Affair of State,* 230–40.

6

Beyond the Procedural Republic
The Communitarian Liberalism of Michael Sandel

Terry Hall

For the better part of two decades the work of John Rawls has provided not only a touchstone for discussions in Anglo-American political theory, but, for many at least, a persuasive vision of liberalism. While there are other strains of liberalism at work in the contemporary mind, we should be mindful that many of the strands of contemporary liberalism come together around Rawls's central idea of the autonomous individual, who chooses his own good, his own "life plan."

These versions of liberal political theory have attracted sustained criticism. One of the most interesting and sophisticated challenges comes from Michael Sandel, who argues that the dominant expressions of liberalism fail to appreciate the extent to which human beings are ineluctably shaped by their communities. Sandel understands liberalism to be claiming that human agency is in a crucial respect unattended by prior attachments or commitments of any sort. Current liberal thinking, Sandel observes, "begins with the claim that we are separate, individual persons, each with our [*sic*] own aims, interests, and conceptions of the good."[1] Rawls, for example, seems to view human agents as essentially independent of what they in fact acknowledge or choose to pursue as good, which contingent commitments can never define them qua human. Sandel's aim is not merely to criticize this account of the "self," which he argues is excessively individualistic, and the theory of justice to which it gives rise; he also wishes to restore to liberalism a notion of the self as essentially constituted by its associations. In short, Sandel champions a liberalism that inspires individuals to identify themselves as citizens committed to realizing the common good. What I call Sandel's communitarian liberalism is, then, the focus of this chapter.[2]

The positions regarding the nature of the self and of political association Sandel attributes to Rawls mark out for the contemporary mind one of the more powerful and attractive ventures in political understanding—regardless of whether we can trace the lineage of this liberalism with definitive accuracy.[3] Sandel seems persuasive when he contends that the liberalism he is calling into question "has a deep and powerful appeal," that for contemporary Americans "it is our vision, the theory most thoroughly embodied in the practices and institutions most central to our public life."[4] I propose, then, to take Sandel's remarks about Rawls at face value, in order to allow the larger issue, the soundness of the liberal view of the self, to be engaged.

DEONTOLOGICAL LIBERALISM

The version of liberalism against which Sandel contends is first described as "deontological liberalism" and subsequently as "rights-based liberalism."[5] Although the most sustained criticism is directed against Rawls, in later writings Sandel widens the scope of his criticism to include Ronald Dworkin and philosophers of libertarian bent, such as Robert Nozick.[6] Whatever description is used, and regardless of the differences among various proponents, the core commitment of this liberalism, according to Sandel, is to a certain sort of political arrangement, namely a just society that "seeks not to promote any particular ends, but enables its citizens to pursue their own ends, consistent with a similar liberty for all; it therefore must govern by principles that do not presuppose any particular conception of the good."[7] Deontological liberalism is incompatible with the public acceptance of a perfectionist understanding of political community, according to which political association is seen as having a particular *telos* or end.

If everyone is free to follow his own conception of the good, and these conceptions are (as they typically seem to be) diverse, the question arises: How are such liberated individuals to live *together?* Where conceptions of human goods are allowed such unfettered liberty of pursuit, will not discord and strife threaten to tear apart political association? Deontological liberalism answers by recommending a view of political life as a neutral framework. Rather than conscript individuals to pursue a common good, the liberal polity will provide them with procedures designed to allow diverse goods to be pursued with a minimum of conflict. The best regime, according to this view, is what Sandel calls the "procedural republic."

Sandel calls this species of liberalism "deontological" to stress its commitment to the priority of the right over the good. This priority means two things: that no one's individual rights may be subordinated to the common good, and that the derivation of these rights cannot make use of any particular under-standing of, or commitment to, what is good for human beings as such.[8]

In Rawls the priority of the right over the good is expressed by the asser-tion that "justice is the first virtue of social institutions."[9] It is "not merely one important value among others, to be weighed and considered as the occasion requires, but rather the *means* by which values are weighed and assessed. . . . With respect to social values generally, justice stands detached and aloof, as a fair decision procedure stands aloof from the claims of the disputants be-fore it."[10]

Justice as a framework of procedures uncommitted to any particular con-ception of the good allows diverse conceptions of the good to be pursued with harmony sufficient to keep the political community together. But how are the principles of justice discovered? And what warrant do we have for excluding the common good as a guiding principle of politics? Why can we not legiti-mately commit ourselves, and our fellow citizens, to an overarching political end?

CHOOSING SELVES

Liberalism's answer to such questions, Sandel argues, involves a certain metaphysical conception of the self. We must recognize that we are persons whose constitution requires such political neutrality among ends. Liberalism demands the procedural republic because it conceives of human agents in a certain way; deontological political theory is buttressed by a distinctively lib-eral psychology. Without this metaphysical conception, Sandel maintains, much of the force of the liberal vision of politics would be diminished.

How, then, does deontological liberalism view the self? In brief, it views the self as radically autonomous. The autonomy of human beings in polit-ical society—their rightful liberty to seek their own good, to direct their life as they choose—is paralleled by a conception of the self as essentially autonomous. This latter conviction is not political in nature, but meta-physical (or ontological), because it involves an understanding of how the self, or human agent *qua* agent, is constituted. It is a view about what the self necessarily is.

Essentially the self is not constituted by the ends it in fact chooses, the at-tachments it makes, or the goods it desires. Rather, the self is simply the ca-pacity to effect these engagements. Speaking about Rawls, Sandel says that "teleology to the contrary, what is most essential to our personhood is not the ends we choose but our capacity to choose them."[11] In Rawls's own formula-tion, the self's capacity to choose means that "the self is prior to the ends which are affirmed by it."[12] There is, then, a double priority within this sort of liberalism: as the right is prior to the good, so the self is prior to its ends.

Therefore, Human beings are essentially and preeminently choosers, agents with the capacity for willing ends. In one sense I shape my identity by the particular choices I make over time; but, in a deeper sense my identity is already given prior to any choices I may make. For I always "stand behind" these choices as the chooser himself. My identity as a human agent consists in just this radical, primordial independence.

We can now perhaps see how, according to Sandel, deontological liberalism's commitment to political arrangements that are neutral toward goods coheres with its conception of the self. We know in fact that particular conceptions of what is good are many, diverse, and evanescent. Furthermore, there seems to be no common conception of the common good. Therefore to install any specific notion of the good as normative for political society would be to impose on some members of that society an alien conception of the good. But this would be to override the essential feature of human agency, that is, the capacity to choose one's own good free of imposition by others. This would be to reverse the priority of the right over the good and the priority of the self over its ends.

A consequence of imposing a conception of the good on political society is that its members are treated instrumentally, as "objects rather than subjects, as means rather than ends in themselves."[13] This recalls the moral writings of Immanuel Kant, to which Sandel in fact traces the lineage of deontological liberalism. The notion of a self that is detached from any particular ends it chooses, inclinations it follows, or attachments it forms is reminiscent of Kant's transcendental subject. It is true that Rawls does not wish to adopt the Kantian account of the human subject. His own theory of justice, he says, "tries to present a natural procedural rendering of Kant's conception of the kingdom of ends, and of the notions of autonomy and the categorical imperative."[14] For Rawls, although the self is quite properly to be conceived as prior to its ends, we must take care not to turn the self into a "ghostly," disembodied subject. Rawls seeks to revise Kant's transcendental self, without divesting it of the autonomy that supports the liberal vision of politics.

UNENCUMBERED SELVES

Rawls's move away from Kant involves placing the human agent—which we shall now call, following Sandel, the "unencumbered self"—in a hypothetical pre-political situation to determine under what political principles such a self would choose henceforth to live. In other words, the question is what sort of regime human agents, operating simply in their capacity as human agents, would choose as being compatible with their status as choosing selves. Rawls calls this hypothetical situation the Original Position. In such circumstances, individuals would choose the procedural republic as that regime which best preserved their freedom of choice.

The original position is a hypothetical choice situation in which human agents identify the basic contours of the political regime in which, given the kinds of agents they are, it is most appropriate for them to live. The original position comes before political activity begins. It is, as it were, a propaedeutic to politics. We must imagine such agents, Rawls says, making their choices under a so-called veil of ignorance, which deprives them of any knowledge of their sex, race, natural abilities (for example, intelligence, physical strength), social and economic class—even the goods, values, and aims to which they will eventually commit themselves.[15]

The original condition of ignorance is meant to accomplish two things. First, it is meant to ensure that the identification of the principles of justice, which will subsequently inform the political association, is made under conditions of equality and fairness. No considerations that could give rise to advantage or superiority in advance are admitted into the original choice situation. Second, the original condition allows human agency to be exhibited in the purest manner. If the human agent is fundamentally just a choosing subject, then only in a situation in which it is unencumbered by prior commitments is human agency most itself.

To say that principles of justice that are subsequently to have probative force are chosen under prepolitical conditions of ignorance is just to say that they are not *discovered* by human beings who possess a given nature but are *originated* by the choices of human agents, "unconstrained by an order of value antecedently given."[16] As Rawls says, "In justice as fairness the principles of justice are not thought of as self-evident, but have their justification in the fact that they would be chosen."[17] Individuals simply *qua* individuals are "self-originating sources of valid claims."[18] Rawlsian liberalism, Sandel writes, thus holds up to individuals a bracing vision of liberation: "Freed from the dictates of nature and the sanction of social roles, the human subject is installed as sovereign, cast as the author of the only moral meanings there are."[19]

Of course, considered in their full amplitude, humans are more than merely choosing agents, and the human estate is more variegated than the original position. Yet how we understand our relationship to our communities, Sandel argues, is shaped in distinctive ways by the liberal ontology of the self. We grasp who we most essentially are, and the character and extent of our communal ties, in the light of how we conceive ourselves essentially to be. He notes that Rawls says that "it is not our aims that primarily reveal our nature but rather the principles that we would acknowledge to govern the background conditions under which these aims are to be formed."[20] As liberal selves, we can certainly participate in communities and associations of all sorts. These are not confined to political affiliations, but can include membership in religious, familial, fraternal, or social communities as well. So long as we view ourselves as essentially unencumbered selves, however, we will almost certainly understand all of our communal attachments to be voluntary. We are not on the liberal view obliged to be members of any community, Sandel points out, and such membership is never constitutive of me. I have not forfeited anything essential as a human agent if I withdraw from a communal attachment.

Sandel goes on to draw out the implications of this consequence of the liberal ontology of the self:

> What is denied to the unencumbered self is the possibility of membership in any community bound by moral ties antecedent to choice; he cannot belong to any community where the self *itself* could be at stake. Such a community— call it constitutive as against merely cooperative—would engage the identity as well as the interests of the participants, and so implicate its members in a citizenship more thoroughgoing than the unencumbered self can know.[21]

That a polity should be seen as neutral among goods and that all communal attachments be understood as voluntary and peripheral to one's identity— these are the implications of the liberal ontology of the self as being prior to its ends. Sandel finds the ontology most strikingly figured in Rawls's conception of the original position. But it is not confined to Rawls; it is part of a more general way of viewing the human self as radically autonomous.

We might put the point Sandel is making, vis-à-vis Rawls, as follows. The original position presents us with a minimal theory of the self which at the same time purports to be the deep truth about human agents. Individuals in their actual careers in political society and other social relationships will of course be to varying extents encumbered (e.g., male or female, white or black, intelligent or stupid, weak or strong, wealthy or poor, benevolent or selfish, communal or solitary). They will be committed to any number of goods and will therefore live according to a great diversity of life plans. What the original position does is to hold up to flesh-and-blood individuals a certain conception of themselves as human agents, such that they will recognize liberal political arrangements and voluntary associations as the only ones consistent with their identity most deeply understood. A just polity need not be in fact excessively individualistic; it may afford scope for a variety of communal pursuits and attachments. It may recognize obligations and fidelities that are incurred as a result of such attachments.

Still, these obligations cannot be incurred in any way other than by our voluntarily accepting them. They are not thrust on us by the accident of birth or by historical contingencies. *We choose* to be so related and so obligated—or we are not related or obligated at all. To think otherwise is to compromise an individual's character as a freely choosing agent. A polity that prescribes such a compromise forfeits its claim to be ordered justly.

SANDEL AND THE DIFFERENCE PRINCIPLE

In *Liberalism and the Limits of Justice* Sandel offers several internal criticisms of Rawls's theory of justice. We shall briefly rehearse his principal objections and then move on to consider his alternative conception of the self and its implications for political and social theory.

Sandel argues that it is difficult to see how on Rawls's "thin" theory of the self any agreement, or contract, among parties to the original position can take place. That there is such a contract Rawls firmly maintains: By virtue of choosing behind a veil of ignorance, individuals in the original position arrive at a unanimous agreement about the principles of justice. They agree, that is, that a procedural republic would give them the best chance of pursuing their particular goods and life plans when they are politically situated. The bargain they strike is a fair one, Rawls says, because no one in the original position has knowledge of himself *as he will be,* sufficient to gain a special advantage over others. All therefore choose neutral, or procedural, principles of justice.

The difficulty with such a view arises when we scrutinize the original choosing agents more closely. Here conceptual incoherences, Sandel argues, come to the fore. Sandel argues that there is no warrant for positing a *plurality* of agents in the original position. And if there cannot be a plurality of agents, there can be no agreement or bargain. For what could individuate such selves given their radical equality as choosers? The capacity for choice is the same in each, and nothing additional is distinctive about them. Rawls wants to say that they all make the same choice; they all choose the same principles of justice. But this is just because they are identical *as agents of choice.* And their capacity to choose exhausts their identity here. In this they are the same, and in nothing are they different. "[O]nce *all* individuating characteristics are excluded, the parties are not merely *similarly* situated (as persons in real life with similar life circumstances and certain overlapping interests), but *identically* situated."[22] A plurality of agents, then, seems ruled out by the sheer uniformity of agency.

Closely related to this difficulty is another, namely, that of seeing how in the original position there can be the discussion, bargaining, even the speaking, that is necessary for understanding a bargain to have occurred. An agreement presupposes a number of agents with (initially) different opinions, different points of view, about the matter under discussion. Again, the selves in the original position, however, are equally, and merely, choosers, which seems to preclude their being conversants altogether.[23] Selves in the original position are not sufficiently "thick" to provide matter for deliberation, bargaining, or agreement. Rawls's characterization of agents in the original position has the paradoxical (and perhaps unintended) consequence of establishing therein but a single speaker.

Moreover, the liberal ontology of the self, Sandel argues, conflicts with the account of how goods in a community are shared according to principles of justice. In any community of individuals, goods will be produced and transactions will be performed. That is to say, what people accomplish by their efforts is distributed one way or another into the community. The question is How shall the distribution be effected in a just manner? Rawls's answer is that just distribution must accord with what he calls the Difference Principle, which stipulates that the scheme of benefits and burdens be arranged so that the least advantaged may share in the resources of the fortunate. The difference principle defines as just only those social and economic inequalities that work to the benefit of the least advantaged members of society. It defines Rawls's conception of democratic equality.[24]

Because the distribution of natural talents, such as intelligence, is arbitrary in the first place (hence not just), the outcome of the exercise of such talents by those fortunate enough to possess them is also arbitrary and not just. Merely setting up more ample opportunities to acquire or perfect natural talents is insufficient to establish justice. What is needed is "an agreement to regard the distribution of natural talents as a common asset" rather than as natural endowments the fruits of which are something to which the one who possesses them is exclusively entitled.[25]

The difference principle, then, provides the warrant for establishing a kind of welfare state. It serves as a rationale for distributing the fruits of our endeavors among our fellow citizens, for including all (and especially the impoverished) within the largesse of the community. "For Rawls, the principles of justice aim neither at rewarding virtue nor at giving people what they deserve, but instead at calling forth the resources and talents necessary to serve the common interest."[26] The difference principle thus represents an attempt to justify what is surely a quintessential liberal concern: that those less favorably endowed by nature or circumstance receive some compensation from their community.

Sandel points out that the difference principle is to some extent supported by the liberal view of the self as unencumbered. If I am not essentially constituted by any of my "possessions", that is, by the talents with which I have been favored by birth and circumstance, and the achievements I have won as a result, then I cannot be said to *deserve* any of these things. I cannot claim the fruits of my achievements as something I own, and which I may use, enjoy, and dispose of however I wish. Rawls, and other liberal thinkers, will not allow "the market" arrangements of "equal opportunity," or chance, to distribute talents and their fruits.

Because individuals cannot be said to own their assets, Rawlsian liberalism says, we must regard them as common goods, owned by the community. They may therefore be distributed and managed for the benefit of all, the least advantaged no less than those more favored. As Sandel notes, the difference principle is a principle of sharing, whereby what would otherwise be understood as individual goods are now understood as common goods. The principal components of deontological liberalism thus all seem to cohere: "[T]he picture so far remains intact; the priority of right, the denial of desert, and the unencumbered self all hang impressively together."[27]

Closer inspection, however, reveals a tension between what the difference principle requires and the notion of the unencumbered self. Located as it is at the very heart of deontological liberalism, this incoherence makes the liberal notion of community impossible to justify.

Sandel observes that it does not follow, from the conviction that an individual's assets do not belong to him (in the strong, constitutive sense), that these assets are *common,* that they belong to the community. To be able to make this claim—which in turn supports the difference principle—one must "presuppose some prior moral tie among those whose assets [one] would deploy and whose efforts [one] would enlist in a common endeavor."[28] The liberal notion of community as an arena for distributing common assets requires a conception according to which human selves are *constituted* by their communal ties. The unencumbered self must be replaced by the situated, communal self. But this is just what the Rawlsian notion of the self rejects. "Short of the constitutive conception, deploying an individual's assets for the sake of the common good would seem an offense against the 'plurality and distinctness' of individuals this liberalism seeks above all to secure."[29] Far from providing support for the liberal notion of community as an association for realizing the common good, the liberal ontology of the self undercuts it. At the heart of Rawlsian liberalism, then, is a debilitating dilemma.

> Either my prospects are left at the mercy of institutions established for "prior and independent social ends," ends which may or may not coincide with my own, or I must count myself a member of a community defined in part by those ends, in which case I cease to be unencumbered by constitutive attachments.

Either way, the difference principle contradicts the liberating aspiration of the deontological project. We cannot be persons for whom justice is primary and also be persons for whom the difference principle is a principle of justice.[30]

THE COMMUNITARIAN SELF

The way to escape the dilemma, according to Sandel, is to reconceive the sense of the self. Instead of seeing the self as unencumbered by prior attachments, values, and so forth, Sandel would have us view the self as essentially constituted by such relationships. He would have us attend to "those loyalties and convictions whose moral force consists partly in the fact that living by them is inseparable from understanding ourselves as the particular persons we are," that is, "as members of this family or community or nation or people, as bearers of this history, as sons and daughters of that revolution, as citizens of this republic."[31]

For Sandel the self is established as a self not by the mere capacity for choice, but by prior attachments, history, interactions, receipts, and engagements of an immensely varied sort. We are thrown into a thick web of such relationships which begin to work on us prior to our choices. As a result of these attachments, we are embedded in "a common vocabulary of discourse and a background of implicit practices and understandings."[32] The self is essentially communal from the very beginning. To attempt to conceive of the prepolitical self as prior to such communal affiliations is a serious and debilitating error.

The thickly constituted, encumbered self gives us a different kind of moral character from the thin, unencumbered self. When an encumbered self deliberates, for instance, it must consider not merely what it wants, what it would choose, but who it *is*—or more precisely, who it already is. Communal selves must take into account the attachments that have already established identity. They will already have incurred obligations and allegiances not of their own origination and choosing. Because such constitutive allegiances have shaped my very identity, my fulfillment of the obligations they impose "go beyond the obligations I voluntarily incur and the 'natural duties' I owe to human beings as such."[33] When I act on behalf of such others, my own identity is engaged, expressed, fulfilled. I can now regard myself not as a mere instrument of the community, to be conscripted to purposes that are alien to me, but as a participant in something to which I essentially belong. In fulfilling the requirements of the common good I am in a sense fulfilling myself.[34]

Liberalism and the Limits of Justice leaves us with many questions. Sandel does not offer anything approaching a comprehensive, or even wide-ranging, political philosophy, perhaps because chief aim has been replacing an ontology of the self he regards as inimical to liberalism with one that supports it (a communal self). By his own admission, he wants to rehabilitate liberalism, not supersede it.

There is much about the nature of the communal self that Sandel leaves unexplored. His account of just how selves are communally constituted, although enticing, is incomplete.[35] He explicitly opposes the teleological commitments of "classical Greek and medieval Christian conceptions" to deontological liberalism,[36] but whether this is for the purpose of provoking a reexamination and appreciation of those conceptions is not so clear.[37]

Near the close of *Liberalism and the Limits of Justice* he writes: "Although there may be a certain ultimate contingency in my having wound up the person I am—*only theology can say for sure*—it makes a moral difference none the less that, being the person I am, I affirm these ends rather than those, turn this way rather than that."[38] Is Sandel suggesting that only in the light of some insight we have into an ultimate, overarching human destiny (through theology) can the communities which are so crucial in shaping our identities themselves be appraised?

Apparently not, for in a review of Richard Neuhaus's *The Naked Public Square,* Sandel appears to recommend the restoration of a sense of community and the common good without having recourse to religious ideals. He finds an alternative basis for communal identity in the tradition of civic republicanism, "a public philosophy concerned less with salvation than with citizenship."[39] His remarks suggest, not that religion is unimportant—it may be very important in our private lives, in family life for example (which Cicero, we may recall, calls the "nursery" of our public life)—but that we must look elsewhere for the resources by which to form our political associations. We must turn to the tradition of political philosophy he terms civic republicanism.

IN DEFENSE OF CIVIC REPUBLICANISM

Responding, in part, to Sandel's criticism, Rawls eventually came to claim that the case for procedural liberalism—which Rawls began to call "political liberalism"[40]—is political not metaphysical. According to this emendation, we are to view the claims that citizens make qua citizens as equally valid, self-authenticating precisely and only inasmuch as it is citizens who make them. Whatever connections these claims might have to higher philosophical or religious principles must be deemed irrelevant to the discussion of such claims in the public domain.

In a review of Rawls's *Political Liberalism* Sandel calls for "more spacious public reason" than Rawlsian liberalism is able to muster. What Sandel hopes to achieve is the articulation of a public philosophy in which religious and philosophical values and principles are taken as legitimate forming agents of public *personae,* and therefore are seen to play a role in debates about the common good. At the same time, this more spacious public philosophy would promote "mutual respect among citizens who hold conflicting moral and religious views."

In *Democracy's Discontent,* Sandel takes up the task of articulating his positive vision.[41] In this work he continues and deepens his criticism of procedural liberalism epitomized by Rawls and others, tracing its history especially as it presents itself in Supreme Court decisions since the 1940s. This strand of understanding of the American polity is contrasted with what Sandel calls civic republicanism, which he finds dominant in the American experience in the run-up to World War II, and which he wishes to restore to our political vocabulary. Essentially, civic republicanism names the kind of regime in which everyone enjoys the prerogative of and takes responsibility for deliberating about the common good. Republican political theory, that is, joins democratic freedom and civic obligation: all are free to deliberate about the common good and the public policies designed to foster it and all are obligated to participate in these engagements. This in turn means that debates about what is good, about what ends are proper to be pursued in the public sphere, be admitted as legitimate, not excluded. The condition for such debates is the rejection of the principle that the right is prior to the good. Civic republicanism involves what Sandel calls the "formative project," which commits a political community to the effort to inculcate certain virtues in citizens in order to foster liberty and self-government. Sandel explains that

> [t]he formative project rejects the idea that government should be neutral toward the values and ends its citizens espouse. It seeks social and political arrangements that cultivate in citizens certain habits and dispositions, or civic virtues. Rather than affirm above all the capacity of persons to choose their own ends, the republican tradition accords the political community an explicit stake in the moral character of its citizens. It makes character a public, not merely private concern.[42]

In contrast to the neutralist ideal of citizens unencumbered with ends and activities they have not chosen for themselves, Sandel's civic republicanism proposes a view of citizenship which imposes "special responsibilities" and "obligations of solidarity" that derive from one's membership in "particular communities."[43] Sharing a common history and incurring special loyalties and moral obligations form the bonds that tie one to the communities of which he is a member. The engagement of self-rule that lies at the heart of the republican concept of citizenship "involves something more than going to the polls every two or four years and expressing interests, values and ends. . . . It also requires a knowledge of public affairs, a sense of belonging, a concern for the whole, and a moral bond with the community whose fate is at stake."[44]

In addition to the coarsening effects on character brought about by popular culture—movies, television, certain sectors of popular music—Sandel emphasizes in particular the deleterious effects of an unfettered economy, and most especially the widening gap between rich and poor. Whereas the procedural liberal would criticize this state of affairs on the grounds that the poor are unable to choose their life plans to the same extent as everyone else, the civic republican would launch a criticism from a different perspective, namely, from the conviction that such severe economic disparities undermine the sense of a shared common life. Sandel says:

> From Aristotle to Rousseau, republicans have worried about too great a gap between rich and poor if it leads to separate ways of life. For if fellow citizens become accustomed to living in separate neighborhoods, shopping in separate stores, taking different forms of transportation, not bumping up against one another in the course of their everyday life, then eventually they will find themselves unable to deliberate about the common good; they won't share enough to be able to think of one another as citizens with mutual obligations.[45]

We should recall that the communities of which Sandel is speaking are not those we choose to join. Rather, we are part of these communities prior to any decision we have made. Consent plays no role here. Thus, we typically just *find* ourselves members of a particular nation, family, race, religion.[46] We are ineluctably "encumbered selves," carrying as part of our identity the values, perspectives, affective affinities, loyalties, and obligations we have acquired as the result of what others have done and chosen who have gone before us.

But how is it that we have these loyalties and these obligations prior to choice? How is it that we are ineluctably connected to these prior communities? To these questions several answers emerge in the course of Sandel's analysis.

First, such loyalties and obligations are constituent features of the membership we enjoy in a given community. That is, to be included as part of a family or a political community means we acquire certain benefits, share in certain goods, as a result of what others have done for us. We are therefore in their debt: we owe at least some degree of loyalty, have incurred some measure of obligation, to those who have made prior arrangements on our behalf.

Second, there is in each of us, Sandel asserts, "the yearning for a public life of larger meaning."[47] Americans are deeply disenchanted with the "naked public square" and its exceedingly thin and impoverished moral discourse. They seek a more fulsome public persona, precisely because they know—if sometimes only inchoately—that merely pursuing their own private, self-chosen ends in isolation from the larger realm of public engagements constitutes less than a fully satisfying life.

Third—and this produces another source of disenchantment and anxiety—citizens often feel powerless to influence the overarching forces (especially, but not only, economic forces) with which they must contend. "The triumph of the voluntarist conception of freedom has coincided with a growing sense of disempowerment. Despite the expansion of rights in recent decades, Americans find to their frustration that they are losing control of the forces that govern their lives."[48] To a significant extent, Sandel thinks, this is because people have been eschewing civic engagement. What we are now, perhaps, in a position to realize is that liberty in the sense of having a tolerable degree of influence over one's environment requires just that civic persona and precisely those republican virtues Sandel is championing. Otherwise, the freedom and mastery over one's life the procedural republic has promised remains illusive. Sandel concludes that

> [o]ur present predicament lends weight to the republican claim that liberty cannot be detached from self-government and the virtues that sustain it, the formative project cannot be dispensed with after all . . . cannot secure the liberty it promises because it cannot inspire the moral and civic engagement self-government requires.[49]

The obligation to think about and act so as to advance the common good of one's civic community presupposes that one is able to do so with at least a minimal level of proficiency. "If sharing self-rule requires the capacity to deliberate well about the common good," Sandel observes, "then citizens must possess certain excellences—of character, judgment, and concern for the whole."[50] That is, citizens of the civil republic must acquire and continually cultivate certain virtues. Absent these virtues, they will be unable to deliberate and act well, which means that they will be unable to exercise the prerogatives and fulfill the duties of being a citizen. If the prerogatives and duties of citizenship are constitutive of human beings, the exercise of republican virtues cannot be viewed as mere options one can legitimately choose to set aside. One might just as well decide not to take nourishment. It is therefore in the interest of a political community to inculcate virtue in its citizens, as well as in the interest of its citizens to participate in the project of virtue acquisition. Their political community cannot leave them completely free to pursue whatever self-chosen ends they decide to pursue, as the neutral liberal regime would do.

A major obstacle to carrying out this formative project of "soulcraft" along republican lines derives from the sheer size of modern political associations, wedded as they are to nations of cumbersome proportions. Modern nations in general, and the United States in particular, are spread out to such a vast extent that establishing a strong sense of communal life is extremely difficult. Granted that citizens are in fact and in many ways interdependent—economically, politically, and in terms of communications technology—they do not share a robust civic identity, a "public life worth affirming."[51] People rarely meet directly, face-to-face, to discuss common political concerns. This results in citizens retreating to the pursuit of their own individual life projects, thinking only intermittently, if at all, about their connection to the common good of the entire political community. Some now emphasize the global context of this problem. Noting the increasing ties between the peoples of the world, these international communitarians wish to promote what they see as lacking, namely, a global community worthy of the name. What is needed, in the words of the Commission on Global Government, is "a universal moral community."[52] Civil society on a global scale, says Richard Falk, must be "premised upon global or species solidarity," on the notion of global citizenship.[53] More than being merely citizens of Russia or Japan or Australia, or any other particular polis, people should think of themselves most emphatically as cosmopolitans, members of a universal city. This sentiment is summed up eloquently in the motto adopted by the nineteenth-century abolitionist, William Lloyd Garrison: "Our country is the world—Our countrymen are all mankind."[54]

Although Sandel acknowledges that this cosmopolitan civic ideal has certain merits—that it can protect one from a narrow and rigid parochialism, for example, and teach people that they have obligations beyond the borders of their own country—he insists that it carries with it dangers as well. Some of these are by now rather well known. One's moral sentiments can, in fact, be so universalized that they effectively eclipse a sense of obligation to those right next door to us. To love mankind while being indifferent to our immediate neighbors, in particular men and women among whom we actually and daily interact, is a classic, perennial evasion. "The love of humanity," Sandel cautions, "is a noble sentiment, but most of the time we live our lives by smaller solidarities," which fact suggests that there are "certain limits to the bounds of moral sympathy" and that "we learn to love humanity not in general but through its particular expressions."[55] Just as Sandel's criticism of the liberal self is that it is inadequately situated, so also does he fault the cosmopolitan self on the same grounds. To claim that my primary allegiance is to "all men" and therefore somehow prior to my moral duties to my own countrymen is simply to reaffirm the unencumbered self on a higher level.

Rather than invest hope in the cosmopolitan ideal, Sandel counsels a reconsideration of American federalism, which embodies the insight that "self-government works best when sovereignty is dispersed and citizenship formed across multiple sites of civic engagement."[56] When citizens enact aspirations of self-determination within a variety of intermediate institutions—that is, associations that stand between the state and the isolated individual—they expose themselves to a civic character formation that is not coercive.[57] In pluralism there is freedom. Sandel criticizes Rousseau's version of civic republicanism for its aspirations of molding citizens to a single, unified and undifferentiated version of the general will; Rousseau wanted no institutions standing between the state and its members.[58] Not Rousseau, but Tocqueville gives us the sort of civic identity that preserves freedom and empowers people to deliberate about how their lives should go. "Tocqueville [Sandel says] stressed the republican benefits of political bodies intermediate between the individual and the state, such as townships. . . . Practicing self-government, Tocqueville observes, impels citizens to larger spheres of political activity as well."[59]

But Tocqueville's township republicanism—as well as Thomas Jefferson's earlier proposal of a ward system to encourage direct political participation—proved not to be enduring, or (in Jefferson's case) feasible, solutions to the problem of bigness.[60] Sandel thinks that the solution already lies ready to hand, to wit, in other intermediate associations such as trade unions, school and workplace groups, churches and synagogues. Here is where the moral character of citizens are most directly and effectively formed. Note that these are typically voluntary associations; as such, they preserve the freedom that procedural republic exalts, but without abandoning people to a debilitating autonomy. The civil rights movement is for Sandel the exemplary instance of this kind of civic engagement. It did more than just secure freedom for disenfranchised Americans to pursue their self-chosen ends; by securing a space for discourse and action in support of the common good, it related citizens to each other in a shared sense of moral transformation: it enabled people to experience a common, public *persona*. It was a formative project, not merely a liberating project. Sandel summarizes this achievement:

> The formative aspect of republican politics requires public spaces that gather citizens together, enable them to interpret their condition, and cultivate solidarity and civic engagement. . . . We commonly think of the civil rights movement as finding its fruition in the civil rights and voting rights laws passed by Congress. But the nation would never have acted without a movement whose roots lay in more particular identities and places.[61]

A note of caution and qualification is appropriate at this juncture. Although he has commonly been located among the communitarians, Sandel has nevertheless been at pains to exclude himself from at least a certain sense of communitarianism, from what he takes to be an essentially historicist strand of this movement. Thus he writes:

> The term "communitarian" is misleading, however, insofar as it implies that rights should rest on the values or preferences that prevail in any given community at any given time. Few, if any, of those who have challenged the priority of the right [over the good] are communitarians in this sense. The question is not whether rights should be respected, but whether rights can be identified and justified in a way that does not presuppose any particular conception of the good. At issue . . . is not the relative weight of individual and communal claims, but the terms of relation between the right and the good.[62]

Instead of taking one's moral bearings by *a* community, Sandel argues that our moral sensibilities are properly formed as a result of our connection to multiple communities. As we have seen, pluralism is the check against acquiring a narrowly encumbered self. Sandelian civic republicanism "requires citizens who can think and act as multiply-situated selves." Our proper task is to cultivate the ability to "negotiate our way among the sometimes overlapping, sometimes conflicting obligations that claim us" and thus to live with the tension this pluralism engenders.[63] This situation can be seen as both a predicament and an opportunity. It is a predicament inasmuch as we cannot evade rival claims to our allegiance, some of which claims will not be easily accommodated. But this predicament also constitutes an opportunity for growth in moral maturity, for the exercise of prudence.

CONCLUSION

To those who are interested in reinvigorating the older philosophical tradition of political theory, Sandel offers helpful guidance. His defense of civic republicanism with its stress on the importance of the common good is a welcome foil to the procedural republic of contemporary liberalism. Having invoked the centrality of the notion of the common good, however, Sandel does not stay to thematize it. The reader never encounters an explication of this most crucial concept. This omission has the unfortunate effect of leaving the impression that the notion is incorrigibly vague, as well as the effect of portraying the common good as mere competitor to the good of individuals, as though one must always sacrifice one's own good for that of the community. The idea that the common good can be the good of individuals acting in concert to bring about a benefit that they would be unable to achieve while acting without coordination is implicit in much of what Sandel says, to be sure; but an exposition of just how, precisely, this can occur is missing.[64] We have a sign pointing in the right direction, but we do not have a detailed map of what the place should look like when we arrive. Still, it is helpful to have the sign.

Sandel should also be commended for being forthright about how deliberation concerning the common good often goes. He wisely points out that such deliberation is quite often beset with disagreement. People who share fundamental philosophical principles can still disagree about particular applications of these principles. Civic republicans committed to advancing the common good can be expected to disagree about just what policy, what course of action, will secure it. "It is often held against republicanism," Sandel says, " that it requires shared values. It doesn't really. It is a tradition teeming with disagreement about what counts as virtue, what kinds of citizens should be formed, what the formative project should aim at."[65] In an elegant gloss on this point, Sandel remarks that

> the case for reviving the civic strand of freedom is not that it would make for a more consensual politics. There is no reason to suppose that a politics organized around republican themes would command a greater measure of agreement than does our present politics. As the reigning political agenda invites disagreement about the meaning of neutrality, rights, and truly voluntary choice, a political agenda informed by civic concerns would invite disagreement about the meaning of virtue and the forms of self-government that are possible in our time. . . . The political divisions arising in response to these issues would probably differ from those that govern the debate over the welfare state. But political divisions there would surely be. A successful revival of republican politics would not resolve our political disputes; at best, it would invigorate political debate by grappling more directly with the obstacles to self-government in our time.[66]

This recognition, I would suggest, is akin to Aquinas's insight that using the principles of the natural law as resource for human (i.e., positive) law involves not deducing a conclusion from premises (a matter of logic) but involves determining a particular arrangement of affairs from general rules (a matter of prudential judgment). Thus for citizens who agree on the general precepts of the law to disagree over their precise instantiation is, for Aquinas, altogether natural and proper. People equally committed to a natural law understanding of political association are not thereby exempt from the process of deliberation, argument, and opposition. To live with such tensions, and to engage them with civility, is part of what it means to be related as citizens.[67]

This being the case, one finds it a bit puzzling that Sandel should persist in judging the republican tradition better able "to deal with a pluralist society, to deal with disagreement" than natural law theory, even as he acknowledges that a natural law jurisprudence furnishes an apt and useful critique of the liberalism he targets. Thus he says:

> It is the openness of argument about virtue, about the conditions of self-government, about qualities of character that democratic life requires, and the competing answers to those questions, that I think we need to restore, not a particular answer to that question. That is why I see the republican tradition as a more apt rival to the reigning public philosophy than the natural law tradition, though I know this could be the beginning of a long argument.[68]

One might reply that Aquinas's natural law understanding is more congruent with Sandel's civic republicanism than he seems prepared to allow. That Sandel appreciates the pertinence of this "long argument" between the two understandings, however, bodes well for the future of the continuing conversation about the proper terms of political life.

NOTES

1. Michael J. Sandel, "Morality and the Liberal Ideal," *New Republic,* May 7, 1984, 16.

2. Sandel is often grouped with other political theorists under the rubric "communitarian critics of liberalism." Although far from constituting a philosophical school, communitarians nevertheless share a cluster of convictions, most notably that human agents are inevitably situated in, and are therefore constituted by, historical communities and traditions. Along with Sandel, perhaps most often mentioned in this connection are Alasdair MacIntyre, Charles Taylor, Robert Bellah, William Sullivan, Benjamin Barber, and William Galston. For a general discussion, see Christopher Lasch, "The Communitarian Critique of Liberalism," *Soundings* 69 (summer 1985): 60–76. For a vigorous critique of the communitarians—whom the author characterizes as "antiliberals"—see Stephen Holmes, "The Permanent Structure of Antiliberal Thought," in *Liberalism and the Moral Life*, ed. Nancy L. Rosenblum (Cambridge, Mass.: Harvard University Press, 1989), 227–53.

3. Whether Sandel is accurate in his reading of Rawls is an issue I cannot enter into here. That Sandel has attempted to read Rawls with care and understanding is to my mind everywhere evident in *Liberalism and the Limits of Justice*. Indeed, Sandel's reading of Rawls is in many respects sympathetic, at least in the sense of trying to think along with him and to identify the nerve of his argument.

4. Michael J. Sandel, "The Procedural Republic and the Unencumbered Self," *Political Theory* 12 (February 1984): 82.

5. For the first description, see *Liberalism,*1 and passim; for the second, see Michael J. Sandel, "The Political Theory of the Procedural Republic," *Revue de métaphysique et de morale* 93 (January–March 1988): 61; and Sandel's introduction to the volume of readings he has edited, *Liberalism and Its Critics* (New York: New York University Press, 1984), 7ff.

6. See Sandel, "The Political Theory of the Procedural Republic," 67, and *Liberalism,* 66–67.

7. Sandel, "The Procedural Republic and the Unencumbered Self," 82.

8. See Sandel, *Liberalism,* 2, and " Procedural Republic and the Unencumbered Self," 82.

9. John Rawls, *A Theory of Justice* (Cambridge, Mass.: Harvard University Press, 1971), 3; quoted in *Liberalism,* 15.

10. Sandel, *Liberalism,* 15–16.

11. Sandel, *Liberalism,* 19.

12. Rawls, *A Theory of Justice,* 560; quoted in *Liberalism,* 19.

13. Sandel, "The Procedural Republic and the Unencumbered Self," 85.

14. Sandel, *A Theory of Justice,* 264; quoted in *Liberalism,* 14.

15. For a more extended discussion of the original position and the veil of ignorance, see Michael Pakaluk's essay on Rawls in this volume.

16. Sandel, "The Procedural Republic and the Unencumbered Self," 86.

17. *A Theory of Justice,* 42; quoted in *Liberalism,* 123.

18. John Rawls, "Kantian Constructivism in Moral Theory," *Journal of Philosophy* 77 (September 1980): 543; quoted in *Liberalism,* 177.

19. Sandel, "The Procedural Republic and the Unencumbered Self," 87.

20. Rawls, *A Theory of Justice,* 560; quoted in "The Procedural Republic and the Unencumbered Self," 86.

21. Sandel, "The Procedural Republic and the Unencumbered Self," 87; emphasis in original.

22. Sandel, *Liberalism,* 131; emphases in original.

23. Sandel, *Liberalism,* 129.

24. Sandel, *Liberalism,* 70.

25. Rawls, *A Theory of Justice,* 101; quoted in *Liberalism,* 70.

26. Sandel, *Liberalism,* 88.

27. Sandel, "The Procedural Republic and the Unencumbered Self," 89.

28. Sandel, "The Procedural Republic and the Unencumbered Self," 89.

29. Sandel, "The Procedural Republic and the Unencumbered Self," 89–90.

30. Sandel, *Liberalism,* 178.

31. Sandel, *Liberalism,* 179.

32. Sandel, *Liberalism,* 172–73.

33. Sandel, *Liberalism,* 179.

34. It should be noted that the communities for which Sandel seems to have the most sympathy are the smaller, subpolitical ("intermediate") communities of family, church, neighborhood, labor union, and municipality. Although Sandel recognizes the penchant for forging a sense of national community—advanced earlier in this century by Herbert Croly and the proponents of the New Deal, and more recently by some

Democrats—he thinks this project has failed to win the allegiance of a majority of Americans. See Sandel, "The Political Theory of the Procedural Republic," 63, 65–66; and "Morality and the Liberal Ideal," 17.

35. Sandel's hint (it is hardly more than this) that language plays a prominent role in establishing one's identity is worth exploring at greater length. See *Liberalism*, 172–73, where his remarks seem to imply that, just as communities are established by the speaking of a common language—not merely the speaking of common tongue, but the sharing of what might be called the language of a culture—so also one's self-identity is formed by participating in a community of speech. Classical authors such as Aristotle (*Politics,* I. 2, 1253a10–17, trans. H. Rackham [London: Heineman, 1932]) and Cicero (*De Officiis* I. 16, trans. Walter Miller [Cambridge, Mass.: Harvard University Press, 1913]) seem especially to have appreciated this wider sense of language and its role in establishing communities. Unfortunately, Sandel does not amplify his discussion of these intriguing features of language.

36. Sandel, *Liberalism,* 175.

37. Sandel need not turn to some version of teleology or the natural law tradition to buttress his notion of encumbered selves. The choice is not simply between unencumbered-selves-without-teleology and encumbered-selves-with-teleology. One could use the account given by those contemporary thinkers who recommend some version of the "historicist" view. Here one would take one's bearings by, and commit one's loyalties to, those communities of which one just happens to find oneself a part. Benjamin Barber argues for this sort of understanding in *Strong Democracy* (Berkeley: University of California Press, 1984). See also Michael Oakeshott's work, notably *Rationalism and Politics* (London: Methuen, 1963) and *On Human Conduct* (Oxford: Clarendon Press, 1975). In any case, Sandel has shown no affinity for this way of thinking.

38. Sandel, *Liberalism,* 180; emphasis added.

39. Michael J. Sandel, "The State and the Soul," review of Richard John Neuhaus, *The Naked Public Square,* and John Diggins, *The Lost Soul of American Politics,* in *New Republic,* 10 June (1985), 40.

40. See John Rawls, *Political Liberalism* (New York: Columbia University Press, 1993), xvi and passim.

41. Michael J. Sandel, *Democracy's Discontent: America in Search of a Public Philosophy* (Cambridge: Harvard University Press, 1996).

42. Michael J. Sandel, "Liberalism and Republicanism: Friends or Foes? A Reply to Richard Dagger," *Review of Politics* 61 (spring 1999): 210. For a thoughtful and provocative critical assessment of Sandel's argument in *Democracy's Discontent,* see the article to which Sandel's remarks here reply, Richard Dagger, "The Sandelian Republic and the Encumbered Self," in the same issue of *Review of Politics,* 181–208, along with Dagger's rejoinder to Sandel, 215–17.

43. Sandel, *Democracy's Discontent,* 15.

44. Michael J. Sandel, "Keynote Address: Democracy's Discontent: America in Search of a Public Philosophy," *Georgetown Law Journal* 85, 2074 (1997). This article forms part of a symposium on *Democracy's Discontent,* and contains, beside Sandel's lead article, critical responses from Hope M. Babcock, Howard F. Chang, Viet E. Dinh, John Hasnas, and Kevin Quinn, S.J., at 2085–187.

45. Michael J. Sandel, "The Constitution of the Procedural Republic: Liberal Rights and Civic Virtues," *Fordham Law Review* 66, 13 (1997).

46. This is not to say that there are just no circumstances in which we choose to become a member, say, of a religion or to become a citizen of a country. One can certainly choose to move from being a member of no religious denomination to being a Roman Catholic, or a Southern Baptist, or a Muslim. One can deliberate about the benefits of becoming a citizen of England. Concerning this last case, however, it is well to bear in mind Michael Oakeshott's remark that one is always and ineluctably a member of some civil association or other, so that were one to extricate oneself from one such community one would inevitably land in another. See "The Vocabulary of a Modern European State," *Political Studies* 28 (December 1975): 411. Still, these are not paradigmatic instances. Typically, one is now an Englishman because one was born such, and one is a Catholic because of choices others have made on one's behalf.

47. Sandel, *Democracy's Discontent*, 322.

48. Sandel, *Democracy's Discontent*, 323.

49. Sandel, *Democracy's Discontent*, 323.

50. Sandel, *Democracy's Discontent*, 318.

51. Sandel, *Democracy's Discontent*, 340.

52. Quoted in Sandel, *Democracy's Discontent*, 341.

53. Quoted in Sandel, *Democracy's Discontent*, 341.

54. The motto appeared in each issue of Garrison's antislavery journal, *The Liberator*, which began publication in January 1831. For Garrison's own gloss on this dictum, see the collection of his speeches and writings in George M. Fredrickson, ed., *William Lloyd Garrison* (Englewood Cliffs, N.J.: Prentice Hall, 1968), 47–48. For a vigorous contemporary defense of cosmopolitanism, see Martha C. Nussbaum, *For Love of Country: Debating the Limits of Patriotism,* ed. Joshua Cohen (Boston: Beacon Press, 1996), and her more substantial treatment, *The Cosmopolitan Tradition,* forthcoming from Yale University Press.

55. Sandel, *Democracy's Discontent*, 342–43.

56. Sandel, *Democracy's Discontent*, 347.

57. For a classic explication of the role played by intermediate institutions, see *Democracy and Mediating Structures,* ed. Michael Novak (Washington, D.C.: American Enterprise Institute, 1980).

58. See, e.g., Jean-Jacques Rousseau, *On the Social Contract,* ed. Roger D. Masters, trans. Judith R. Masters (New York: St. Martin's Press, 1978), II. 3.

59. Sandel, *Democracy's Discontent*, 347.

60. For Sandel's brief discussion of Jefferson's ward system, see *Democracy's Discontent,* 347–48.

61. Sandel, *Democracy's Discontent*, 349.

62. Review of John Rawls, *Political Liberalism, Harvard Law Review* 107 (1994): 1767.

63. Sandel, *Democracy's Discontent,* 350. Sandel notes here that classical republicanism, of, say, Aristotle's Athenian polis, saw self-government as entrenched "in a particular place, carried out by citizens loyal to that place and the way of life it embodies." However, "self-government today . . . requires a politics that plays itself out

not in a single place—whether nation or town or family or neighborhood or some transnational political community. It requires instead a politics that plays itself out in a multiplicity of settings, from neighborhoods, to nations, to the world as a whole. Politics today requires citizens who can live with the ambiguity of complex identities." *The Constitution of the Procedural Republic,* 14.

64. For a nuanced explication of the concept of the common good, see Yves R. Simon, *Philosophy of Democratic Government* (Chicago: University of Chicago Press, 1951), 36–71; and *A General Theory of Authority* (South Bend, Ind.: University of Notre Dame Press, 1962), 23–79. See also the perceptive remarks by John Oesterle, *Ethics: The Introduction to Moral Science* (Englewood Cliffs, N.J.: Prentice Hall, 1957), 198–201; and Charles Taylor, "Cross-Purposes: The Liberal-Communitarian Debate," in *Liberalism and the Moral Life,* 167–72.

65. Sandel, "The Constitution of the Procedural Republic," 15.

66. Sandel, *Democracy's Discontent,* 337–38.

67. For Aquinas's analysis see *Summa Theologiae* Ia-IIae, 95, 2; also 96, 1, ad 1. For a discussion of this issue, see Terry Hall, "Legislation," in *Natural Law and Contemporary Public Policy,* ed. David F. Forte (Washington, D.C.: Georgetown University Press, 1998), 135–56. Cf. Thomas Gilbey, one of Aquinas's most perceptive expositors, who finds at the heart of the latter's political thought the engagement of *civilis conversatio,* civil conversation. *The Political Thought of Thomas Aquinas* (Chicago: University of Chicago Press, 1958).

68. Sandel, *The Constitution of the Procedural Republic,* 15.

7

Alasdair MacIntyre

Recovering the Rationality of Traditions

David M. Wagner

Liberalism, accustomed to swinging the axe of skeptical criticism at other traditions of moral philosophy, has been coming under attack itself of late years from Alasdair MacIntyre (formerly of Vanderbilt, Notre Dame, and Duke, now returned to Notre Dame). The core of his argument is that the attempt to ground morality in tradition-independent rationality leads only to emotivism; rational morality must rest on the practices of human communities, which give rise to traditions of enquiry. Rationality subsists within intellectual traditions, not outside them. This theory has been developed in *After Virtue* (1981, 2nd ed. 1984), *Whose Justice? Which Rationality?* (1988), and *Three Rival Versions of Moral Enquiry: Encyclopedia, Genealogy, and Tradition* (1990).[1]

For MacIntyre, liberalism is in crisis because, in all its forms, it is an attempt to carry on a fundamentally flawed tradition of enquiry, namely, that of the Enlightenment. The Enlightenment, of course, did not look upon itself as a tradition but rather as an emancipation from tradition. From this emancipation would come new modes of moral thinking, which would be independent of all tradition. In *After Virtue,* MacIntyre details the failures of this project and argues that it was inevitable.

The view that such failure was *not* inevitable has led to various attempts to make it work; these attempts (by John Stuart Mill, John Rawls, Ronald Dworkin, et al.) constitute the subsequent history of the liberal tradition.[2] In *After Virtue,* MacIntyre argues that these, too, have failed, and in *Whose Justice? Which Rationality?,* he pursues the point that the Enlightenment and its liberal progeny, although conceived as antidotes to tradition, are themselves merely one more tradition of enquiry. MacIntyre's position throughout is that, contrary to the

Enlightenment's pretensions, no rationally conclusive, tradition-independent standards exist for choosing any one tradition of moral enquiry rather than another.

Yet MacIntyre rejects relativism. Instead, he adopts a test that consists of asking which tradition is best able to repel challenges and deal with the "epistemological crises" that arise when one tradition is challenged by another. On the last page of *Whose Justice? Which Rationality?* MacIntyre suggests that the winner under this robustness test is the Thomistic tradition.

When we look at his 1988 Gifford Lectures at the University of Edinburgh, published as *Three Rival Versions of Moral Inquiry,* we find that MacIntyre's universe of credible options—which in *After Virtue* boiled down to Nietzsche or Aristotle—now boils down to Nietzsche or Thomas Aquinas.

It is fundamental for MacIntyre—and essential before we go further—that the word "tradition" signifies not merely inherited beliefs or practices but also an ongoing, transgenerational discussion based on inherited beliefs and capable of amending and reformulating those beliefs when necessary. Thus what MacIntyre means by "tradition" is a tradition of enquiry; or, as he clarifies in *Three Rival Version of Moral Enquiry,* philosophy as a craft, in which apprentices must learn the rudiments from a master.

THE STARTING POINT: EMOTIVISM

MacIntyre begins his argument in the first book we are considering, *After Virtue,* by observing something about contemporary moral argument that must have struck anyone who has observed it or participated in it: whatever rational and analytic elements it may contain, it soon boils down to "Well, I just feel. . . ." This, says MacIntyre, is emotivism:

Emotivism is the doctrine that all evaluative judgments and more specifically all moral judgments are *nothing but* expressions of preference, expressions of attitude or feeling, insofar as they are moral or evaluative in character.[3] Emotivism fills the void left by the breakdown of earlier forms of moral enquiry, which had certain features that MacIntyre considers crucial: they proceeded from the actual practice of human communities and were therefore historically contingent; and they had a definite view of the human *telos.* The Enlightenment acted, and was meant to act, as a solvent to both teleology and religion: away with the personalist God whose will matters in human affairs; away, too, with any notion of human purpose beyond what the individual chooses for himself (or, for Rousseau, what the community, detached from both God and tradition, chooses for him). Away, as well, with mere historical contingency: the Enlightenment project was a search for rational morality as such.

What this project has left us with in the field of moral argument is some-times called pluralism, but this reassuring word masks a troubling reality:

> The notion of pluralism may equally well apply to an ordered dialogue of inter-secting viewpoints and to an unharmonious melange of ill-assorted fragments. The suspicion—and for the moment it can only be a suspicion—that it is the lat-ter with which we have to deal is heightened when we recognize that all those various concepts which inform our moral discourse were originally at home in larger totalities of theory and practice in which they enjoyed a role and function supplied by contexts of which they have now been deprived.[4]

The foregoing passage is a brief preview of much of the rest of the book and its two sequels, in which certain "larger totalities of theory and practice" are looked at in great detail. MacIntyre's purpose in doing so is to support his thesis as to why moral argument has degenerated to its present state: the proj-ect of deriving morality from pure reason, while rejecting experience,[5] reve-lation, and teleology, had to fail, and its failure has left in its wake nothing but emotivism and indeterminacy.

THE IS–OUGHT PROBLEM AS KEY TO THE FAILURE OF THE ENLIGHTENMENT

David Hume argued (and modern legal positivists are fond of repeating) that there is no logical connection between a premise framed around "is" and a conclusion framed around "ought." You cannot get from a descriptive prem-ise to a prescriptive conclusion. MacIntyre sees this dilemma as a typical product of the Enlightenment and as evidence of its fundamental errors, es-pecially its rejection of teleology.

To use MacIntyre's two examples, we know what a good watch or a good farmer is, because we know what a watch or a farmer is supposed to be. Thus we may safely assert that, if some amended version of the "No 'ought' con-clusion from 'is' premises" principle is to hold good, it must exclude argu-ments involving functional concepts from its scope. But this suggests strongly that those who have insisted that *all* moral argument fall within the scope of such a principle may have been doing so because they took it for granted that *no* moral arguments involve functional concepts. Yet moral ar-guments within the classical, Aristotelian tradition—whether in its Greek or in its medieval versions—involve at least one central functional concept, the concept of *man* understood as having an essential nature and an essential purpose or function; and it is when and only when the classical tradition in its integrity has been substantially rejected that moral arguments change their character so that they fall within some version of the "No 'ought' conclusion from 'is' premises" principle.[6]

As MacIntyre sees it, the Enlightenment severed morality from the only bases it had ever had—which were the only bases it ever could have. People today who emote about how they "feel" about grave moral issues and people today who must listen to them are the heirs of the confusion to which the Enlightenment project has led.

THE ENLIGHTENMENT AND NIETZSCHE

The nineteenth century saw many attempts to shore up the Enlightenment. One of these was the profound certainty of the Victorian rationalists that their intellectual community was uniquely able (as against past eras of human enquiry) to discern "facts" from "values" and to engage in a dispassionate search for objective truth. MacIntyre analyzes the Victorian rationalist worldview in *Three Rival Versions of Moral Enquiry.* Viewing them as a man of the late twentieth century, MacIntyre punctures the pomposity of the late Victorians, but it is important to his overall argument that he was not the first to do so. That honor belongs to a man of the late nineteenth century—Nietzsche.

In MacIntyre's work, Nietzsche is not only a powerful critic of all rationalism but also a symbol of ultimate ruin. *This*—Nietzscheanism, with its radical denial of truth and affirmation of will—is what happens when you make the mistakes the Enlightenment made. Like Alberich in Richard Wagner's *Ring of the Nibelung,* Nietzsche appears at intervals in MacIntyre's recent books, cursing the gods and predicting the day he will storm Valhalla with Hella's hordes.

MacIntyre credits Nietzsche's moral philosophy with being "one of the two genuine theoretical alternatives confronting anyone trying to analyze the moral condition of our culture."[7] Indeed, Nietzsche is "*the* moral philosopher *if* the only alternatives to Nietzsche's moral philosophy turn out to be those formulated by the philosophers of the Enlightenment and their successors."[8] Nietzsche is the only game in town, if the Enlightenment and its successors are the only *other* game in town. But are they?

We find the above-quoted statements in a chapter called "Nietzsche or Aristotle." These are the alternatives, as seen in *After Virtue*—although MacIntyre also is concerned that we may need a new St. Benedict, apparently feeling that a new dark age is upon us and that the Aristotelian tradition can be conserved only through retreat from the world. MacIntyre joins Nietzsche in criticizing the Enlightenment for failing to answer—or even to ask—the question, "What sort of person am I to become?" Instead of conceiving of morality as a derivative of the process of answering this question, as an Aristotelian would, the Enlightenment redefined morality as self-existing rules, and took as the initial question of moral enquiry, "What rules ought we to follow, and why ought we to obey them?" This shift from virtues-first to rules-first analysis dominates liberal thinking today.

Ronald Dworkin has recently argued that the central doctrine of modern liberalism is the thesis that questions about the *good life for man* or the ends of human life are to be regarded from the public standpoint as systematically unsettleable. On these questions individuals are free to agree or disagree. The rules of morality and law hence are not to be derived from or justified in terms of some fundamental conception of the good for man. In arguing thus Dworkin has, I believe, identified a stance characteristic not just of liberalism but also of modernity. "The virtues are sentiments, that is, related families of dispositions and propensities regulated by a higher-order desire, in this case a desire to act from the corresponding moral principles," asserts John Rawls, one of the latest moral philosophers of modernity [*Theory of Justice,* 1971, 192] and elsewhere he defines "the fundamental moral virtues" as "strong and normally effective desires to act on the basic principles of right" (436).[9]

So the problem is, you grasp the rules end of the stick, and you find Nietzsche on the other end. But long ago, humankind grasped the other end of the stick, that of the virtues.

FORWARD INTO THE PAST

So saying, MacIntyre begins two separate tours of the history of moral enquiry: one in *After Virtue,* the other accounting for the bulk of *Whose Justice? Which Rationality?* For each tradition and philosopher that he looks at, he describes a way of thinking about justice, and a corresponding way of thinking about practical rationality. Links between the philosophers and the historical circumstances are stressed.[10]

The object of these tours is to show us the origins and development of what MacIntyre calls "tradition-constituted, tradition-constitutive enquiry."

> Of what did the Enlightenment deprive us? What the Enlightenment made us for the most part blind to and what we now need to recover is, so I shall argue, a conception of rational enquiry as embodied in a tradition, a conception according to which the standards of rational justification themselves emerge from and are part of a history in which they transcend the limitations of and provide remedies for the defects of their predecessors within the history of that same tradition.[11]

It should be emphasized that history and philosophy are intertwined throughout MacIntyre's survey; it is part of his argument that modern departmental boundaries within universities—boundaries that are part of the heritage of the Enlightenment—are arbitrary and tend to falsify our view of the past:

> There ought not to be two histories, one of political and moral action and one of political and moral theorizing, because there were not two pasts, one populated only by actions, the other only by theories. Every action is the bearer and expression of more or less theory-laden beliefs and concepts; every piece of theorizing and every expression of belief is a political and moral action.[12]

It is outside the scope of this chapter to convey the richness of detail and analysis in both of these excursions. But in outline, this is what we see (note that the focus is sometimes on the communities themselves, and sometimes on the individual philosophers who conducted moral enquiry from within the life of those communities):

Homeric Greece: a world in which human functions are very well defined, and every person is judged in terms of how well he fulfills the function in which he finds himself, especially those of soldier and king.

Periclean Athens: a polis animated by Homeric notions of virtue as function well performed, but increasingly torn by a split between what MacIntyre calles "the goods of excellence" and "the goods of effectiveness."

Aristotle: systematizes the enquiry begun by Socrates and Plato, in a manner that not only incorporates the practices of Athens but later interacts fruitfully with Judaism, Islam, and Christianity.

Augustine: amends the Aristotelian concept of the will to account for the fact that the human person sometimes wills one thing yet does another, as St. Paul pointed out.

Aquinas: overcomes the epistemological crisis caused in Christianity by Christendom's encounter with Aristotle; synthesizes Augustine and Aristotle and thereby inaugurates a powerful new tradition.

The Scottish Enlightenment: an uneasy synthesis of Calvinist Christianity and Aristotle.

David Hume: as an "Anglicizing" Scotsman rejects the Scottish Enlightenment in favor of an English concept of reciprocal rights in a society based on landed property.

The Enlightenment: an attempt to replace and supersede tradition by means of rationalism, but it fails to overcome its inherent tendency toward nihilism and merely inaugurates another tradition.

THE DEMISE OF LIBERALISM

The tradition inaugurated by the Enlightenment is that of liberalism, and Mac-Intyre's argument that this tradition has failed is central to his overall thesis.

The Enlightenment was an attempt to overcome tradition, religion, and particularity; in moral philosophy, its goal was "to construct a morality for tradition-free individuals."[13] Over the past two hundred years, this has been attempted "by an appeal to one out of several conceptions of universalizability or to one out of equally multifarious conceptions of utility or to shared intuitions or to some combination of these,"[14] but the only result is "a history of continually unresolved disputes, so that there emerges no uncontested and incontestable account of what tradition-independent morality consists in and consequently no neutral set of criteria by means of which the claims of rival and contending traditions could be adjudicated."[15] As evidence, MacIntyre points to the book review pages of the professional philosophical journals, which are "the graveyards of constructive academic philosophy."[16] He might also have cited certain Supreme Court decisions in which the clashes of opinion and dissent reveal fundamental clashes of moral outlook (e.g., *Bowers v Hardwick*[17] and *Michael H. v Gerald D.*[18]).

At all events, hardly anyone would dispute that our epoch is characterized by moral clashes that seem not to be publicly resolvable. Does that mean the failure of moral rationalism as such? More precisely: must we conclude that the Enlightenment experiment in moral philosophy has failed because its intellectual heirs have failed to produce moral arguments that persuade all rational persons to whom they are made?

Yes, says MacIntyre—because the Enlightenment set itself just such a goal. What else can a project of deriving rationally based, tradition-independent morality mean, if not that the work-product of that enquiry will be compelling to all rational hearers? Those who have tried to carry out the Enlightenment project (in this passage MacIntyre specifically cites Kant and Rawls, and alludes to Mill by referencing the utility standard[19]) may protest at being held to such a high standard of success, but it is not MacIntyre who has imposed this standard on them. His test, as we shall see, is not the power to persuade all rational listeners, but the power to express and carry forward a tradition capable of overcoming the epistemological crises that it faces as its history unfolds.

The failure of the intellectual project that the Enlightenment set for itself has led to paradoxes in the social order constructed under its dominion, namely, that of liberal individualism. The perpetual inconclusiveness of liberal moral argument means that the liberal social order must treat moral questions as perpetually open. Appeal to revelation or tradition may solve them for individuals or for some types of groups, but cannot solve them for the liberal public order as a whole. Thus, liberal political philosophy becomes (to borrow a standard term that MacIntyre does not himself use) antiperfectionist. "An indeterminability which was from the standpoint of an earlier liberalism a grave defect to be remedied as soon as possible has become, in the eyes of some liberals at least, a kind of virtue."[20]

But this retreat to antiperfectionism leads to a sort of new perfectionism. Appeals to tradition and/or revelation are banned from the public sphere by liberal principles—and this ban is experienced by members of tradition- and/or revelation-based communities within a liberal society as a very heavy burden.

> Any conception of the human good according to which, for example, it is the duty of government to educate the members of the community morally, so that they come to live out that conception of the good, may up to a point be held as a private theory by individuals or groups, but any serious attempt to embody it in public life will be proscribed. And this qualification of course entails not only that liberal individualism does indeed have its own broad conception of the good, which it is engaged in imposing politically, legally, socially, and culturally wherever it has the power to do so, but also that in so doing its toleration of rival conceptions of the good in the public arena is severely limited.[21]

MacIntyre here has his finger on a paradox that may be observed in action in many arenas today. A possible example would be a scene that is occasionally played out in public elementary schools: materials chosen by school authorities for classroom use are offensive to the conservative values of some parents; the parents consider the use of such materials in the public schools (private schools would be a different matter) to be an imposition by the liberal social order, and they complain; the school authorities (who, in this parable, represent the liberal social order), instead of respecting the autonomy of the tradition of which the parents are a part, consider the parents' complaints to be an imposition by a tradition- and/or revelation-based group. The question of who is imposing on whom in such situations is incapable of value-neutral resolution.[22]

Caught in such embarrassing postures, liberalism does not look much like the great rationalistic reconstruction of morality that the Enlightenment tried to inaugurate. Instead, in MacIntyrean terms, it looks a lot like a tradition of enquiry—and one experiencing an uncommonly severe epistemological crisis at that. It derives stability from its ability to subsume its internal conflict under procedures, political and legal, "in which conflict resolution takes place without invoking any overall theory of human good."[23] Nonetheless, "liberalism can provide no compelling arguments in favor of its conception of the human good except by appeal to premises which collectively already presuppose that theory."[24]

And what, finally, is the liberal conception of the human good? MacIntyre's answer has to be inferred from his narrative as a whole. It is apparently this: the human good according to the Enlightenment was to embark, free from tradition and revelation, on a search for the human good. This search proving inconclusive, the human good under liberalism became the preservation of the political and cultural arrangements necessary to a tradition- and revelation-free search for the human good. The circularity of this concept of the human good leads to the paradoxically illiberal behavior of the liberal social order whenever it must react to a community within itself that asserts a nonliberal concept of the human good.

THE ROAD TO RECOVERY

It is no wonder, then, that some philosophers have begun looking for alternatives to liberalism. But abandoning the liberal tradition cannot mean simply looking for moral principles superior to those developed by liberalism, for that would be a recapitulation of the Enlightenment project of seeking a morality based on reason alone. That project presupposed that a neutral ground exists, outside of all traditions, from which a moral system can be built up, and from which competing traditions can be judged. That project failed because, MacIntyre maintains, there is no such neutral ground. There is no neutral rationality-as-such. Instead, MacIntyre would seek to recover "what the Enlightenment deprived us of," that is, the rationality of traditions.[25]

Basing himself on his earlier narrative descriptions of various traditions of enquiry and the concepts of justice and rationality that they gave rise to, MacIntyre sketches a view of traditions of enquiry as modes of knowing.

The mechanism of the rationality of traditions proceeds in three stages:[26]

1. Pure historical contingency: the circumstances and practices that a given community has as a matter of historical happenstance. This is the starting point.
2. A challenge to the practices and beliefs of the community: This challenge may be external or internal. It reveals a lack of resources for confronting new questions.
3. Rejection, emendation, or reformulation. This is the fish-or-cut-bait stage of a tradition. The challenge of step 2 must be dealt with. If it cannot be overcome, then the tradition has been rejected. But if the

challenge can be met by either amending or reformulating the tradition, then it survives, stronger than before.

MacIntyre has three criteria for a successful emendation or reformulation: It must solve previously intractable problems; it must explain the earlier inability of the tradition to cope with the challenge; and it must maintain continuity with the tradition as it was before the challenge.

This is a neat enough way to generalize from the history of traditions of moral enquiry, but the real question is, how does one deny the existence of a rational means of choosing among competing traditions, and yet avoid the charge of relativism?

Or, if MacIntyre can avoid that charge, how can he avoid the charge of irrationalism? When, near the end of *Whose Justice? Which Rationality?* he finally explains the process of choosing a tradition, he describes a typical experience thus:

> Upon encountering a coherent presentation of one particular tradition of rational enquiry, either in its seminal texts or in some later, perhaps contemporary, restatement of its positions, such a person [i.e., a person who has not yet given allegiance to any tradition] will often experience a shock of recognition: *this* is not only, such a person may say, what I now take to be true but in some measure what I have always taken to be true.[27]

At this point MacIntyre is so anti-Nietzschean that he is actually Wagnerian: what he describes sounds like Sieglinde's famous exclamation in *Die Walküre* of sudden recognition of kinship with another.[28] But is this mode of recognition not as irrationalist as anything in Nietzsche?

This is perhaps the most heavily criticized link in MacIntyre's chain. But I believe that when he denies "rationality as such," he does not mean to deny the possibility of the mind gaining and possessing real knowledge. His argument, rather, goes to the question of what comes first. The Enlightenment project, and those doctrines of objective morality that are traceable to that project, was to *start* with rationality, and *then* use it to choose, or build, a moral system. No, says MacIntyre: tradition is the horse, not the cart.

MacIntyre blasts Edmund Burke for seeing in tradition "wisdom without reflection."[29] For MacIntyre, "rational theorizing"[30] is both possible and important, but it is, and can only be, "a work of and within tradition."[31] To engage in rational theorizing, one must enter into a tradition—a process that MacIntyre describes in terms such as "transformation"[32] and even "conversion."[33]

"What kind of transformation is required? It is that which is involved in making oneself into an apprentice to a craft, the craft in this case of philosophical enquiry."[34]

It should be clear, therefore, that MacIntyre's skepticism about "rationality as such" is not a denial of the possibility of philosophy. But there is still the question of how would-be inquirers are to choose the tradition in which they wish to seek an apprenticeship.

The answer, basically, is a robustness test: Which traditions have, historically, demonstrated the greatest capacity to overcome epistemological crises, and to carry on, strengthened rather than weakened by the challenges they have faced?

Drawing on the totality of the history he has narrated in *Whose Justice? Which Rationality?*, MacIntyre, in the penultimate paragraph of that book, declares that in Thomism we find

> an Aristotelian tradition with resources for its own enlargement, correction, and defense, resources which suggest that *prima facie* at least a case has been made for concluding first that those who have thought their way through the topics of justice and practical rationality, from the standpoint constructed by and in the direction pointed out first by Aristotle and then by Aquinas, have every reason at least so far to hold that the rationality of their tradition has been confirmed in its encounters with other traditions and, second, that the task of characterizing and accounting for the achievements and successes, as well as the frustrations and failures, of the Thomistic tradition in the terms afforded by the rival traditions of enquiry, may, even from the point of view of the adherents of those traditions, be a more demanding task than has sometimes been supposed.[35]

MacIntyre's next book, a reader might have thought, would have been an elaboration of that paragraph. *Three Rival Versions of Moral Enquiry* is not that book—although it does do at least two valuable things: It carries forward the analysis of moral enquiry as a craft, making the case that authority, far from being inimical to rational enquiry, is its precondition; and it compares the Thomistic tradition in great detail with two rivals: late-nineteenth-century rationalism (or "encyclopedia," because this tradition is exemplified for MacIntyre by the ninth edition of the *Encyclopaedia Britannica*), and Nietzscheanism (or "genealogy," because MacIntyre's focus within Nietzsche's work is on *Toward a Genealogy of Morals*).

CONCLUSION

MacIntyre describes a philosophical world being turned upside down. A philosophy that has presented itself since its inception as the haven of rational persons rejecting the hoary myths of the past is shown to be something of a hoary myth itself. A philosophy that took iconoclasm as its style is itself seen as a tottering idol. And the solution to the crisis arising from the fall of that idol is shown to lie along the lines of the very ideas and traditions that the idol tried to destroy.

Questions, however, remain. MacIntyre's attempted escape from the relativism problem, what I have called the robustness test, remains problematic. Is that test rationally defensible? If not, why use it? Why is a robust tradition necessarily to be preferred to an evanescent one? But if the robustness test *is* defensible, then is it not a neutral, tradition-independent criterion for judging between traditions—something MacIntyre has said does not exist?

The very least that MacIntyre can be said to have achieved is to have directed enquiry at one of the main problems of contemporary moral argument, namely, its ultimate indeterminacy. We can argue from premises, but how do people go about choosing premises, and how *should* they do so? MacIntyre has engaged the debate at that level.

At the other extreme, that of the maximum characterization of MacIntyre's achievement, we may have here the seeds of a new way of conducting moral debate, a way that could vindicate many communities of practice and belief that have been trampled by the long reign of the Enlightenment and its successors—the dawn of a Counter-Enlightenment.

Adding the Virtues of Dependence to the Rationality of Traditions

In the years since the period covered by the previous portion of this chapter, Alasdair MacIntyre has deepened his commitment and reputation as a Thomist, continued the effort (begun in *After Virtue* and continued in *Whose Justice? Which Rationality?*) to achieve escape velocity from "emotivism" by grounding ethics on something firmer than intuition; and to recover, for this purpose, the wisdom of communities of practice (AV) and traditions of inquiry (*Whose Justice? Which Rationality?*). This continuation has confirmed his commitment to Thomist Aristotelianism and the Catholic faith against their principal modernist and postmodernist competitors (*Three Rival Versions of Moral Inquiry*), and led him in his latest book to a new appreciation of the moral implications of humankind's enfleshed nature (*Dependent Rational Animals: Why Human Beings Need the Virtues*).

For MacIntyre, the Enlightenment project was doomed to fail because the neutral vantage point, which it presupposed and from which all competing traditions and truth-claims can be judged, does not in fact exist. No human being, philosopher or not, is so completed independent of the historical situation in which he exists, thinks, and writes that he can bring the Enlightenment project to fulfillment. As noted in the earlier portion of this chapter, the Enlightenment promised liberation from tradition but turned out to be just one more tradition, and not a very robust one at that.

In *Whose Justice? Which Rationality?* MacIntyre developed a theory of rival traditions competing with each other over time, and either growing by surviving, or perishing. The great "survivor" tradition, he maintains, is Catholic Christianity clad in the armor of Thomist metaphysics. Thanks to St. Thomas Aquinas, Christianity survived its clash with rediscovered Aristotelianism in the thirteenth century, and now stands heir apparent to the mantle that the Enlightenment, with its deceptive hopes of universally accessible objectivity, has been forced to lay aside.

MacIntyre's critique of the Enlightenment sets up an interesting, yet largely unexplored, conflict with the followers of Leo Strauss. As critical of Enlightenment pretensions as MacIntyre himself, the Straussians nonetheless argue that escape from Plato's "cave" to a point of knowledge of things as such is at least notionally possible. MacIntyre, by contrast, seems to maintain that all thought has inescapably historical roots. On the other hand, commentator Kelvin Knight reads MacIntyre as holding that ultimately, "rationality can be articulated in ways that are no longer simply cultural but also philosophical and critical."

Despite his greater emphasis on tradition as compared to Strauss, MacIntyre too believes that philosophy can escape the orbit of history. A tradition of enquiry starts in history: it has predecessors and successors, and it has limitations imposed by its historical situation. But, as MacIntyre further explained in an interview: "It is insofar as it transcends the limitations and corrects the mistakes of its predecessors, and insofar as it opens up new possibilities for those successors, that it achieves rational justification."

MacIntyre's constant attention to history, in apparent defiance of Strauss's strictures on "historicism," have given rise to charges that MacIntyre is, after all, a relativist. What else can one be (the argument goes) if one denies, as MacIntyre does, the possibility of a "neutral" vantage point from which competing traditions of enquiry can be judged? The answer is found in part in the theory of clashing traditions described in *Whose Justice? Which Rationality?*

Furthermore, MacIntyre confronts the relativism issue again in another interview. He admits that he goes with the relativist part-way: to the point of denying that there is any referee for competing traditions that is not itself merely another tradition. But the relativist takes two further steps where MacIntyre refuses to follow. The first is to maintain that the existence of competing traditions "provides grounds for putting in question and altering one's view of the justification of one's own reasoning and conclusions." In other words, the old sophist's trick "Some people disagree with you, therefore you're wrong" is a non sequitur. The second stage at which MacIntyre refuses to accompany the relativist consists of a similar sophist's trick: "people disagree about truth, therefore truth cannot exist." Comments MacIntyre: "Neither of these stages in the relativist argument is justified and it is of course only by having pursued the argument to this unwarranted point that the relativist lays her or himself open to those types of self-referential refutation which have so often been deployed against relativism."

Three Rival Versions of Moral Inquiry

After *Whose Justice? Which Rationality?* MacIntyre published *Three Rival Versions of Moral Inquiry* (the Gifford Lectures of 1988), in which he compared and contrasted the Enlightenment (represented by the eleventh edition of the *Encyclopaedia Britannica,* with its late-Victorian faith in science and progress; hence the moniker "Encyclopedia" instead of "Enlightenment"); Nietzsche (represented by the term "genealogy," as in . . . *of Morals*); and Thomist Catholicism (represented by the term "Tradition," thus carrying forward his earlier project as vindicating "the rationality of traditions"). Thus, *Three Rival Versions of Moral Inquiry* compares modernity, postmodernity, and premodernity through these particular representatives.

As MacIntyre has moved from the emphasis on "practices" in *After Virtue* to the stratospheric intellectual clashes of *Three Rival Versions,* he may have concluded that his philosophy had lost its former contact with the real, the bodily, the physical. After all, he has never been inclined to go the way of John Finnis and Germain Grisez, deducing an ethical system from first principles known to practical rationality and disclaiming any derivation of an "ought" from an "is." As early as his 1959 essay "Notes from the Moral Wilderness," from his post-Stalinist but not yet post-Marxist period, he rejected the claim of the "liberal tradition" that "morality is to be taken as autonomous," and protested against the "isolation of the moral from the factual."

Instead, in *After Virtue,* he looked to social roles (in Homer) and practices (in Athens) to arrive at conclusions about human nature that could at least boast of being rooted in actual humans at actual times and places. Aristotle, too, preferred to start his ethical inquiries about asking what ordinary people do and say. So it is not surprising that MacIntyre's most recent book, *Dependent Rational Animals: Why Human Beings Need the Virtues,* is an effort to take seriously to the bodily aspects—especially the bodily limitations—of human nature, and a proclamation of the consequences of these aspects and these limitations for ethics.

Dependent Rational Animals

MacIntyre remains a "recoverist" in the sense that he continues to inspect a ruined ethical city and considering how it may be rebuilt. In *After Virtue,* invoking the *Canticle for Leibowitz* metaphor, he surveyed the moral wreckage left by the failure of the Enlightenment project, and he sought to recover a program of historically rooted ethics in ancient Athenian praxis and Aristotle's ethics. He continued this project in *Whose Justice? Which Rationality?* this time elaborating the theory of clashing traditions outlined in the earlier part of this chapter, and tentatively pronouncing Thomist Aristotelianism the winner of the Tradition Derby that he has intricately described.

Though this recoverist project has inevitably endeared MacIntyre to conservative political theorists, he has steadfastly avoided affiliation with any actually existing political movement. Kelvin Knight goes so far as to call MacIntyre's conception of politics "revolutionary," since liberalism (exposed in *Whose Justice? Which Rationality?* as just one more tradition among many, rather than an escape from tradition) "legitimates the institutions of state and capitalism, and, in turn, is sustained by them." Certainly MacIntyre's Aristotelian approach to politics gives him little in common with "the liberalism of contemporary American and English conservatives," who defend primarily the conservative side of liberalism, that is, the free market and the minimalist state.

On the other hand, a long process of reflection has brought MacIntyre to a position that will resonate very positively with another wing of today's conservatism: the wing that undertakes to defend the institution of the family against the remarkable array of contemporary challenges to its legitimacy.

We may put the question this way. Is the social unit of mother-plus-father-plus-children a natural phenomenon essential to human flourishing, the abolition or weakening of which can only lead to totalitarian forces emerging in its place? Or is it a social construct, reflecting the victory of, and oppression by, the patriarchal class, propped up by an ideologically laden culture, and needing to be deconstructed in both theory and practice, so as to make way for alternative possibilities?

A long chain of reflection has brought MacIntyre to the point of endorsing the former view. But unlike pro-family advocates who start there and defend their position as a *partie prise,* MacIntyre has taken the long road, and is therefore in a sense a more candid spokesman. Briefly, in *After Virtue,* seeking to re-ground morality in "practices," he accepted Aristotle's political construct (the polis seeking the good life for man as such), but sought to distance himself from Aristotle's teachings on biology, and so avoided inquiry into what may or may not be "natural." *Whose Justice? Which Rationality?* shows MacIntyre embracing Aristotle more fully, thanks in large part to St. Thomas. Then, in Dependent Rational Animals, he announces a rather dramatic further step: "Although there is indeed good reason to repudiate important elements of Aristotle's biology, I now judge that I was in error in supposing an ethics independent of biology to be possible." Biology-free ethics fails to account for "the nature and extent of human vulnerability and disability." Re-reading Aquinas as an "adapter" of Aristotle, not just an interpreter, MacIntyre found "an account of the virtues that reckoned not only with our animal condition, but also with the need to acknowledge our consequent vulnerability and dependence."

Much of *Dependent Rational Animals* unfolds as a description of the lives and natures of the more intelligent animals, with an eye not toward "animal rights" but toward showing that enfleshedness as an irreducible aspect of human nature gives us more in common with animals than we are accustomed to thinking.

What is most glaringly missing from the tradition of Western moral philosophy, MacInyre argues, is any serious grappling with the inevitability of illness, disability, and dependence. Not that the sick, the disabled, and the dependent are entirely absent from this tradition—it's just that when they show up there, "it is almost always exclusively as possible subjects of benevolence by moral agents who are themselves presented as though they were continuously rational, healthy and untroubled." Patroclus gets killed, but Achilles— the model for pre-philosophical Greece—is never seen on camera in any state short of physical perfection. Socrates, until hemlocked, is never prevented by headache or catarrh or just plain off-peak performance from pursuing the exact chain of questioning needed to turn a young interlocutor's soul inside out. Aristotle's ethical ideal, the *megalopsychos* or "great-souled man," seems endowed with a body that is never less than "mega." Adam Smith acknowledges that his moral/economic system has less to offer to those "in the languor of disease and the weariness of old age," but, in MacIntyre's words, "to allow our attention to dwell on this is, on Smith's view, misguided."

Dependent Rational Animals is in part a cry of protest against Smith's, and the tradition's, omission of inevitable dependence as a factor in ethics. Seeking to repair the omission, MacIntyre examines many forms of behavior common to humans and other animals. Those interested in the *status questionis* regarding the border-line between the human and the non-human will find the central chapters of *Dependent Rational Animals* a true feast, as will those with a passion for dolphins. Here, I mean to call attention to MacIntyre's discovery (for such it almost seems) of the family, and my point is that MacIntyre's appreciation of the family is very much a conclusion and not a premise: it falls into place *only after* two decades of reflection on practice-based ethics, Aristotle, Aquinas, the clash of traditions, the dialogue of Thomist Aristotelianism with the Enlightenment and with Nietzsche, the recognition of human vulnerability and dependence as ultimate facts in the ethical equation, and the observation and analysis of practice in the animal kingdom.

The discovery takes shape in chapter 8 of *Dependent Rational Animals,* entitled "How Do We Become Independent Practical Reasoners? How Do the

Virtues Make This Possible?" Echoing his earlier protest at moral philosophers who assume a permanently healthy and rational individual, MacIntyre here objects that with dubious exceptions such as Rousseau, moral philosophers have also assumed "mature independent practical reasoners whose social relationships are the relationships of the adult world." The next paragraph is worth quoting at length because it illustrates succinctly both the conclusions and the methodology of *Dependent Rational Animals* as a whole:

> To become an effective independent practical reasoner is an achievement, but it is always one to which others have made essential contributions. The earliest of these relate directly to our animal existence, to what we share in our development with members of other intelligent species. We owe to parents, especially mothers, to aunts, grandparents, and surrogates for these, that care from conception through birth and infancy to childhood that dolphins also owe to elders who provide maternal and other care. And in human as in dolphin life there are patterns of receiving and giving, enduring through and beyond the life-span of particular individuals. Dolphins, having been cared for, care for others, sometimes extending such care beyond their own species to human beings. So Plutarch, in a dialogue comparing the excellences of sea creatures to those of land animals, ascribed to dolphins—in contrast with what he took to be the narrow self-interest of swallows—"that virtue so much sought after by the best philosophers: the capacity for disinterested friendship." (*Moralia* LXIII, "Whether Land or Sea Animals Have More Practical Intelligence.")

I venture the guess that among today's productive philosophers, only MacIntyre could join practical reason, Plutarch, and dolphins as seamlessly as that.

Nonetheless, human beings can do at least one thing that eludes even the dolphins: we can "look back to infancy or forward to aging and death." This capacity means that what we do by nature (form sexually complementary unions, have children, raise them, and teach them the virtues) can be done also by reflection and precept; that is, in MacIntyrean terms, it can become a "practice," which is high praise.

And what does this practice—the family—produce? Something that has preoccupied political philosophy since *The Republic:* the education of desire; or, as MacIntyre puts it, "external reasons also become internal."

Chesterton wrote the fable of the English sailor who "discovered" England; it may be said of MacIntyre—with reservations that I will explain in a moment—that he started with Marx, went to Troy with Achilles and to Athens with Aristotle, joined the school of St. Thomas, and ended up at the Cleavers' house.

One necessary reservation is that while MacInyre has discovered—and, in discovering, defended—the basic structure of the Cleaver household, he would no doubt remains critical of its unreflectiveness. Any form of self-satisfaction is anathema to the MacIntyrean conception of political life. Yes, a polis needs "an inherited cultural tradition" around which to form, but:

> [T]hese requirements have to serve the ends of a society in which individuals are always able to put in question through communal deliberation what has hitherto by custom and tradition been taken for granted both about their own good and the good of the community. A *polis* is always, potentially or actually, a society of rational enquiry, of self-scrutiny.

He would also be critical of the Cleaver household's tendency to consumerism, or, not to make this too hard on Ward and June, to the consumerism endemic to the society of which they were a part. For MacIntyre, "households," along with other associations such as "workplaces, schools, [and] parishes," are loci "in which resistance to the goals and norms of a consumer society is recurrently generated." But consumerism—and with it, veneration of the nation-state—were plainly not banished from 1950s America; therefore, that society would fall short of the quasi-Utopian goals that MacIntyre sketches in chapter 11 of *Dependent Rational Animals*.

In that quasi-Utopia, the nation-state is not rejected (after all, with its "blundering and distorted benevolence" it can still do some good), but at the same time, we avoid "the communitarian mistake, [which is] to attempt to infuse the politics of the state with the values and modes of participation in local community." At the same time, local community is not to be worshiped as such. It is valuable only as a means to achieve those "face-to-face encounters and conversations [that] are necessary for the shared achievement of the common goods of those who participate in the rational deliberation necessary to sustain networks of giving and receiving." Apart from this, local community is corrupted "by narrowness, by complacency, by prejudice against outsiders, and by a whole range of other deformities, including those that arise from a cult of local community." One hopes that he includes in these "other deformities" the squads of neighborhood bossy-boots whose idea of civic revival is to fine people for decorative choices that threaten to reduce resale values. Local community? It's the polis, or it's spinach.

But MacIntyre is not reluctant to step up to the brink of Utopianism. He recommends, for instance, "self-imposed limits to labor mobility for the sake of the continuities and the stabilities of families and other institutions." "Self-imposed," one assumes, so that state power is not being brought to bear to prevent people from seeking honest economic self-betterment by moving to where the better jobs are; they just don't, because their communally informed analysis of the virtues of justice and generosity informs that they should not. As I said, Utopian. "But," MacIntyre suggests disarmingly, "trying to live by

Utopian standards is not Utopian, although it does involve a rejection of the economic goals of late capitalism."

NOTES

1. Alasdair MacIntyre, *After Virtue* (Notre Dame, Ind.: University of Notre Dame Press, 1981); Alasdair MacIntyre, *Whose Justice? Which Rationality?* (Notre Dame, Ind.: University of Notre Dame Press, 1988); Alasdair MacIntyre, *Three Rival Versions of Moral Inquiry: Encyclopedia, Genealogy, and Tradition* (Notre Dame, Ind.: University of Notre Dame Press, 1990).

2. Although most of the theories that lie in the path of MacIntyre's scythe are liberal ones, conservative attempts to revivify the Enlightenment tradition are equally threatened. See for example, H. Arkes, *First Things* (Princeton, N.J.: Princeton University Press, 1986).

3. MacIntyre, *After Virtue,* 12 (emphasis in original).

4. MacIntyre, *After Virtue,* 10.

5. MacIntyre speaks of "historical contingency," a more subtle concept than experience in the everyday sense. To derive morality from historically contingent circumstances means more than simply to learn from experience: it means to construct a morality on the basis of "what our people do" or "what a person who has such-and-such a role in our community must do to fulfill that role well." The Enlightenment, which viewed tradition as per se oppressive, could not but despise any morality so derived, preferring to ground morality on what must be apparent to any rational person, that is, (MacIntyre would say), on what was apparent to Denis Diderot and his friends.

6. MacIntyre, *After Virtue,* 58 (emphasis in original).

7. MacIntyre, *After Virtue,* 110.

8. MacIntyre, *After Virtue,* 114 (emphasis in original).

9. MacIntyre, *After Virtue,* 119 (emphasis in original).

10. These links do not amount to "historicism" in the sense condemned by students of Leo Strauss, that is, the notion that past philosophy is conditioned by its historical circumstances and is therefore of no present interest. MacIntyre calls himself an historicist and asserts explicitly that no philosophy can be understood apart from its historical circumstances. However, for him, the historically contingent nature of philosophy argues for trying to understand past ages as a participant (to learn their language as a new first language, as he likes to put it—see chapter 19, entitled "Traditions and Translation" in *Whose Justice?* (370–88)—rather than for discarding their philosophical work product).

11. MacIntyre, *Whose Justice?,* 7.

12. MacIntyre, *After Virtue,* 61.

13. MacIntyre, *Whose Justice?,* 334.

14. MacIntyre, *Whose Justice?,* 334.

15. MacIntyre, *Whose Justice?,* 334.

16. *Whose Justice?* 334.

17. 478 U.S. 186 (1986).

18. 109 Sup. Ct. 2333 (1989).

19. MacIntyre, *Whose Justice?*, 334

20. MacIntyre, *Whose Justice?*, 335.

21. MacIntyre, *Whose Justice?*, 336.

22. The liberal lobby People for the American Way assimilates parental complaints of the type discussed here to a category that it calls "attacks on the freedom to learn." Thus, for the type of liberal that PAW represents, interference with liberal coercion is an attack on rationality as such. PAW in this instance exemplifies anti-perfectionist theory turning into perfectionist practice. See *Attacks on the Freedom to Learn: People for the American Way 1989–1990 Report* (1990).

23. MacIntyre, *Whose Justice?*, 344.

24. MacIntyre, *Whose Justice?*, 345.

25. MacIntyre, *Whose Justice?*, 7.

26. What follows is a summary of the chapter entitled "The Rationality of Traditions" in MacIntyre, *Whose Justice?*

27. MacIntyre, *Whose Justice?*, 394.

28. In Act I of *Die Walküre,* Sieglinde says to Siegmund: "You are the spring that I longed for in the frosty time of winter. My heart greeted you in holy fear when my glance first beheld you. I was a mere stranger from of old; all around me was friendless. . . . But you I recognized, shining and clear. As soon as I saw you, you were my own. What I hid in my breast, what I am, bright as the day shone forth, and like a resounding cry fell on my ear, when in the frosty friendless emptiness I first beheld my friend."

29. Edmund Burke, *Reflections on the Revolution in France* (New York: Liberal Arts Press, 1955). See MacIntyre, *Whose Justice?* 353.

30. MacIntyre, *Whose Justice?*, 353.

31. MacIntyre, *Whose Justice?*, 353.

32. MacIntyre, *Whose Justice?*, 396.

33. MacIntyre, *Whose Justice?*, 396.

34. MacIntyre, *Three Rival Versions,* 61.

35. MacIntyre, *Whose Justice?*, 402–403.

8

Inescapably a Liberal
Richard Rorty as Social Theorist

Gerard V. Bradley

Richard Rorty's *Philosophy and the Mirror of Nature*[1] was probably the most significant event in American philosophy since John Rawls's *A Theory of Justice* came out in 1971. Acclaimed for its breadth of learning and its charming prose, *Philosophy and the Mirror of Nature* can nevertheless be unnerving to read, as unnerving as intellectual vertigo. One commentator laments that "Rorty disturbs and astonishes like the spring weather. His pages mount like cumulus clouds in our intellectual sky, saturated by the past and promising (ambiguously) either to irrigate or inundate the present fields of our culture. Almost everybody complains about him, but can anything be done?"[2]

Why all the fuss? Those unfamiliar with the book may assume that Rorty makes a powerful case for the professed aim of *Philosophy and the Mirror of Nature*: "to undermine the reader's confidence in 'the mind' as something about which one should have a philosophical view, in 'knowledge' as something about which there ought to 'be a theory' and which has 'foundations,' and in 'philosophy' as it has been conceived by Kant."[3] Rorty wants us to set aside—permanently and without anointing a successor discipline—the epistemology-centered philosophy of the past four centuries. Accepting his invitation means changing "our image of humanity, our concept of rationality, and abandonment of epistemic objectivity."[4] No wonder Bernard Williams says that "it matters to what extent [Rorty] is right."[5]

Philosophy and the Mirror of Nature said almost nothing about social theory. In the mid-1980s Rorty produced a series of articles and lectures on the topic, many of them collected in his 1989 book *Contingency, Irony and Solidarity*.[6] These efforts established Rorty as a liberal—he said so repeatedly—with a superficial resemblance to recent Rawls, the Rawls whose liberalism

141

is grounded not in the universalistic plane of *A Theory of Justice* but in a deep historical particularism.[7]

Despite their recent vintage, these writings have already figured prominently in accounts of "legal pragmatism" by various academic authors. In my view, Rorty is also Laurence Tribe's philosophical mentor, the shadow philosopher of the second edition of Tribe's *American Constitutional Law*.[8] Rorty's social theory is one step removed (ahead, actually) from the engine powering recent constitutional law: the right to autonomous control over the development and expression of one's intellect and personality—the sovereign self, commanding a "facilitative" society. Most broadly, Rorty's "pragmatism"—his antifoundationalist critique of reason and disinterested thought—is an effective apology for legal realism of the left (Critical Legal Studies) and of the right (Law and Economics), and stands athwart many attempts to rebut them both. This chapter endeavors to describe in detail Rorty's "social theory," his term of choice for an enquiry that, for most readers, comprises ethics, political theory, legal philosophy, and the social sciences. Rorty's social theory turns out to be only superficially Rawlsian. It is really a unique, Rortyan construction that is just as arresting as *Philosophy and the Mirror of Nature*.

RORTY'S PHILOSOPHY

The target of *Philosophy and the Mirror of Nature* is Philosophy (with a capital "P"), the foundational discipline that investigates knowing as such, and therefore can adjudicate among all other claims—religious, political, artistic—to "know." Rorty takes naive realism as the linchpin of this discipline. "To know [the tradition held, according to Rorty] is to represent accurately what is outside the mind."[9] Truth consists of correspondence of the "picture" within the "knowing" subject's mind to a mind-independent reality outside it. Bernard Lonergan called this realism a matter of "taking a good look," the spectator theory of knowledge.

The philosophical heroes of *Philosophy and the Mirror of Nature* are an unlikely trio: Ludwig Wittgenstein, Martin Heidegger, and John Dewey. According to Rorty, each was dismayed by the professional philosophy about him, and each initially sought to replace a failing foundation with a new, sturdier one. Of the "late" work of Heidegger, Dewey, and Wittgenstein, Rorty observes,

[e]ach . . . came to see his earlier effort as self-deceptive, as an attempt to retain a certain conception of philosophy after the notions needed to flesh out that con-

ception had been discarded. Each . . . broke free of the Kantian conception of philosophy as foundational, and spent his time warning us against those very temptations to which he himself had once succumbed. Thus their later work is therapeutic rather than constructive, edifying rather than systematic, designed to make the reader question his own motives for philosophizing.[10]

Rorty's own presentation is self-consciously modeled on the trio's strategies. "They set aside epistemology and metaphysics as possible disciplines." "Set aside" rather than "argue against" because "they do not devote themselves to discovering false propositions or bad arguments in the works of their predecessors (though they occasionally do that too). Rather, they glimpse the possibility of a form of intellectual life in which the vocabulary of philosophical reflection inherited from the seventeenth century would seem as pointless as the thirteenth-century philosophical vocabulary had seemed to the Enlightenment."[11]

A central support of the argument in *Philosophy and the Mirror of Nature* is "the linguistic turn" (not coincidentally, the title of Rorty's first book). Rorty, closely following Wittgenstein here, says that "truth" and "objectivity" are entirely intralinguistic affairs. Rorty means that such notions are useful only within a particular tradition of discourse and are otherwise unintelligible. Truth is a property of sentences and is a matter of agreement with the beliefs that serve as the evidential rules of the language game and *not* with some extramental reality. Truth is "what is good in the way of belief,"[12] another name for the familiar and the conventional, for the overlapping parts of vocabularies.[13] This is "normal discourse." "Abnormal discourse" is the unfamiliar, the strange, the uncanny. People we call "mad" are simply folks we don't understand because their vocabularies are peculiar. But the distinction "does *not* coincide with any distinction of subject matter (for example, nature versus history, or facts versus values), method (for example, objectivation versus reflection), faculty (for example, reason versus imagination), or any of the other distinctions which systematic philosophy has used to make the sense of the world consist in the objective truth about some previously unnoticed portion or feature of the world."[14] This complex of ideas he calls "epistemological behaviorism."

Because Rorty capitalizes so powerfully on the "linguistic turn," let us carefully note what he means by it. He is *not* saying, with virtually all religious thinkers, that reality, especially transcendent reality (God, the supernatural) ultimately confounds and escapes our concepts and description. Rorty is no mystic either. He does not hold that the way to apprehend and attune oneself to Being is a *via negativa,* to rid oneself of language. Rorty does not join two of his heroes—Hans Gadamer and (in my view but perhaps not Rorty's) Heidegger—both of whom were convinced that although traditional philosophy obscured Being, ontology survived the linguistic turn. Rorty opines that the world does not speak. Only we do. Heidegger, for instance, thought that Being spoke to us through language.

Rorty is definitely a historicist but he is stalking bigger game than the usual prey of historicists, which is the "ahistorical" or Archimedean point of observation, which is exempt from the situatedness of human thought. We are all historicists now, says Rorty; we all concede that thought is "thunk" by finite, historically situated human beings. But neither Rorty's "historicism" nor his "nominalism" (roughly, that only individual and not abstract or general entities exist) without additional premises, explain *Philosophy and the Mirror of Nature* or its abrupt linguistic turn. There are some foundationalists who are nearly historicists; Thomas Hobbes, Martin Luther, and William of Ockham were all nominalists, and none ended up where Rorty has.

One criticism of Rorty is that he disregards more differentiated, nuanced accounts of the relation between human understanding and reality. This oversight (or strategy) permits him to crown his "epistemology" by default.[15] Rorty's "linguistic turn" collapses the related but separate inquiries of alethiology (theory of the nature of truth) and ontology (theory of what there is) into "epistemology" (roughly, the study of human knowing).

Charles Taylor puts the criticism nicely: Rorty is still operating within the tradition he would escape, precisely because Rorty's perception of the alternatives is commanded by the tradition.[16]

In any event Rorty builds upon his displacement of the correspondence theory. He moves on to claim that vocabularies are ultimately "incommensurable." They cannot be reduced to an Esperanto (a universal language) or to various expressions of universal experiences. By "incommensurable" Rorty means that disputes about what there is cannot be arbitrated by criteria drawn from outside the warring vocabularies. Rorty does not argue for that position, so much as he (as Taylor suggests) presumes it follows from his demolition work. But Taylor rightly questions Rorty's suggestion that nonarbitrability is shown by the perpetual inconclusiveness of debates about some "weighty matters."[17] Lack of consensus is an observation about people. From it no conclusion of invincible disagreement may be drawn. Besides, some issues — such as the injustice of racism — have been settled by rational agreement.[18]

RORTY'S LAUNDRY LIST OF LIBERALISM

We can more directly approach Rorty's social theory by recounting some virtues of the linguistic turn. It connected knowing and doing by bringing philosophy into contact with the everyday realities of life. That is, it forced philosophical speculation into an arena defined by a particular culture because language was so defined and limited. The historicist touch prevents "philosophers" from solving "eternal" problems—according to Rorty, yesteryear's problems—irrelevant to today's issues. Also, the linguistic turn made truth an intrinsically public affair, the outcome of an ongoing conversation. For these reasons, we may plausibly view Wittgenstein's efforts, and Dewey's, as communitarian in effect and intention.

Rorty capitalizes upon this plausibility. His articles explicitly oppose "Solidarity" to "Objectivity," "Democracy" to "Philosophy." It seems that Rorty's social theory is characterized by an overriding commitment to communitarianism or social solidarity. Were Rorty to follow this trajectory, he might well have ended up (in jurisprudence) like Dworkin, committed to the *deep* conventionalism displayed in *Law's Empire,* a kind of constitutional law by common-law method. This piles Burke upon Wittgenstein: the turn to linguistic practices accompanied by a deep sociality. But Rorty is no Burke. He takes Wittgenstein and adds the fervid individualism of the libertarian Robert Nozick.

Rorty's individualism is perhaps the efficient cause of his liberalism. But whether as simple "liberal," as "postmodernist bourgeois liberal," as "tragic liberal," or as "liberal ironist" (all *his* self-descriptions), Rorty says very little about the content of his liberalism. What he does say is quite casual. In the introduction to *Contingency, Irony and Solidarity* Rorty lays down the "harm" and (something like Rawls's) difference principles as foundations for his own political opining.[19] At the same time he takes Judith Sklar's sine qua non—avoid cruelty—as the linchpin of liberalism.[20] On another occasion Rorty adopted Rawls's suggestion that liberalism be grounded in cultural givens like religious tolerance and the wrongness of slavery.[21] But Rorty has never attempted to deduce anything from, or even to elaborate the meaning of, his condemnation of slavery. And he wants to expand "religious tolerance" so that virtually all meaning is privatized in the way religion has been.

Throughout the Rortyan opus, one nevertheless encounters laundry lists of liberalism's ingredients. In no particular order and virtually without commentary, Rorty champions "free press," "free speech," "free universities," "free elections," market economies, interest group politics, "free judiciary," democracy. The list is not exhaustive. None is thought problematic, singly or in combination. Rorty evinces no misgivings about the risks to democracy of "free speech" and "free press" in "market economies" with media monopolies. He is blind to the tensions between "democracy" and "free judiciary" that Dworkin, among others, sees. Many liberals array the judiciary—the principled, apolitical protector of individual rights—against an intrinsically intolerant majority pursuing mere "collective interests." Rorty never explores issues such as abortion, capital punishment, affirmative action, drug abuse, feminism, pornography, crime. He is not interested in jurisprudence or distributive justice. He does not mention the Constitution.

QUESTIONING LIBERALISM

What's going on here? In an inconspicuous footnote Rorty bares his "epistemology" of political discourse and suggests why he is uninterested in liberalism's menu. He abjures "rationality" in politics because he thinks it never supplies reasons for action. "[W]e figure out what practices to adopt first and then expect our philosophers to adjust the definition of 'human' or 'rational' to suit."[22] The footnote supports the textual proposition (no surprise after *Philosophy and the Mirror of Nature*) that although "reason" may have been useful in creating democratic societies, "it can now be dispensed with—and *should* be dispensed with, in order to help bring the liberal utopia [he favors] into existence."[23] The original citation continues:

> [W]e know that we should not kill a fellow human, except in our official capacity as soldier, hangman, abortionist or the like. [Query: does Rorty presume there is one "liberal" answer to all these moral questions?]. So are those whom we do kill in those capacities—the armies of the invading tyrant, the serial murderer, the fetus—not human? Well, in a sense, yes and, in a sense, no—but defining the relevant senses is an after-the-fact, largely scholastic exercise. We deliberate about the justice of the War, or the rightness of capital punishment or of abortion, first, and worry later about the "status" of the invader or the murderer or the fetus! When we try to do the opposite, we find that our philosophy offer no sufficient conditions for humanity or rationality less controversial than the original practical questions. . . . The large several principles wait portionently for the outcome and then the crucial term which they contain or redefined to accord with that outcome.[24]

Neither "reason" nor any particular language game can tell us how to think—much less can they affect our actions—in the liberal polity.

As I apprehend Rorty, he is saying basically this: Reason cannot explain why we are or should remain liberals, any more than it can tell us what to think about killing, any more than it can persuade communists or fascists to become liberals. Persons are born liberals—that is, at the dawn of consciousness they find themselves in the liberal language game. Beyond the linguistic border is either helpless passivity or resort to force. This arresting claim explains Rorty's review of Roberto Unger's recent trilogy in social theory. As a "tragic" North American liberal—one whose institutions are in extremis—

Rorty can only observe Unger's vision of politics and hope that, perhaps, his great grandchildren will find themselves in its grips. But for now, that Unger is a Brazilian and Rorty is an American takes the discussion as far as it can be taken. "Our only excuse is, once again, to appeal to national differences— to say in effect, 'Maybe it's easier in Brazil, but it's pretty hard here.' . . . To imagine great things is to imagine a great future *for a particular community.* . . . In the modern world, this usually means one's nation."[25]

Rorty doubts whether arguments play much of a role in political changes. But arguments are not just impotent. They are destructive. Their premises, phrased in familiar vocabularies, "get in the way of attempts to create an unfamiliar vocabulary, a new *lingua franca* for those trying to transform what they see around them."[26] Language is the condition of the real, so that revolutionaries propose new vocabularies. "[W]e humans are lords of possibility as well as actuality—for possibility is a function of a descriptive vocabulary, and that vocabulary is as much up for political grabs as anything else."[27] Revolutions, it seems for Rorty, are gigantic exercises of some noncognitive faculty. Some are dictated over the barrel of a gun. But others—probably most— are spasms: an ecstatic coupling between society and a vocabulary/persona, a delirious mass embrace. An interphenomenal "zap." Unger's thought seems to have enticed Rorty, but not seduced him. And he doubts it will seduce us.

In his 1987 "Thugs & Theorists," Rorty regretted previously describing himself as a "post-modernist bourgeois liberal."[28] Obviously disturbed by critics (like his friend Richard Bernstein) who found his articles "frivolous in tone, pointlessly extreme, and paradoxical in formulation, and likely to give aid and comfort to the wrong people (and, in particular, to neoconservatives),"[29] Rorty endeavored to rephrase his position. Now a "social democrat," he attempted to satisfy his critics by calling "the shadowy millionaires" manipulating Reagan "thugs," just like the KGB, the Boers, and the Ayatollah.

The difficulty is that these harsh judgments were no less flip and insouciant than the prior formulations they were supposed to remedy. In my view, that is because, for Rorty, insouciance is the correct approach to politics. Politics are supposed to be flaccid, frivolous, paradoxical, complacent, inert. That's the point, and the only kind of politics Rorty can hold given what else he holds. "Liberal disclosure *should* remain untheoretical and simple-minded (emphasis mine).[30]

Can we say *anything* about "social theory," other than description? Rorty thinks that "solidarity"—for him, *the* problem of politics—can be brought to some level of consciousness as a question. Rorty retreats therefore not to a linguistic Esperanto but to an experiential one: the capacity to feel pain, which we share not only with each other but with the beasts. We are Sklarian liberals.[31]

How should this work ideally? According to Rorty, by reading. The more we read other vocabularies the more tolerant and the less cruel we will be. Here is a glimmer of synthesis of public and private in the ideal world: the perpetually redescribing-itself-self is the model citizen. But, as Rorty says in "Thugs and Theorists," the ideal has nothing to do with here and now.

Here we need add one piece of laundry purposely left off prior lists: procedural justice. *It* is Rorty's only account of justice at all. As Jo Burrows writes, Rorty "thinks that the identification of political problems is a fairly straightforward, empirical exercise, that it is *means* rather than ends which are generally in dispute."[32] Borrowing from the like thinking of Gordon Graham, Burrows phrases Rorty's view this way:

> We can conduct political argument on the grounds of what will or will not be successful. . . . Political action is possible without recourse to grand conceptions of history and society. . . . The pragmatist operates with no conception of history or vision of the future. . . . The pragmatist policy is neither short term nor long term. It is simply needed for the moment and just how long that moment is . . . is something contingent circumstances will determine.[33]

This might be a prudential move. That is, Rorty does not want a "thick" conceptual description of politics—even of our liberalism—because it will tend to enlist or entrench upon our private vocabularies.[34] Its writ—like Unger's—might run into the imagination. "Thin" political discourse would ensure maximum freedom in the private sphere. That might be true, but that is not the important point. The "foundation" is this: political discourse is inert for the same reason that the perfection of life is a task for the imagination. But that takes us to the depths of Rorty's entire scholarly project. Which is to say, Rorty's "social theory" is the product of, and only comprehensible when seen with, his existentialism.

THE POLITICAL SELF

Here is a passage from a short *New Republic* review of Jean-Paul Sartre's wartime diaries, which cuts to the core of Rorty's concern. The diaries

> argue [the] "existentialist" thesis that human life is "a useless passion": the attempt to be both capable of objective moral knowledge and radically free, to be subject to an unyielding code although fully aware that it is only one of many, equally plausible, codes.
>
> Sartre thought of this passion as the inevitable and doomed effort to be simultaneously hard and soft, completely committed and completely open to alternative

possibilities, simultaneously slick and porous. He saw philosophy as the paradigmatic expression of this self-deceptive attempt to have everything both ways: the attempt to pull one's decisions up by their bootstraps, so that they might be absolutely obligatory (expressing "the will of God," or "human nature," or "the moral law") and also be the product as of perfect, rational freedom.

Sartre knew that such fantasies, [about the rugged American individualist] as well as Marxist doctrines about "the march of history," were just further attempts to synthesize necessity and freedom, to be both perfectly hard and perfectly soft. But he was no more immune from this useless passion than are any of the rest of us.[35]

Now we can see that for Rorty "politics" is the realm of necessity and determinism, controlled by forces that we do not control, even as we know it is we that are the stuff of politics. Rorty has effectively severed political behavior from the realm of autonomous action. Politics is like nature, a mechanized operation, a Darwinian struggle of opposing forces whose outcome can be only observed, post hoc, by "participants," some of whom feel a need to discourse about it. Hence, we should take deadly seriously Rorty's conception of the political "self," from "Post Modernist Bourgeois Liberalism:

> The crucial move . . . is to think of the moral self . . . as a network of beliefs, desires, and emotions with nothing behind it—no substrate being the attributes. For purposes of moral and political deliberation and conversation [that is, for purpose of interpersonal life] a person just is that network, as for purposes of ballistics she is a point-mass, or for the purposes of chemistry a linkage of molecules. She is a network that is constantly remeaning itself . . . in the hit-or-miss way in which cells readjust themselves to meet the pressures of the environment.[36]

No wonder Rorty can reduce "social theory" to the descriptive discourses of sociology and political history. No wonder too that we shouldn't care whether Heidegger was a thug who, like Nietzsche, was a sordid piece of work.[37] Of course Heidegger was a thug—a Nazi—but he was no more responsible for his politics than we are for ours. Was it his fault to have come of age in Hitler's Germany? Presumably when the final scientific book is written, we will comprehend fully the *causes* of Heidegger's thuggery just as we will comprehend the causes of Mother Teresa's charity, just as we will comprehend the *causes* of our postmodernist bourgeois liberalism. One should assume, writes Rorty, that Heidegger "was as mixed up as the rest of us." Our job is not to fret or rush to judgment about Heidegger, but to read Heidegger as Heidegger "would not have wished to be read: in a cool hour, with curiosity, and an open tolerant mind."[38] Otherwise, we risk being Heidegger, someone who, like Hitler, took philosophy and himself seriously.

DISENCHANTED POLITICS

Rorty grants that his chilly, Sartrean view of politics disenchants the world.[39] And his ultimate defense of "frivolous" social theory is that it, too, helps along the disenchantment.[40] To those (like the early Unger and Alasdair Mac-Intyre) who would re-enchant it, Rorty poses the decisive question: "Whether disenchantment has, on balance, done us more harm than good."[41] With little reticence Rorty joins Dewey in coughing up the coins: "communal and public disenchantment is the price we pay for individual and private spiritual liberation."[42]

One might say that Rorty offers a pragmatic apology for disenchanted politics. This would be an exaggeration of a standard move in liberal legal theory: not that there *is* no God, but better for religious freedom if we all act in public life as if there is not. Rorty's world *is* disenchanted. That is why we should think of it that way. Our only hope is to act, in the tiny cubicle of the imagination where it is possible to do so, to fantasize as if it were not.

In *Philosophy and the Mirror of Nature,* Rorty asserted the following:

> Every speech, thought, theory, poem, composition, and philosophy will turn out to be completely predictable in purely naturalistic terms. Some atoms-and-the-void account of micro-processes within individual human beings will permit the prediction of every sound or inscription which will ever be uttered. There are no ghosts.[43]

Were we enthralled by scientism, there would be no hope. But we are not, at least after *Philosophy and the Mirror of Nature.* We are able to see ourselves as "strong poets" precisely by stripping science of its privileged epistemological position. But Rorty, though no scientist, *is* a materialist. So, more exactly, we need to dethrone scientistic discourse, out of which the Enlightment threatened to fashion a science of human goodness, truth, and beauty, to license the poets.

ONE'S OWN VOCABULARY

Freud is the necessary link between Rorty's profound materialism and his guarded humanism. Lengthy quotation is unavoidable:

> It has often seemed necessary to choose between Kant and Nietzsche, to make up one's mind—at least to that extent—about the point of being human. But Freud gives us a way of looking at human beings which helps us evade the choice. After reading Freud we shall see neither Bloom's strong poet nor Kant's

dutiful fulfiller of universal obligations as paradigmatic. For Freud himself es-
chewed the very idea of a paradigm human being. He does not see humanity as
a natural kind with an intrinsic set of powers to be developed or left undevel-
oped. By breaking with both Kant's residual Platonism and Nietzsche's inverted
Platonism, he lets us see both Nietzsche's superman and Kant's common moral
consciousness as exemplifying two out of many forms of adaptation, two out of
many strategies for coping with the contingencies of one's upbringing, of coming to terms with a blind impress. There is much to be said for both. Each has
advantages and disadvantages. Decent people are often rather dull. Great wits
are sure to madness near allied. Freud stands in awe before the poet, but describes him as infantile. He is bored by the merely moral man, but describes him
as mature. He does not enthuse over either, nor does he ask us to choose between
them. He does not think we have a faculty which can make such choices.

But there is a difference between Nietzsche and Freud which my description
of Freud's view of the moral man as decent but dull does not capture. Freud
shows us that if we look inside the *bien-pensant* conformist, if we get him on
the couch, we will find that he was only dull on the surface. For Freud, nobody
is dull through and through, for there is no such thing as a dull unconscious.
What makes Freud more useful and plausible than Nietzsche is that he does not
relegate the vast majority of humanity to the status of dying animals. For Freud's
account of unconscious fantasy shows us how to see every human life as a
poem—or, more exactly, every human life not so racked by pain as to be unable
to learn a language nor so immersed in toil as to have no leisure in which to generate a self-description. . . . What Freud takes to be shared by all of us relatively
leisured language-users—all of us who have the equipment and the time for
fantasy—is a faculty for creating metaphors.

When a metaphor is created it does not *express* something which previously
existed, although, of course, it is *caused* by something that previously existed.
For Freud, this cause is not the recollection of another world but rather some
particular obsession-generating cathexis of some particular person or object of
word early in life. By seeing every human being as consciously or unconsciously acting out an idiosyncratic fantasy, we can see the distinctly human, as
opposed to animal, portion of each human life as the use for symbolic purposes
of every particular person, object, situation, event, and word encountered in later
life.[44]

This Wittgensteinian attitude, developed by [Gilbert] Ryle and [Daniel] Dennett
for minds and by [Donald] Davidson for languages, materializes mind and language by making all questions about the relation of either to the rest of universe
causal questions, as opposed to questions about adequacy of representation of
expression.[45]

The effect is to disrupt the connection between intention and determinism,
so that the seat of subjectivity might be that faculty with which we play

language games—the imagination, awash in a sea of Derridaen text toys. Not the ghost in the machine—as Rorty says, there *is* no ghost—but a machine programmed with a capacity for distraction so edifying that it can induce forgetfulness of the wheels turning within. The *summum bonum* of an individual human life is a "final vocabulary," not in the sense of a best or consummate or "true" language but a vocabulary all one's own.[46] Rorty's social hero is the "strong poet." Few persons ever so perfect themselves but a few (Proust, Derrida) have. "Thus I willed out," according to Rorty, is the eulogy we ought covet.[47]

From these foundations, we can work outward and reappropriate yet another of Rorty's expressions for his social theory. That theory is "bourgeois" precisely because peace, wealth, and "the standard bourgeois freedoms of the leisured class" are preconditions for distraction. "Equality of opportunity" is the password: the "social glue" holding together Rorty's ideal society is "our" conviction to let "everybody have a chance at self-creation to the best of his or her abilities."[48] We can all start together in the race to be Derrida. The masters would be the intellectuals, the "ironist" class. The great mass of regular folks would be "common-sensically nominalist and historicist"; contented not by platitudes about God or the universe, but by the intellectuals' insistence that there are no viable concrete alternatives to liberalism.[49]

Rorty courageously confesses that being Derrida holds no appeal and makes no sense to the man on the street, who might well prefer the sorts of things Orwell wanted: getting more air down into the mine shafts. "The ironist is the typical modern intellectual. The only societies which give her the freedom to articulate her alienation are liberal ones." So, how do ironists pay their way?[50] Rorty hopes there is some service rendered by spinning out possible redescriptions, which might sensitize persons to the suffering and humiliation of those around them. But that is little more than vain hope. It is so little that Rorty is obliged to conclude that "ironist" philosophy has not done, and will not do, much for freedom and equality."[51] They are "private philosophers—philosophers concerned to intensify the irony of the nominalist and the historicist. Their work is ill-suited to public purposes, of no use to liberals *qua* liberals."[52]

There is not much to say after a "social theorist" privatizes his work.

Rorty's Secular Humanism

Richard Rorty has turned often since 1990 to questions of political life and social cooperation more generally. He remains a resolute, self-professed man of the left, a liberal, a romantic. The old stances and prescriptions remain in their places. Among them are:

An undiminished, spirited opposition to "correspondence" theories of truth. Rorty rejects without qualification the notion that something "out there" has to do with the validity or worthwhileness of our desires, projects, ideals. The pragmatic test of "truth" is what satisfies human needs and interests; "truth is about what bears fruit for us, here and now.[53]

Rorty favors "coherence" accounts of validity, and holds, too, that social projects (like law, science) require, as a precondition to their successful pursuit if not to their intelligibility, intersubjective agreement.[54] The "test" of validity for public initiatives is their capacity to gain the assent of the relevant population;[55]

Insouciance in political discourse. "Philosophical superficiality and light mindedness helps along the disenchantment of the world. It helps make the world's inhabitants more pragmatic, more tolerant, more liberal, more receptive to the appeal of instrumental rationality."[56]

Instrumental rationality, or the utilitarian outlook, is the only "reason" available in public decisions. Ends—individual and communal—are scarcely amenable to conscious deliberation and to choice guided by reason. "[T]hough objectivity is a useful goal when one is trying to calculate means to ends by predicting the consequences of actions, it is of little relevance when one is trying to decide what sort of person or nation to be."[57] "The frequent complaint that a philosopher who holds the pragmatic theory of truth cannot give you a reason not to be a fascist is perfectly justified. But neither can that person give you a reason to be a fascist."[58]

The pivotal role of avoiding "cruelty" in all that one does, and in all that one's community does. "Cruelty" is, for Rorty, the *summum malum* of politics.[59] Rorty is nevertheless enough of a utilitarian to concede that, in extreme cases, *anything* at all—including torture—might rightly be done.[60]

A Millian principle of political morality. "Mill's *On Liberty* provides all the ethical instruction you need. . . . [H]uman perfection becomes a private concern, and our responsibility to others becomes a matter of permitting them as much space to pursue these private concerns—to worship their own gods, so to speak—as is compatible with granting an equal amount of space to all."[61]

Rorty's political writings in the last decade are best described as those of a *deeply* secular, *passionate* humanist. Though he explicitly abjures nothing of

substance which my original essay attributed to him, Rorty's earlier, pro-
nounced materialism—and determinism—have been muted. The earlier glib-
ness is gone, too. (Rorty even thanks Matthew Festenstein for suggesting that
Rorty is "neither complacent nor frivolous" about political questions, "two
adjectives which are still frequently applied."[62]) Rorty's recent writings on
matters political are serious, nuanced, and passionate. He is more willing to
explain and defend his (hitherto, glib) positions. He takes contrary positions,
and counterarguments, more seriously than he used to.

The recent writings are motivated by deep concern for the temporal welfare
of human beings, and they extend Rorty's case against public religion. He maintains, in prose packed dense with learning and cleverness, that religion must be
kept private if society is to have any chance of being decent, safe, humane.

Rorty's work also exhibits a strengthened commitment to lunch-bucket,
New Deal liberalism. He calls this program "Reformist" liberalism; it is
preached by the "Old left." The new "cultural left" specializes in the "'politics of difference,' or 'of identity' or 'of recognition.'" The "cultural left
thinks more about stigma than about money."[63]

In Rorty's most sustained recent treatment of politics—his Massey Lectures at Harvard, published as *Achieving Our Country*—Rorty chided fellow
academic liberals in particular for worrying more about stigma than about
selfishness, for their complacency about economic redistribution.

Rorty has certainly not gone soft on stigma. Freedom from degrading
stereotypes and humiliation is still the nerve center of his politics. Rorty believes, however, that the battle against stereotypes has been largely won or, at
least, that a winning strategy is in place for inevitable victory. "Except for a
few Supreme Court decisions, there has been little change for the better in our
country's laws since the Sixties. But the change in the way we treat one another has been enormous."[64] Having defined "sadism" as speech (and, sometimes, other acts) which "humiliate" groups such as African-Americans, gays,
and women, Rorty observes: "During the same period in which socially accepted sadism has steadily diminished, economic inequality and insecurity
have steadily increased."[65]

Rorty scolded the new Left in his Massey Lectures for leaving working
class resentments to be exploited by "scurrilous demagogues like Patrick
Buchanan." Rorty persuasively argues that globalization of the labor market
has made the American worker a nervous cog in the industrial world order,
and calls—again, plausibly, if not cogently—for liberals' reengagement of
economic politics. "I think that the Left should get back in the business of
piecemeal reform within the framework of a market economy."[66]

Rorty's main concern in the political reflections has been secularism.
His case for the privatization of religion has been extended; it is sharper,

more poignant. He states approvingly that the "secularization of public life [w]as the Enlightenment's central achievement."[67] He characterizes (again, with unqualified approbation) the "compromise" wrought during the Enlightenment as "privatizing" religion as a condition of "religious liberty." This *religious* liberty is actually a set of uses of a broader liberty of all persons to a commodious private life, consistent with a like accommodation of others.[68]

Religion is a particularly suspect resident of the private zone. That is because religious believers characteristically consider their commitments—their religious life—to include the experience of faith, considered as a relationship with a greater than human source of meaning and value. Rorty carries no brief against this faith apart from creedal commitments implicating Truth. He likens it, without criticizing it, to the role which being in love with another human being has in so many persons' lives. Faith, like love, may supply a reason to live, to persevere, to fight on in the face of darkness and sorrow.[69] Poetry, literature, or sex may play a similar role in the lives of others. Paul Tillich's attempt to treat religious faith as "symbolic," and thereby to treat religion as poetry (and vice versa) "is on the right track."[70] If poetry (or the rosary or masturbation) helps us get through the night, who is to say nay?

It is here to be noted that Rorty's optimism about human progress contributes to his secularism. "In past ages of the world, things were so bad that 'a reason to believe, a way to take the world by the throat' was hard to get except by looking to a power not ourselves."[71] But if hardscrabble peasants needed god to get trough their days, we do not. "In those lucky parts of the world where wealth, leisure, literacy, and democracy have worked together to prolong our lives and fill our libraries," people do not need an "afterlife." They need not look beyond nature, but "only beyond the human past to the human future."[72]

Religious believers have also characteristically asserted propositions concerning what is really out there, about who God is, and about what God expects of persons. These "creedal" components of religion Rorty arraigns for crimes against humanity, for accumulated barbarisms. What Rorty calls "religious fundamentalism" is a "private project which has gotten out of hand." Along with "scientific realism," they "are attempts to make one's own private way of giving meaning to one's life—a way which romanticizes one's relation to something starkly and magnificently nonhuman, something ultimately true and real—obligatory for the general public."[73] The results are dismal; the prospect of pleasing the Deity, of securing a place in the hereafter, of avoiding complicity in sin all prompt the believer to ignore the (obvious) well-being of real persons, and to mistreat others, even to kill them.

Rorty does not quite assert that religious propositions are false. He confesses that, raised an atheist, he finds talk about God "merely confusing."[74] He declares of religious "truths": [i]t is never an objection to a religious belief that there is no evidence for it. The only possible objection to it can be that it intrudes an individual project into a social and cooperative project, and thereby offends against the teachings of *On Liberty.* Such intrusion is a betrayal of one's responsibilities to cooperate with other human beings, not of one's responsibility to Truth or Reason."[75]

Rorty's hostility to public religion is probably unsurpassed by any contemporary writer. Wariness, if not outright opposition, to public religion is characteristic of liberal political theory. Almost all liberals nevertheless recognize *some* socially beneficial effects of belief, even of public promotion and recognition of faith. (Often enough, "conservatives" who favor public religion do so entirely for faith's politically useful effects.) Liberals characteristically hold, though, that benefits of public religion are marginal, or at least that the dangers of public religion outweigh any prospective benefits.

Rorty is an exception. While "faith," construed generally as described above, is a valuable component of individuals' lives, religion portends *only* trouble, in Rorty's opinion, when introduced into the public square.

Rorty's extreme secularism is best evidenced by his strained attempt to defeat the claim that the Christian emphasis on human fraternity—"the idea that for Christians there is neither Jew nor Greek, and the related idea that love is the only law"[76]—constitutes a welcome public use (so to speak) of religion. Rorty surely wishes to embrace universal fraternity. Just as surely, much of what he otherwise holds weighs against any reasonable grounds, or warrants of any type, for treating all persons across the face of the earth as brothers and sisters.

Space does not permit elaboration of Rorty's argument, or of its implausibility. One brief observation is nevertheless in order. Throughout his work Rorty avoids the question of power. More exactly, he never confronts the fact that, once public "deliberation" about ends is no longer deliberation about the *common good,* but a more or less stable consensus on an agenda—as it is for Rorty—public life is exposed as a field of unremitting power. The political is not, and cannot be, for Rorty, a matter of common *reasoning* about what to do. "Ends" are simply givens, or "can't helps"; "means" are, in principle, immense technical calculations with a single correct answer. *Reasonable* disagreement about ends is strictly impossible. So, too, about means. Since we cannot imagine unanimity about public matters, raw *division,* and not *disagreement,* would characterize our life together on the Rortyan construal of it. And Rorty's long sojourn to the privatization of religion may end up back where it started.

NOTES

1. R. Rorty, *Philosophy and the Mirror of Nature* (Princeton, N.J.: Princeton University Press, 1979).

2. T. Jackson, "The Theory and Practice of Discomfort: Richard Rorty and Pragmatism," *Thomist* 51 (1987): 270.

3. Rorty, *Philosophy and the Mirror of Nature*, 7. The only comparably arresting claim I can recall is the penultimate sentence of Harold Berman's *Law and Revolution* (Cambridge, Mass.: Harvard University Press, 1983), 558: "Without the Last Judgment and the fear of purgatory, the Western legal tradition could never have come into being." Berman wonders how long our institutions can survive without the deep spiritual foundations we long ago undermined because we have just about consumed the last of our inherited moral capital. Berman seeks a new "integrative" jurisprudence—synthesizing historicist, positivist, and natural law strands—to ground out institutions anew. Rorty is no jurisprude, and only lately a social theorist. Still, he bemoans not the demise of our institution's theological (and metaphysical and philosophical) foundations. They are otiose illusions, however useful at one time.

4. Baynes et al., eds., *After Philosophy* (Cambridge, Mass.: MIT Press, 1987), 221.

5. B. Williams, "Auto-da-Fe: Consequences of Pragmatism," in A. Malachowski, *Reading Rorty* (Cambridge, Mass.: Basil Blackwell, 1990), 26–27.

6. R. Rorty, *Contingency, Irony, and Solidarity* (New York: Cambridge University Press, 1989).

7. See for example, J. Rawls, "Justice and Fairness: Political Not Metaphysical," *Philosophy & Public Affairs* 14 (1985): 225; J. Rawls, "The Domain of the Political and Overlapping Consensus," *New York University Law Review* 64 (1989): 233.

8. Laurence Tribe, *American Constitutional Law,* 2nd ed. (Mineola, N.Y.: Foundation Press, 1989).

9. Rorty, *Philosophy and the Mirror of Nature,* 3.

10. Rorty, *Philosophy and the Mirror of Nature,* 5–6.

11. Rorty, *Philosophy and the Mirror of Nature,* 162.

12. Rorty, *Philosophy and the Mirror of Nature,* 162.

13. Rorty, See *Philosophy and the Mirror of Nature,* passim, for various formulations of Rorty's invincibly conventionalist account of truth.

14. Rorty, *Philosophy and the Mirror of Nature,* 387.

15. For example, Rorty has *never* considered *Insight* (London: Longmans, 1958), Bernard Lonergan's monumental effort to identify an invariant stratum of human knowing, beyond epistemology, in cognitive theory. (I have looked in vain for *any* reference to Lonergan in his writings). Rorty's pragmatism—truth is what works—implicitly denies Lonergan's project, a project that presupposes an activity of "pure" knowing, the erotic quest of the mind for knowledge.

16. C. Taylor, "Rorty in the Epistemological Tradition," in *Reading Rorty,* 264.

17. Taylor, *Reading Rorty,* 262.

18. Taylor, *Reading Rorty,* 262.

19. Rorty, *Contingency,* chap. 14.

20. Rorty, *Contingency,* chap. 15.

21. R. Rorty, "The Priority of Democracy to Philosophy," in *Reading Rorty,* 284.

22. Rorty, *Contingency,* 194, n. 6.

23. Rorty, *Contingency,* 194.

24. Rorty, *Contingency,* 194, n. 6.

25. R. Rorty, "Unger, Castoriodis, and the Romance of a National Future," *Northwestern Law Review* 82 (1988): 335, 343.

26. Rorty, *Unger,* 339.

27. Rorty, *Unger,* 344.

28. R. Rorty, "Thugs and Theorists: A Reply to Bernstein," *Political Theory* 15 (1987): 564.

29. Rorty, "Thugs and Theorists," 564.

30. Rorty, *Contingency,* 121.

31. See Rorty, *Contingency*, 141–98.

32. J. Burrows, "Conversational Politics: Rorty's Pragmatistist Apology for Liberalism," in *Reading Rorty,* 322, 330.

33. Burrows, "Conversational Politics," 330.

34. See J. Rawls, *A Theory of Justice* (Cambridge, Mass.: Harvard University Press, 1971).

35. R. Rorty, "Finding His Way" (review of *The War Diaries of Jean-Paul Sartre,*" trans. Q. Hoare), *New Republic,* April 15, 1985, 32–34.

36. R. Rorty, "Postmodernist Bourgeois Liberalism," *Journal of Philosophy* 80 (1983): 563.

37. See R. Rorty, "Taking Philosophy Seriously" (review of V. Farias, *Heidegger et le Nazisme*), *New Republic,* April 11, 1988, 31–34.

38. Rorty, "Taking Philosophy Seriously," 34.

39. See Rorty, "Priority of Democracy," 294.

40. Rorty, "Priority of Democracy," 293.

41. Rorty, "Priority of Democracy," 294.

42. Rorty, "Priority of Democracy," 294.

43. Rorty, *Philosophy and the Mirror of Nature,* 387.

44. Rorty, *Contingency,* 36.

45. Rorty, *Contingency,* 15.

46. Rorty, *Contingency,* 97.

47. Rorty, *Contingency,* 37, 97.

48. Rorty, *Contingency,* 84.

49. Rorty, *Contingency,* 87.

50. Rorty, *Contingency,* 88–89.

51. Rorty, *Contingency,* 94.

52. Rorty, *Contingency,* 95.

53. The most pointed recent treatment by Rorty of "epistemology" is R. Rorty, "Religious Faith, Intellectual Responsibility, and Romance," in *The Cambridge Companion to William James,* ed. R. Putnam (New York: Cambridge University Press, 1997) (hereafter, "Romance"), 84–102.

54. R. Rorty, "Pragmatism and Romantic Polytheism," in *The Revival of Pragmatism*, ed. M. Dickstein (Durham, N.C.: Duke University Press, 1998) (hereafter, "Polytheism"), 21, 28.

55. See R. Rorty, "Religion as Conversation Stopper," 3 *Common Knowledge* 1, 5 (1999) (hereafter "Conversation").

56. R. Rorty, *Objectivity, Relativism and Truth: Philosophical Papers 1*, 193–94 (1991).

57. Rorty, *Achieving Our Country*, 11 (1998) (hereafter, "Achieving").

58. Rorty, "Polytheism," 25.

59. R. Rorty, "Response to Owens," in *Rorty and His Critics*, ed. R. Brandom (Malden, Mass.: Blackwell, 2000), 111.

60. Rorty, "Response to Owens," 114.

61. Rorty, "Polytheism," 24.

62. R. Rorty, "Response to Matthew Festenstein," in *Richard Rorty: Critical Dialogues*, ed. M. Festenstein and S. Thompson (Cambridge: Polity, 2001), 219.

63. Rorty, *Achieving*, 76–77.

64. Rorty, *Achieving*, 81.

65. Rorty, *Achieving*, 83.

66. Rorty, *Achieving*, 105.

67. Rorty, *Conversation*, 1.

68. Rorty, See *Conversation*, passim.

69. Rorty, "Romance," 94.

70. Rorty, *Polytheism*, 28.

71. Rorty, "Romance," 97.

72. Rorty, "Romance," 97.

73. Rorty, "Romance," 93.

74. Rorty, "Romance," 98.

75. Rorty, *Polytheism*, 28–29.

76. Rorty, *Polytheism*, 26.

9

The Unorthodox Liberalism of Joseph Raz

Robert P. George

[I]t is the goal of all political action to enable individuals to pursue valid conceptions of the good and to discourage evil or empty ones.[1]

Where, in contemporary writing, would one expect to find such a claim? Perhaps the last place one would be tempted to look is in a book described by its author as "both an introduction and a contribution to the political theory of liberalism."[2] After all, is it not the distinctive claim of modern liberals, as against ancient and medieval political thinkers, that political authorities ought, to the extent possible, to remain *neutral* as between citizens' competing conceptions of what makes for a valuable and morally worthy way of life?[3]

No less orthodox a liberal moralist than the late Justice William J. Brennan captured the spirit of mainstream liberalism nicely in his notion that the political order established by the Constitution of the United States is "facilitative."[4] According to a facilitative conception of politics, government—whether federal, state, or local—has no authority to judge matters of "personal" morality. The question of whether a conception of the good is "valid" or "evil" is for individuals to decide for themselves free of governmental intrusion. The proper concern of government is to preserve the freedom of individuals to pursue *whatever* conceptions of the good they happen to favor (so long as they do not violate the rights of others).

The quotation with which I began this chapter leaves no doubt that the "liberalism" of Joseph Raz departs radically from the Brennanite orthodoxy. In Raz's view, a morally sound political order cannot be neutral about which ways of life are good and which are evil: the very point of political action is to encourage pursuit of what is truly worthwhile and discourage pursuit of what is morally unworthy.

Just as fifteen years earlier John Rawls's *A Theory of Justice*[5] helped to reorient the discussion of liberal political philosophy by challenging the utilitarian premises of pre-Rawlsian liberalism, Raz's *The Morality of Freedom* is
helping to reorient the debate by challenging the prevailing assumptions of
post-Rawlsian liberalism. What Raz proposes, however, is not a return to utilitarianism, but the adoption of a political morality that is not only nonutilitarian and nonneutralist but also, at least in some ways, preliberal.

If the modern approach to political theory is distinguished from the ancient
and medieval approaches above all by the modern commitment to a neutralist or "facilitative" politics, the position Raz adopts in *The Morality of Freedom* places him in the company of Plato, Aristotle, and Aquinas rather than in
the camp of Locke, Rawls, and Brennan. In what sense, then, can Raz's political theory qualify as liberal?

PLURALISTIC PERFECTIONISM AND THE VALUE OF AUTONOMY

Mainstream liberal political theory is antiperfectionist. Antiperfectionism is
the view that government is either (1) required to remain neutral on controversial questions of what makes for, or detracts from, a morally good life, or
(2) forbidden to act on the basis of controversial ideals of moral goodness.
Rawls's adoption of antiperfectionism in *A Theory of Justice* has been fol-
lowed by many of the most influential contemporary liberal political theorists, including Robert Nozick, Ronald Dworkin, Bruce Ackerman, and David
Richards.

Raz, however, breaks sharply with these theorists by utterly rejecting antiperfectionism. He devotes two chapters of *The Morality of Freedom* to criticizing the various arguments that these authors and others have put forward
in support of governmental neutrality and the exclusion of ideals. His conclusion is that antiperfectionist principles of political morality are neither
warranted nor, strictly speaking, even possible.

He proposes, therefore, to construct a theory of political morality on perfectionist premises. He denies, however, that perfectionist political theories
must be illiberal. If there are, as Raz believes, good grounds for supposing
that liberty is humanly and morally valuable, then a sound perfectionist theory will not leave the good of liberty out of account.[6] A perfectionist liberal
political theory will give liberty a certain pride of place among the human
goods.

In concluding his critique of antiperfectionist liberalism, Raz makes two
points that foreshadow his adumbration of a perfectionist alternative. First, he
observes that "not all perfectionist action is a coercive imposition of a style

of life. Much of it could be encouraging and facilitating[7] action of the desired [i.e., morally upright] kind, or discouraging undesired [i.e., immoral] modes of behaviour."[8] Second, he notes that "[p]erfectionism is . . . compatible with moral pluralism, which allows that there are many morally valuable forms of life which are incompatible with each other."[9]

The second point is critical to Raz's project. From the perspective of anti-perfectionist critics, Raz's perfectionism renders his claim to be presenting an authentically liberal theory of political morality dubious or at least highly suspect. In reply to these critics, Raz would maintain that what qualifies his theory of political morality as "liberal" is the pride of place it gives to individual liberty. He must, therefore, give some account of why liberty should enjoy this pride of place. Any such account will, in turn, depend upon an understanding of the value of liberty.

According to Raz, something is valuable insofar as it contributes to human well-being. And things can contribute to human well-being in two ways. Some things are instrumentally valuable; they are worth having as means to other valuable things. Other things are intrinsically valuable; they are worth having for their own sakes. Instrumental values have their value as means ultimately to things that are intrinsically valuable.

In Raz's theory of practical reasoning, values, including intrinsic values, are reasons for action. They are not reducible to desires. On the contrary, desires are, he says, "reason-dependent."[10] It is the reason-dependent character of desires that grounds a person's reasonable wish not to have his false desires satisfied. "Want-satisfaction *qua* want-satisfaction," Raz concludes, "is not intrinsically valuable."[11] We do not necessarily do people a favor, then, by helping them to get whatever they happen to want. If they happen to want what is evil or empty, they have reason not to have their desires fulfilled and others may have reason to frustrate, or even help to alter, the desires they happen to have.

Now, how does Raz conceive of the value of liberty? Is liberty intrinsically valuable? Or is it merely instrumentally valuable? If it is intrinsically valuable, is the value of liberty realized in every act in which liberty is exercised? Or is it realized only when someone exercising liberty chooses what is morally good?

Raz takes the position that liberty, or what he prefers to call "autonomy,"[12] is intrinsically valuable. It is an aspect of human well-being. A rich and full human life is made even richer and fuller when the values realized in that life are realized in and through acts in which the agent freely chooses what to do.[13] Of course, an autonomous agent does not ordinarily choose for the sake of autonomy. Rather, his autonomous choice is ordinarily motivated by some other value. Thus, "the value of freedom depends on the other values which the freedom to perform such actions serves."[14] Autonomy or freedom, in Raz's philosophy, is not the only intrinsic value. Many other things are intrinsically good; and inasmuch as autonomy is ordinarily exercised in choosing for reasons other than autonomy, it would not be valuable *unless* there were other intrinsic goods.

It is clear, then, that Raz's perfectionism is pluralistic. There are many human perfections. Thus, frequently, there are many possible morally valuable possibilities among which people must choose. In choosing, one realizes not only the values that motivate one's choice; one realizes the value of autonomy as well.

Is it not the case, however, that one may autonomously choose possibilities that are morally bad? Are such choices somehow redeemed by the freedom one exercises in making them? Raz faces these questions squarely. His position is that although one may autonomously choose what is morally bad, "[a]utonomy is valuable only if exercised in pursuit of the good."[15] "Indeed," he says, "autonomously choosing the bad makes one's life worse than a comparable non-autonomous life is." Raz himself takes note of some of the political implications of this view: "[s]ince autonomy is valuable only if it is directed at the good it supplies no reason to provide, nor any reason to protect, worthless let alone bad options."[16]

Raz argues that the good of autonomy requires that people have available to them for choice a range of morally worthy options. A perfectionist political order will, therefore, concern itself with the provision of such options. On the basis of this conclusion, Raz rejects familiar notions of liberalism as a theory of limited government. "While not denying that governments can and often do pose a threat to individual liberty," he says "there is another conception which regards them also as a possible source of liberty."[17] It is the latter conception that he embraces.

In rejecting the former conception, Raz also rejects the individualism so characteristic of antiperfectionist liberal political philosophy. Near the beginning of *The Morality of Freedom,* he says that "[i]f there is one common thread to the argument of this book it is its critique of individualism and its endeavour to argue for a liberal morality on non-individualistic grounds."[18] How does Raz square his antipathy to individualism with his central concern for individual freedom?

The answer to this question is most interesting. Raz argues that the existence of certain social institutions, practices, and conventions (what he generally refers to as "social forms") are often critical to making available to people morally valuable opportunities for choice. The opportunity to marry, for example, is only available in circumstances where the institution of marriage exists. Marriage simply is not a realistic option for people in a society that is lacking that social institution. And although the institution of marriage differs in certain respects from society to society, there are limits to the pluralism that any society can bear with respect to that institution. The concrete legal and symbolic significance of the institution of marriage as it exists (where it exists) is not an individual matter.[19] Raz illustrates the point with the example of monogamous marriage:

> Monogamy, assuming that it is the only morally valuable form of marriage, cannot be practised by an individual. It requires a culture which recognizes it, and which supports it through the public's attitude and through its formal institutions.[20]

Thus, according to Raz, in promoting and protecting social forms such as marriage public authorities—far from violating individual liberty and autonomy—enhance these goods. By contrast, a political order that neglects to provide such support fails to make available to its members the morally valuable opportunity afforded by, for example, the institution of monogamous marriage.

Moreover, Raz notices that certain social forms that are important for human well-being and fulfillment need not themselves even provide opportunities for choice. In remarking on this fact, Raz draws out further implications of his conception of individual liberty that run contrary to liberal orthodoxy.

The relations between parents and their children are an example of a relationship that is not based upon choice of partners. It shows that an environment can be supportive of autonomy and yet include forms not based on choice. It has to be admitted though that even here choice has tended to creep more and more into the relations. Parents have greater control over whether and when to have children, and to a certain extent over which children to have. The widespread use of contraception, abortion, adoption, in vitro fertilization and similar measures has increased choice but also affected the relations between parents and their children. The impact of the increased choice on the character of the family is just beginning to be felt.

> It would be a mistake to think that those who believe, as I do, in the value of personal autonomy necessarily desire the extension of personal choice in all relationships and pursuits. They may consistently with their belief in personal autonomy wish to see an end to this process, or even its reversal.[21]

I have quoted Raz at length here to highlight both his thoroughgoing anti-individualism and, relatedly, his rejection of the common liberal belief that the expansion of individual choice, or its extension into new areas of human activity, is inevitably desirable. For Raz, everything depends on the moral evaluation of the options being made available for choice. Where a choice is between morally worthy but incompatible possibilities, one realizes (in addition, perhaps, to other goods) the intrinsic good of autonomy simply by choosing for oneself. The opportunity to make the choice is therefore one that it is in principle valuable for one to have. By contrast, it may not be valuable for one to have the choice of immoral possibilities. Raz insists that the choice of an immoral option, despite its autonomous nature, is valueless. The opportunity to make such choices is valuable only to the extent that confronting and overcoming the temptation to choose immorally is necessary for one to build a good moral character. As Raz observes, however, no particular immoral possibility need be available to serve this function.[22] Life is filled with ineradicable temptations against which one may form one's moral backbone and test one's mettle.

Let us take stock: Raz's pluralistic perfectionism allows for a range of choices between morally valuable but incompatible possibilities. In making these choices, individuals uniquely realize a particular intrinsic good (or human perfection), namely, personal autonomy. This good provides the moral ground for the liberal political commitment to individual liberty. At the same time, in its perfectionist concern for the moral well-being of citizens, government ought to support those social institutions that help to make morally valuable opportunities available for choice. It should eschew neutrality with respect to marriage and family life, for example. In promoting and protecting these valuable social forms, government does not violate people's autonomy; rather, it extends autonomy by enriching the morally valuable opportunities for choice. As between morally valuable but incompatible possibilities, however, government must, for the sake of autonomy, respect individual liberty. Autonomy requires that government abstain from dictating to people in morally neutral matters. Tyrannical governments, insofar as they deprive people of morally worthy options, harm them by violating their autonomy. On the other hand, government need not, and indeed should not, remain neutral as between morally upright and immoral options. It should play an active role in encouraging morally valuable activities and discouraging activities that are morally evil.

LIBERAL TOLERATION AND THE HARM PRINCIPLE

None of what I have said thus far is likely to provide much reassurance to orthodox liberals. By the same token, more traditionally minded philosophers may be wondering just what, if anything, separates their positions from Razian liberalism. To be sure, Raz's political theory is not illiberal; it places a great emphasis on the importance of individual liberty. Contemporary natural law theorists and other traditionally oriented conservative critics of liberalism, however, typically defend alternatives to liberalism that are in no way illiberal. They too are pluralistic perfectionists.[23] They too believe that people ought to shape their own lives by choosing for themselves whether, or whom, to marry, for example. They agree that government ought to support social institutions that make morally valuable opportunities available to people but abstain from dictating to people in matters that are morally indifferent. Their perfectionism is no more sympathetic to tyranny than is Raz's perfectionist liberalism. So, the question lingers: What is distinctively liberal about Raz's political philosophy?

The answer may lie in Raz's endorsement of a modified version of J. S. Mill's "harm principle."[24] In Raz's hands, this principle forbids the government from using coercive means to discourage people from committing "harmless" or, better, "victimless" immoralities.[25]Although his perfectionism authorizes the government to use noncoercive methods of combatting immoralities of this sort, he argues that a due regard for the value of autonomy forbids the government as a matter of principle from criminalizing immoral acts unless those acts are harmful, or at least potentially harmful, to others.

It is worth emphasizing that Raz opposes the legal prohibition of victimless immoralities as a matter of moral principle. He is not merely making a prudential or pragmatic argument against morals legislation. Thus, his position can be distinguished from the position of Aquinas, for example. In his famous reply to the question of whether the criminal law ought to repress all vices, Aquinas held that human law should concern itself mainly with those vices that cause harm to others.[26] He did not, however, rule out in principle the use of the criminal law to protect the community's moral environment against the corrupting influences of vice. He treated the matter as one for prudent legislative judgment.

Raz, by contrast, wishes to show that the use of the criminal law to combat victimless immoralities is itself morally wrong. Here he adopts, I submit, a distinctively liberal position. He supports that position with an argument meant to show that "victimless crimes" are ruled out by a proper concern for autonomy. He recognizes, however, that this claim is problematic in view of his perfectionism. Noting that his general argument is "that it is the function of governments to promote morality," he says that

> that means that governments should promote the moral quality of the life of those whose lives and actions they can affect. Does not this concession amount to a rejection of the harm principle? It does according to the common conception which regards the aim and function of the principle as being to curtail the freedom of governments to enforce morality. I wish to propose a different

understanding of it, according to which it is a principle about the proper way to enforce morality.[27]

He then sets about the task of "deriv[ing] the harm principle from the principle of autonomy."[28]

Raz's proposed derivation of the harm principle begins with yet another reminder of a concession entailed by his perfectionism. He then makes two distinct claims by which he purports to establish that this concession does not undercut the principle of his liberal opposition to morals laws.

> Pursuit of the morally repugnant cannot be defended from coercive interference on the ground that being an autonomous choice endows it with any value. It does not (except in special circumstances where it is therapeutic or educational). And yet the harm principle is defensible in light of the principle of autonomy for one simple reason. The means used, coercive interference, violates the autonomy of its victim. First, it . . . expresses a relation of domination and an attitude of disrespect for the coerced individual. Second, coercion by criminal penalties is a global and indiscriminate invasion of autonomy. Imprisoning a person prevents him from almost all autonomous pursuits. Other forms of coercion may be less severe, but they all invade autonomy, and they all, at least in this world, do it in a fairly indiscriminate way. That is, there is no practical way of ensuring that the coercion will restrict the victim's choice of repugnant options but will not interfere with other choices.[29]

It must be said that liberal critics of legal moralism, no less than its nonliberal defenders, have found Raz's argument in defense of the harm principle to be fragile.[30] His claim that coercion necessarily "expresses a relation of domination and disrespect" seems gratuitous. He offers no evidence for the claim and many people, including myself, see no reason to credit it. As the antiperfectionist liberal theorist Wojciech Sadurski has correctly observed, "more radical perfectionists than Raz have argued that it is precisely the respect for a person which should trigger our coercive interference with morally repugnant actions."[31] Sadurski goes on to argue that, in light of Raz's perfectionist conception of autonomy (i.e., the conception in which autonomy is valuable only if exercised in the pursuit of what is morally valuable), it is hard to perceive any violation of the value of autonomy in legal prohibitions of victimless wrongs. "And this raises the suspicion that Raz smuggles into his argument a nonperfectionist notion of autonomy."[32]

As for Raz's claim that "coercion by criminal penalties is a global and indiscriminate invasion of autonomy," it is hard to quarrel with Sadurski's judgment that "[t]his argument is surprisingly inadequate to the burden it is supposed to carry, namely the defence of the harm principle."[33] Criminal prohibition and punishment in the case of morals laws are certainly no more "global and indiscriminate" than prohibition and punishment in other areas of the criminal law. If preventing self-corruption is as valid a reason for political action as preventing theft, as Raz concedes it is, then there seems to be no *moral* principle that forbids the use of the criminal law to combat vice. *Prudential* considerations may tip the balance against legal prohibition in many (or even most) cases; the force of such considerations, however, will vary with the circumstances. In any event, as Sadurski observes, "Raz's argument is, at best, an autonomy-based argument against the penalty of imprisonment for morally repugnant actions, but is not sufficient to justify rejection of all coercive prohibitions of immoral [though victimless] behaviour."[34]

Even apart from the difficulties it creates for his argument in the area of morals legislation, there is something peculiar in Raz's claim that autonomy is intrinsically valuable, yet devoid of value in the case of morally evil choices. Indeed, Donald Regan maintains that Raz's position on the matter is internally inconsistent.

> [T]here is no inconsistency in saying that autonomy is autonomy even when it chooses the bad, and saying also that autonomy is valuable only when it chooses the good. But there is an inconsistency in asserting both of these propositions and in supposing also (as Raz does) that autonomy, *tout court*, is valuable. These three propositions taken together entail that autonomy which chooses the bad both is and is not valuable.[35]

Regan's advice to Raz is that, "strange as it may sound," he should abandon the claim that autonomy is autonomy even when it chooses the bad. The less-desirable alternative, according to Regan, is to give up the claim that autonomy as such is valuable.

I think that Regan is on to something here, but that he gives Raz the wrong advice. If something is intrinsically valuable, its realization in immoral acts does not negate its value. By the same token, its value does not redeem the immoral choices by which it is realized, at least if consequentialism is false (as Raz agrees it is).[36] If therefore autonomy is conceived to be intrinsically valuable, we must recognize its value even when exercised immorally. And we can do so without jeopardizing the belief that some autonomous acts really are immoral.

Nevertheless, I think that Raz is both mistaken in his understanding of autonomy as intrinsically valuable and correct in his view that nothing of value is realized in wicked choices by virtue of their having been made autonomously. Autonomy *appears* to be intrinsically valuable because something really does seem to be more perfect about the realization of goods when this realization is the fruit of one's own practical deliberation and choice. The additional perfection, however, is provided not by autonomy, but by the exercise of one's reason in self-determination. Autonomy, in some sense, is surely a condition for such exercise, and thus for the realization of the value of bringing reason to bear in deciding what to do. Practical reasonableness, however, and not the autonomy on which it is conditioned, is the intrinsic good in play here. Thus, we may validly conclude that practically reasonable choices are perfective of human beings (i.e., are intrinsically valuable); practically unreasonable (i.e., immoral) choices, by contrast, realize no value in respect of the autonomy exercised in making them.

PATERNALISTIC COERCION AND TRUST

In an essay published a decade after the appearance of *The Morality of Freedom,* Raz introduced a new argument for rejecting paternalistic coercion—at least where the harm from which paternalistic legislation is designed to protect people is *moral* harm.[37] Nothing in the argument alters his view that autonomy is intrinsically valuable or revises his belief that morally repugnant, albeit autonomous, choices are generally valueless. The argument is offered to supplement, rather than replace, the antipaternalistic arguments he advanced in earlier writings.

Raz's new argument pivots on the importance of *trust* in justifying paternalistic coercion:

> Paternalistic coercion is justified when it meets two cumulative conditions: first, it is undertaken for a good reason, one sufficient to make reasonable a partial loss of independence. Secondly, barring emergencies, it comes from the hands of someone reasonably trusted by the coerced.[38]

It is worth emphasizing that Raz is here concerned with the conditions justifying *paternalistic* coercion. The second condition does not apply in the case of non-paternalistic legislation. "Naturally, trust is not a condition of the legitimacy of an authority in stopping people from violating the rights of others or unjustifiably harming them."[39] But why, one might ask, in the case of paternalistic legislation is trust imposed as a special condition over and above the requirement of reasonableness? Raz's answer seems to be that the interests of the person coerced for paternalistic reasons cannot be truly advanced where he is not in a relationship of trust with the coercer. It is possible for one to retain one's self-respect when prevented for one's own good from doing as one pleases or sees fit by a trusted friend whose benevolence and good intentions are "beyond doubt." Raz suggests that the same is not true, however, in the case of coercion at the hands of strangers—including government officials. In the latter case, one will likely experience the coercion as a form of manipulation that reduces the person coerced to the status of a "tool [ ] in the hands of others." One will not be able reasonably to accept it in the way one might reasonably accept having one's own will overridden by the coercive intervention of someone whose good judgment and benevolence one trusts.

In a reply to this line of argument, Christopher Wolfe maintains that Raz fails to provide "any principled argument as to the need for trust, over and above good reasons, as a ground for moral paternalism."[40] Wolfe concedes that trust is a *factor* in evaluating paternalistic legislation. But he views it as one among many *prudential* considerations bearing on the question whether the legislation is likely to achieve the good ends for which it is designed. The greater and more widespread the lack of faith in the goodwill or moral competence of legislators and other governmental officials, the less likely the law is to accomplish its moral goals. In Wolfe's judgment, however, what matters at the level of principle is not whether persons coerced *happen to* trust or distrust the government; rather, it is whether the government is *worthy* of trust. He argues that well-intentioned and morally competent legislators need not refrain from enacting laws to prevent moral harm on the basis of an *unwarranted* distrust of them by persons who disagree with the moral views embodied in the paternalistic laws they enact and who wish to behave in ways that such laws would forbid.

For Wolfe, the question is an objective one: Is the government worthy of trust? For Raz, the question is, by his own description, "semi-objective": "It turns not on how people actually feel, but on how it is reasonable for them to feel."[41] But this raises an important question. Is it possible for people *reasonably* to object to (or feel victimized by) paternalistic laws that meet the first of Raz's conditions for justified paternalistic coercion? Could there be situations in which distrust of the government's paternalism is reasonable despite the fact that its legislation is fully supported by good justifying reasons? What could be the reasonable grounds of subjective distrust of objectively reasonable paternalistic laws?

Fundamentally, Raz seems to be concerned that moral paternalism will undercut or erode "the status of citizenship which makes it rationally possible for people to regard themselves as fully belonging to the political community, and similarly to regard its law as their law, and its government as their government."[42] Apparently his belief is that citizens who disagree with the moral grounds of laws restricting their freedom for the sake of their own moral welfare will have a reasonable basis—even if the moral grounds of the laws are objectively sound—for distrusting the government and feeling as though they are being treated as something less than full citizens. "To feel part of a society," Raz says, "to be a full citizen of it one must be able to profess one's basic beliefs, and conduct one's life in accordance with one's deepest feelings without fear of criminal sanctions, legal or social discrimination, or social ridicule or persecution."[43]

As Wolfe points out, however, laws protecting other people's rights and the interests of the community in protecting public health, safety, and morals, frequently subject people to fear of criminal sanctions, not to mention social discrimination and even ridicule—think of racists, smokers, environmental polluters, pedophiles, and many others. If the morality of the laws is sound, we ordinarily consider that sufficient to justify them irrespective of their impact on the deepest feelings or even the self-respect of people who dissent, however conscientiously, from that morality. If feelings or self-respect are harmed, the fault is not with the law, but rather with the defective moral understandings of those dissenting from them. Why should anything be different in the case of paternalistic laws? Of course, if the morality embodied in the laws is defective, then the laws should be abolished or revised—but that is true of all laws, not just paternalistic ones. Moreover, the need for abolition or revision in such cases is not rooted in the paternalistic character of the laws; rather, it follows from their substantive moral defectiveness.

One might additionally ask why paternalistic laws should give anyone reason to feel that they are being treated as less than full citizens. After all, in seeking to protect people from their own moral failings and misjudgments, the law is expressing concern for their well-being. (Of course, the particular concern may be misguided, but that raises a different issue.) Dissenters may criticize and even resent the content of the law. It may subjectively offend their deepest feelings and, to be sure, damage their self-respect. But if it does so in holding people to sound moral standards of behavior, then it is prohibiting acts or practices that people should not, in fact, respect themselves for performing or engaging in. In that event, the path to a self-respect worth having is in the way of personal moral reform, not the abolition of paternalistic laws forbidding truly immoral conduct.

CONCLUSION

Raz's claim to be operating within the tradition of liberalism seems strongest where his arguments on the merits seem weakest. Whatever else is to be said for and against antiperfectionism (and I think that Raz is correct to think that there is much to be said against it), its premises clearly provide more solid support for the principled rejection of morals legislation than Raz is able to muster.

Of course, Raz could abandon his strong claims against legal moralism and repair to prudential objections to most (or even all) morals laws. In response to critics who might then accuse him of abandoning liberalism, he could say that the coincidence of his political theory with the theories of philosophers who think of themselves as outside the liberal tradition simply reveals the extent to which liberal pluralism has influenced virtually all contemporary political thinkers. In the world of ideas, he might argue, the liberal view of the importance of individual liberty has triumphed.

NOTES

1. Joseph Raz, *The Morality of Freedom* (Oxford: Clarendon Press, 1986), 133.
2. Raz, *The Morality of Freedom,* 1.
3. See Ronald Dworkin, "Liberalism," in *A Matter of Principle* (Cambridge, Mass.: Harvard University Press, 1985), 191.
4. See *Michael H. v Gerald D.,* 109 Sup. Ct. 2333, 2351 (1989) (Brennan, J., dissenting).
5. John Rawls, *A Theory of Justice* (Cambridge, Mass.: Harvard University Press, 1971).
6. John Finnis makes the same point: "liberty and authenticity are goods, too. They will find their place in any accurate (i.e., 'full,' non-emaciated . . .) theory of human good." *Fundamentals of Ethics* (Oxford: Oxford University Press, 1983), 50.
7. Obviously, Raz's use of the term "facilitating" here implies no Brennan-like notion of a "facilitative" political order that abstains from treating people's personal moral welfare as a reason for political action. Raz is simply proposing that there are sometimes noncoercive means of encouraging and enabling people to do what is morally good and avoid what is morally evil.
8. Raz, *The Morality of Freedom,* 161.
9. Raz, *The Morality of Freedom,* 161. Raz's notion of "moral pluralism" has nothing to do with moral relativism. In speaking of "many morally valuable forms of life which are incompatible with each other," he is not supposing that there are actions that are "morally wrong" for people who happen to think that they are morally wrong but "morally right" for people who happen to think otherwise. Nor is he supposing that there are actions that are "morally right" for people who wish to perform them but "morally wrong" for others. He has in mind, rather, the idea that there are certain morally valuable possibilities (e.g., actions and ways of life), the choosing of which is incompatible with the choosing of certain other morally valuable possibilities. For example, the choosing of a life of consecrated celibacy, while morally valuable, is incompatible with the choosing of marriage despite the fact that marriage is morally valuable. Or again, the choice to devote an evening to conversation with friends, while morally valuable, is incompatible with the choice of spending that evening reading Shakespeare, reflecting on human finitude, or praying for wisdom despite the fact that these activities are morally valuable.
10. Raz, *The Morality of Freedom,* 140–44.
11. Raz, *The Morality of Freedom,* 143.

12. Raz distinguishes autonomy in his sense, namely, "personal autonomy" from "the only very indirectly related notion of moral autonomy." *The Morality of Freedom,* 370, n. 2. Cf. David Richards's reduction of moral autonomy to personal autonomy in various of his writings, e.g., *Sex, Drugs, Death and the Law* (Totawa, N.J.: Rowman & Littlefield, 1982). For a critique of Richards see John Finnis, "Legal Enforcement of Duties to Oneself: Kant v. Neo-Kantians," *Columbia Law Review* 87, § 3, (1987): 433.

13. Raz explains that "[t]he ruling idea behind the ideal of personal autonomy is that people should make their own lives. The autonomous person is (part) author of his own life. The ideal of personal autonomy is the vision of people controlling, to some degree, their own destiny, fashioning it through successive decisions throughout their lives." *The Morality of Freedom,* 369. "Autonomy," he says, "is opposed to a life of coerced choices. It contrasts with a life of no choices, or of drifting through life without ever exercising one's capacity to choose." *The Morality of Freedom,* 371.

14. Raz, *The Morality of Freedom,* 16.

15. Raz, *The Morality of Freedom,* 381.

16. Raz, *The Morality of Freedom,* 411.

17. Raz, *The Morality of Freedom,* 18.

18. Raz, *The Morality of Freedom,* 18.

19. According to Raz, "[t]he very relationship between spouses depends . . . on the existence of social conventions. These conventions are constitutive of the relationship. They determine its typical contours. They do this partly by assigning symbolic meaning to certain modes of behavior." *The Morality of Freedom,* 350.

20. Raz, *The Morality of Freedom,* 160.

21. Raz, *The Morality of Freedom,* 393–94.

22. Raz, *The Morality of Freedom,* 410.

23. For an example of a pluralistic perfectionist natural law theory, see John Finnis, *Natural Law and Natural Rights* (Oxford: Oxford University Press, 1980). In *The Morality of Freedom,* 395–99, Raz usefully distinguishes between "weak" and "strong" forms of pluralism. "Strong" pluralism, which he endorses, is marked by the recognition of incompatible virtues that (1) "are not completely ranked relative to each individual," and/or (2) "are not completely ranked by some impersonal criteria of moral worth," and/or (3) "exemplify diverse fundamental concerns." Raz explains that the incommensurability of values supports (1) and (2), and renders (3) highly plausible. It is noteworthy that Finnis's natural law theory is fully compatible with Raz's "strong" pluralistic perfectionism. This compatibility is undoubtedly to be accounted for in large part by Finnis's own belief in the incommensurability of the basic forms of human good that provide ultimate reasons for choice and action. Raz and Finnis both reject utilitarianism—even the "two-level" and "indirect" forms of utilitarianism that may be morally pluralistic in a weaker sense and, as Raz points out, "may also accept the first two strong forms of pluralism [but] are incompatible with the third." *The Morality of Freedom,* 397.

24. According to Wojciech Sadurski, who criticizes Raz's political philosophy from an antiperfectionist point of view, "[t]he major point of convergence between Raz's book and the 'conventional' liberal theory is the acceptance of the harm princi-

ple as a basis for restraining the exercise of coercive powers of the state." "Joseph Raz on Liberal Neutrality and the Harm Principle," *Oxford Journal of Legal Studies* 10 (1990): 122–33, 130.

25. Raz's references to "harmless" immoralities in *The Morality of Freedom* created some uncertainty as to the scope of his critique of morals legislation. Recently he has clarified the matter by making clear that he objects to the criminalization of "victimless" immoralities generally. See "Liberalism, Skepticism, and Democracy," *Iowa Law Review* 74 (1989): 761–86.

26. *Summa Theologiae* I–II, q. 96, a. 2, reply. Joel Feinberg has recently claimed that Aquinas's position qualifies him as a "liberal" on the question of the moral limits of the criminal law. Inasmuch as Aquinas clearly does not rule out morals legislation as a matter of moral principle, however, Feinberg's claim is mistaken. See Robert George, "Moralistic Liberalism and Legal Moralism," *Michigan Law Review* 88 (1990): 1415–29; 1421–22.

27. *The Morality of Freedom*, 415.

28. *The Morality of Freedom*, 415.

29. *The Morality of Freedom*, 418–19.

30. Compare the criticisms of Raz's argument made in Sadurski, "Joseph Raz on Liberal Neutrality," 130–33, with those I offered in "Justice and Public Morality," *The World and I* 5 (1990): 517–45, 537–43.

31. Sadurski, "Joseph Raz on Liberal Neutrality," 132. For examples of "more radical perfectionists" making precisely the argument mentioned by Sadurski, see Finnis, "Legal Enforcement of 'Duties to Oneself,'" 437; and Robert George, "Individual Rights, Collective Interests, Public Law, and American Politics," *Law and Philosophy* 8 (1989): 245–61, 256–58.

32. Sadurski, "Joseph Raz on Liberal Neutrality," 132.

33. Sadurski, "Joseph Raz on Liberal Neutrality," 132.

34. Sadurski, "Joseph Raz on Liberal Neutrality," 133.

35. Donald Regan, "Authority and Value: Reflections on Raz's *The Morality of Freedom*," *Southern California Law Review* 62 (1989): 995–1085, 1084.

36. Raz rejects consequentialism on the ground that consequentialist methods of moral judgment rely on the mistaken assumption that basic values are commensurable in a way that would make aggregation and comparison of values possible. See *The Morality of Freedom*, chap. 13. For a more radical critique of consequentialism based on the "incommensurability thesis," see John Finnis, Joseph M. Boyle, Jr., and Germain Grisez, *Nuclear Deterrence, Morality and Realism* (Oxford: Clarendon Press, 1987), 254–60.

37. Joseph Raz, "Liberty and Trust," in *Natural Law, Liberalism, and Morality,* ed. Robert George (Oxford: Clarendon Press, 1996), 113–29.

38. Raz, "Liberty and Trust," 122.

39. Raz, "Liberty and Trust," 123.

40. Christopher Wolfe, "Being Worthy of Trust: A Response to Joseph Raz," in *Natural Law, Liberalism, and Morality,* 131–50, 138–139.

41. Raz, "Liberty and Trust," 124.

42. Raz, "Liberty and Trust," 124.

43. Raz, "Liberty and Trust," 126.

10

William Galston's Defense of Liberalism
Forging Unity Amid Diversity

J. Brian Benestad

William Galston is a political theorist who has dedicated most of his writings to the defense of liberalism. Using a self-described quasi-Aristotelian approach, he has explained the deficiencies in the thought of major liberal theorists and defended liberalism on the basis of a substantive account of the good. Galston has published articles criticizing the approaches of Michael Walzer, Roberto Unger, Amy Gutmann, Jeremy Waldron, and especially John Rawls. Galston's own defense of liberalism is premised on his belief in the genuine possibility of arriving at an understanding of truth through the discipline of political philosophy. He believes that liberalism can be defended on the basis of truth claims. In other words, the liberal state is the best possible regime given the fact of pluralism and a proper understanding of the good.

Galston seeks a *via media* between perfectionist liberalism and pragmatic liberalism. Galston's *via media* is a minimal perfectionism. The liberal state is not and cannot be neutral with respect to an understanding of the good. Citizens in a liberal regime do and must share agreement on some limited notion of what is good in order to form a cohesive community. In his writing, Galston puts forth a "liberal" conception of the good and specifies the virtues needed even in a pluralistic democracy. The shared agreement on the good and liberal virtues would still allow wide scope for a pluralism of ends. Hence, minimal perfectionism.

Crucial to Galston's project is the preservation of the "metaphysical" or "transcendental" impulse in political philosophy. Like Plato and Aristotle, Galston believes in "the systematic comparison and testing of opinion." Political philosophy begins from and seeks to get behind the common opinions held by the citizens of a nation. It has the potential of transcending the bias of

177

a particular culture and justifying the truth of at least a minimal code of public morality, which all citizens should accept. Without shared agreement on some moral principle, Galston believes the social unity of a liberal regime will be in danger.

Galston is very critical of John Rawls's political philosophy because its attempt to forge a consensus on justice doesn't allow for a transcultural standard of right. In the 1980 "Dewey Lectures," Rawls, according to Galston, argues that political philosophy should simply attempt to discern and spell out the latent and explicit principles and practices of a specific culture. Galston comments: "it follows that there are no general principles or particular judgments *external* to the shared understanding of a public culture that can be employed to judge the worth of that culture, taken as a whole."[1] This Rawlsian political philosophy needs a finely attuned antenna because "the content of its principles is provided by the shared beliefs of the democratic community."[2] Galston adds: "If our principles are valid for us only because we (happen to) believe them, then they are not even binding for us."[3] There is no compelling reason to abide by principles that are only valid because they are accepted. Still another objection to Rawls is that he fails to perceive the shared beliefs of Americans. Galston contends that "justice as fairness departs so sharply from our shared understanding that Rawls cannot plausibly claim to be making our intuitions explicit, or to be providing a foundation for what we already believe."[4]

GALSTON'S DEFENSE OF THE LIBERAL STATE

Contemporary liberal theorists, says Galston, have defended the liberal state on the grounds that it is neutral with respect to the question of the good life. The liberal state does not rest on a substantive or thick theory of the good and is therefore open to different ways of life. To the question why neutrality justifies the liberal state, theorists give two answers. "First it may be argued that there is in fact no rational basis for choosing among ways of life."[5] If rational knowledge of the good is inaccessible to citizens and political leaders, then state neutrality is the only proper response. Galston formulates the second argument as follows: "even if knowledge about the good life is available, it is a breach of individual freedom—the highest value—for the state to impose this knowledge on its citizens."[6] Only in the neutral state will freedom have priority over the good.

Contemporary liberals such as John Rawls invoke John Locke's doctrine of religious toleration to justify neutrality on moral questions.[7] Just as no one can prove that a particular religion is true, so no one can demonstrate the truth of any moral position.

Galston convincingly shows that Locke is far from neutral on important moral questions. Although civil authority may not coerce people to believe a religious truth, it may offer persuasive arguments on behalf of that truth. Second, Locke's rational knowledge of morality "undergirds both the critique of religious intolerance and the principles governing the relations between religion and the public order."[8] Thirdly, Locke does not hold that the state must tolerate all religious practices. The state may prohibit religiously grounded actions when they conflict with the civil order. For Locke "a core morality is politically essential,"[9] says Galston.

The liberal state does not necessarily or logically follow if knowledge of the good is inaccessible. "Full skepticism about the good," says Galston, "leads not to tolerance, not to liberal neutrality, but to unconstrained struggle among different ways of life, or struggle in which force, not reason, is the final arbiter."[10] Without some moral convictions about the good, people will not have any solid reason to respect human rights or other ways of life. Of course, fear or self-interest could lead to tolerance but passions are not a very reliable ground on which to create and maintain social unity.

Although contemporary liberal theorists claim to do without a substantive theory of the good, in fact, says Galston, they all "covertly rely on the same triadic theory of the good: first, the worth of human existence; second, the worth of human purposiveness and of the fulfillment of human purposes; and finally, the worth of rationality as the chief constraint on social principles and actions."[11] In Galston's view, an adequate defense of the liberal state requires making explicit the notion of the good upon which it is based. Galston stresses that "every polity embodies a more than minimal conception of the good that serves to rank-order individual ways of life and competing principles of right conduct."[12]

Galston does not think that leading contemporary liberal theorists offer an adequate defense of the liberal state. Not only do they fail to make explicit the substantive notion of the good upon which their writings depend but also they do not draw out "the full theory of the good latent in liberal practice."[13]

In his book *Liberal Purposes* Galston proposes "a liberal conception of the individual human good."[14] More precisely he tries to discern the concept of good that adequately provides a foundation for the functioning of a liberal social order. There seems to be a consensus, according to Galston, that the following are the key dimensions of the good accepted by citizens in a liberal polity: life, normal development of basic capacities, fulfillment of interests and purposes, freedom, rationality (e.g., belief in argument), society (family, friends, acquaintances, and associates in voluntary organizations), and subjective satisfaction.[15] This theory of the good, constituting a minimal perfectionism, rules out certain approaches to social life as a basis of public action.

(1) Secular nihilism—the belief that human life and purposiveness are without moral significance; (2) theological withdrawalism—the belief that what happens here on earth doesn't matter because the real action is in the afterlife; (3) moral monism—"one size fits all" accounts of the good, (4) Nietzschean irrationalism; (5) barbarism—deliberate or heedless deprivation of minimal goods.[16]

Agreement on a theory of the good provides citizens with a common basis for public policy initiatives. For example, without the proper education of children the fulfillment of purposes is in jeopardy. Galston discerns two kinds of public policy in a liberal polity, reflecting respect for persons and a shared conception of the good.

The distinction between public policy directed toward capabilities and opportunities on the one hand, and the conduct of individual life-plans on the other, reflects the fact that liberalism embodies a respect for individual agency as well as a conception of the good.[17]

A liberal theory of the good keeps at a minimum the attempt to forge a consensus on common ends for the polity. Rather, it directs attention toward creating and ensuring possibilities for individuals to make choices that seem fitting to them. Allowing scope for a pluralism of ends is characteristic of minimal perfectionism. A more fully perfectionistic understanding of the good would regard desires as acceptable when consistent with some objective standard such as Aristotelian excellence or the divine law.[18]

Galston justifies the liberal state on the grounds that it promotes a number of goods: social peace; the rule of law; the recognition of diversity by providing opportunity for all to develop their talents and pursue their life plans according to their conceptions of the good; "the tendency to treat steadily increasing percentages of their members as full and equal citizens"; reduction of wanton brutality and desperate poverty; affluence for many people; equality of opportunity created especially by means of universal education; approximate justice through response to need-based claims in the political area and desert-based claims in the economy; openness to truth through such instruments as universities, the press, and political institutions; and protection of "an autonomous sphere of private sentiments and affections" against encroachment by social and political powers.[19]

In a liberal society "the full development of each individual is equal in moral weight to that of every other. . . . Thus a policy that neglects the educable retarded so that they do not learn how to care for themselves and must be institutionalized is, considered in itself, as bad as one that reduces extraordinary gifts to mere normality."[20] This is an example of equality in practice. Liberal society, furthermore, provides an extraordinary degree of freedom. Citizens even have the opportunity to acquire "a reflective distance" from the principles undergirding their own regime.

Although Galston celebrates the freedom allowed individuals in a liberal society, he does not defend a doctrine of rights independent of duties. There is no right to do wrong.[21] An individual's freedom is circumscribed by duties to self and to others.[22] Galston affirms that rights actually have as a foundation some concept of right and wrong. For example, if an individual has an absolute negative right—that is, "the right not to be the recipient of certain kinds of acts," then "everyone must have the duty to refrain from that act in all circumstances."[23] That duty rests on some notion of what is right and wrong that binds all people.

In his criticism of Robert Unger's *Politics,* Galston reveals another angle of his conception of the good society. In responding to four Unger theses, Galston makes the following points. First, "human beings are naturally drawn together into political communities whose goals, moreover, include such natural ends as survival, security and material adequacy."[24] These goals necessarily "impose certain constraints" on the shape of political institutions and policies. Second, Galston defends the benefits of hierarchies, namely, "the authority of parents over children, teachers over students, skilled artisans over apprentices, and more generally the authority of those who have special knowledge or competence."[25] Third, Galston defends "revision-resisting contexts" such as indissoluble marriage because of the way it fosters intimacy and personal growth. Fourth, political change is not analogous to scientific change. "Without the practical familiarity born of habit, political propositions cannot be rendered effectively binding on a community. Excessive openness to revision undermines the very foundation of law, and with it, the very possibility of a community not ruled by force."[26] Finally, in a general comment on Unger's modernist theory, Galston counsels against cultivating infinite longing for finite things. "It is sounder," Galston writes, "to eschew the idolatry of this world, to insist that infinite longing can find its satisfaction only in an infinite object, and to acknowledge that in the absence of such an object, man truly is a useless passion."[27]

What sets Galston apart from many defenders of liberalism is his frank admission that liberalism is a regime and thus a political community with a certain bias. "Aristotle was right," says Galston, "core political principles shape the character of every aspect of the community."[28] Liberal principles do have an impact on the lives of individuals, families, and groups. Galston gives six examples to illustrate his point. First, the definition of what will remain in the private sphere "is largely a public, political determination." For example, constitutional law extends "the sway of liberal public values throughout the society."[29] Liberal elites, says Galston, even use constitutional law at times and other means to override the public influence of the traditional moral convictions held by ordinary Americans. As examples of this tendency, Galston cites the "dismantling [of] long-established practices such as school prayer, restraints on pornography, and prohibitions against homosexuality and abortion—a process that has evoked strong passions."[30] Liberal elites are persuaded, says Galston, that a liberal state can survive quite well without some public recognition of religion and traditional morality.[31] This is the reason why elites see no danger in flouting the long-standing moral convictions of many Americans.

Second, liberal principles exert an "informal gravitational influence on individuals and institutions."[32] Galston believes that the Roman Catholic Church in the United States has been significantly influenced by the liberal public culture.

> Witness the extraordinary recent meeting in the Vatican between U.S. Catholic bishops and representatives of the Pope: The Roman prelates inveighed against what they saw as the laxity of the American Church. American bishops responded with a fascinating disquisition in which they pointed out, *inter alia,* that liberal political culture encourages rational criticism of all forms of authority, a tendency the American church is not free to disregard. The notion of unquestioned authority . . . is almost unintelligible to U.S. Catholics and the American Church has been significantly reconstructed in response to the influence of liberal public culture.[33]

Galston means, I think, that Catholics tend to look at authoritative teachings on faith and morals through the prism of such concepts as autonomy, choice, rights, subjectively held "values," and "historical consciousness." Another example: "The core liberal notion of free choice and contractual relations have permeated the previously sacramental understanding of marriage and the family. The notion of an irreversible, constitutive commitment has been corroded by notions of liberation and autonomy; 'till death do us part' has been replaced by 'till distaste drives us apart."[34]

Still another example of the way liberal principles exercise a harmful gravitational pull on religion becomes immediately evident when reflecting on the implications of one key principle in Rawls's political theory, namely, the moral power "to form, to revise and rationally pursue a conception of the good."[35] As already mentioned, belief in revealed religion requires the willingness to receive God's truth rather than to form a conception of the good for oneself.

Third, "ways of life that require self-restraint, hierarchy, or cultural integrity are likely to find themselves on the defensive, threatened with the loss of both cohesion and authority."[36] If Galston is correct, then revealed religions will necessarily experience difficulty in maintaining the purity of their teachings and practice in a liberal society. Recall that even John Rawls now admits that some worthy ways of life may lose out in a liberal society.[37]

Fourth, even in a liberal society, the political still has primacy, often in the area of religion. Locke clearly subordinates practices mandated by religious belief "to the requirements of civil peace and order."[38] Galston points out that the U.S. Supreme Court has done the same.[39] Furthermore, it is important to note that liberalism does not remove religion from public scrutiny. "Indeed, twentieth-century First Amendment litigation is a testimony to the multifaceted tension between particular religions and the common polity."[40]

Fifth, the "cultural reflection" fostered by liberalism may have negative effects on people's ability to maintain commitments resting on tradition, unquestioned authority, and faith. . . . Any liberal commitment to key elements of both Socratic and Enlightenment rationalism has important corrosive effects on a wide range of psychological and social structures."[41]

"In short," says Galston, "liberal public principles should be seen as more than simply overriding but less than fully pervasive," but still "pervasive in the sense that they structure a set of influential tendencies in reference to which all activities and choices are compelled to be defined."[42] There is absolutely no doubt that the liberal state is not neutral but is a regime that endorses a substantive notion of the good but "consistent with a very considerable measure of social diversity."[43] The scope for diversity does allow even very traditional groups such as Orthodox and Hasidic Jewish groups to survive and even thrive. In his article on Tocqueville, Galston says that Christianity has been considerably weakened since the 1830s under the influence of liberal principles.[44] This weakening is not irreversible, according to Galston, because "key features of liberal societies make possible a substantial measure of withdrawal and insulation for dissenting groups."[45] Religious institutions, Galston implies, must become aware of liberalism's influence and take appropriate measures to maintain their integrity.

Liberal society should attempt "to mute the coercive consequences of its own unavoidable biases."[46] For example, public education in the liberal state need not infuse all students with a Socratic critical attitude toward the ways of life in which parents have educated their children. "On the level of political practice ways must be found to de-escalate the conflict between traditionalism and juridical liberalism. On the level of political theory an authentically liberal version of morality and the good must be rearticulated and linked—so far as possible—with the traditionalist understanding."[47] For example, juridical liberal theory would support Justice Harry Blackmun's argument in *Bowers v Hardwick* (1986) that the right to commit sodomy is one of the fundamental liberties guaranteed by the Constitution. Galston disputes this contention and suggests that state-level relaxation of antisodomy laws would generate much less controversy between juridical liberalism and traditional morality. At least for the sake of progressive politics, Galston insists, liberal elites must not alienate Americans who have a traditional understanding of morality.

Besides muting the antagonism between juridical liberalism and traditional morality, contemporary liberals have the theoretical task of specifying the virtues required by a liberal polity and of linking those liberal virtues with religiously grounded traditional morality. In a 1988 article Galston spelled out his version of liberal virtues. He began by saying that every political community needs courage, law-abidingness or the settled disposition to obey the law, and loyalty or "the developed capacity to understand, to accept and to act on the core principles of one's society."[48] Virtues specific to a liberal society are independence, tolerance, and respect for individual excellences and accomplishments. Education to independence requires strong family life, which in turn requires self-restraint, fidelity, and the willingness to make sacrifices for the sake of bringing up children. "Tolerance," says Galston, "does not require belief that every life-plan is equally good." Rather, it rests on the conviction that the pursuit of the better course should be (as in many cases can only be) the consequence of education or persuasion rather than coercion."[49]

A liberal economy demands the entrepreneurial virtues of imagination, initiative, drive, and determination; the organizational virtues of punctuality, reliability, "civility toward co-workers and a willingness to work within established frameworks and tasks;" and three generic virtues required by any market economy, namely, the work ethic, the capacity to delay gratification, and the ability to adapt, for example, to change jobs and place of residence.

The virtues of liberal politics are "the capacity to discern and the restraint to respect the rights of others," "the capacity to evaluate the talents, character and performance of public officials," and "the ability to moderate public desires in the face of public limits."[50] Liberal virtues are not republican virtues. Citizens have neither a duty to participate in politics nor a duty "to subordinate personal interest to the common good systematically."[51]

The virtues of leadership within a liberal polity are as follows: the "patience to work within the limits imposed by social diversity and constitutional limitation," the "capacity to forge a sense of common purpose," the "strength to resist the temptation to pander to the public whim," and the "capacity to narrow the gap between public preference and wise action and between principles and practices," and lastly "the disposition—and developed capacity—to engage in public discussion."[52]

An indispensable means of engendering the liberal virtues is civic education. Whereas the purpose of philosophic education, says Galston, is "the pursuit of truth," the goal of civic education is "rather the formation of individ-

uals who can effectively conduct their lives within, and support, their political community."[53] This education, Galston affirms, should be "far more
rhetorical than rational."[54] Liberal civic education must not only engender the
requisite virtues "but also the widest possible acceptance of the need for such
excellence in the conduct of our public life."[55] Tension between civic education and parental education should be minimized by the state. Galston argues
against Amy Gutmann's view that civic education should be so structured as
"to foster in children skeptical reflection on ways of life inherited from parents or local communities."[56] Galston believes that education in the home will
ultimately benefit liberal society. In fact, he says that "the greatest threat to
children in modern liberal societies is not that they will believe in something
too deeply, but that they will believe in nothing very deeply at all. Even to
achieve the kind of free self-reflection that liberals prize, it is better to begin
by believing something."[57]

While liberal institutions must attempt to provide a civic education in the
liberal virtues, Galston expects educational help from the family and to some
extent from religion. Galston is well aware that modern morality and Christian morality converge in some areas and diverge in others. In an article on
Tocqueville and religion, Galston implicitly admitted that Christian morality
restrains the passions whereas modern morality tends to indulge them. He
also sees that the latter legitimates self-interest, while the former teaches people to love their neighbor as themselves. Modern morality indulges public
opinion, while religious leaders such as Pope John Paul II see it as a very
great danger to faith and morals.[58]

In several articles Galston argues that the liberal tradition itself does provide
a foundation for virtue. "Indeed it suggests three conceptions of intrinsic individual excellence, overlapping yet distinct."[59] These conceptions are derived
from Locke, Kant, and from Romanticism through John Stuart Mill, Ralph
Waldo Emerson, Henry David Thoreau, and Walt Whitman. Locke's understanding of excellence is that of rational liberty or self-direction. Certain unspecified traits are needed to be independent and to exercise liberty informed by
reason. The Kantian conception of excellence, Galston says, is "to make duty the
effective principle of personal conduct and to resist the promptings of passion
and interest insofar as they are incompatible with this principle."[60] The Romantic conception of excellence is simply "the full flowering of individuality."[61] In
commenting on these liberal conceptions, Galston admits that the Lockean and
Romantic conceptions—especially the latter—can lead "to a wide range of de-
liberative outcomes." The only common core of these liberal positions is "a vision of individuals who, in some manner, take responsibility for their lives."[62]

The presentation of liberal virtues or "collectively held moral convictions"
is a difficult enterprise. It depends on the proper civic education, character

formation in the family, and some respect for religion.[63] Respect for binding moral standards, Galston adds, also depends upon behaving decently toward foreign nations. "If we apply the pure principle of collective selfishness in our dealings with the rest of the world, then the moral and psychological foundations of domestic cooperation are eroded."[64]

IS LIBERALISM ENOUGH?

Galston has made a significant contribution to contemporary liberal theory by his penetrating criticisms of leading liberal theorists such as John Rawls, and by offering a very thoughtful defense of liberalism. In showing that the liberal state is a regime with a gravitational pull on nonpublic principles, he has offered valuable insights to political leaders, political theorists, theologians and church leaders. Finally, his advocacy and explanation of liberal virtues is a good beginning. Galston, however, has not persuaded me that the liberal tradition has the philosophical resources to ground a theory of virtue adequate to the needs of a liberal polity.

In my judgment Galston does not adequately demonstrate that any strand of the liberal tradition provides a solid foundation for all the virtues required by a liberal regime. Galston's writings are usually very specific and concrete; however, in this area of moral foundations, he remains general and abstract. Laying a philosophical foundation is especially important because Galston does not place any great hope in the vitality of the Christian tradition as support for the liberal virtues, much less the classical or Christian virtues. Galston explains: "If America is no longer now as it was in Tocqueville's time, a Christian nation, then Tocqueville's linkage between Christianity and the moral basis of liberalism—however historically accurate—cannot serve as our point of departure. Liberalism must examine its innate resources without recourse to specific theological support."[65] Galston believes that Christian teachings in tension with liberal principles tend to lose their grasp on the mind and hearts of Christians. A Christianity that accommodates itself to the spirit of the age loses something of its leavening power in a liberal society. A modified Christianity cannot oppose disordered passions and immoderate self-interest with the same effectiveness as a vital orthodox Christianity.

Moreover, Galston notes, liberal elites have been successful in progressively excluding the influence of religiously grounded beliefs from public life.[66] These elites operate from the proposition that a liberal polity can make do without some public recognition of religion and traditional morality.[67] Because of the internal weakening of Christianity and the general opposition of educated elites to the influence of religion on public and civil life, Galston does not expect Christianity to play a significant role in providing moral foundations for the liberal state. He does, however, try to persuade liberal theorists to lessen their opposition to the public influence of religion for the sake of recovering progressive politics. A liberal regime must respect traditional religion and moral sensibilities to avoid a divisive backlash from ordinary American citizens.[68]

In raising a doubt about whether there is a solid foundation for the liberal virtues in the philosophy of Locke, Kant, and others, I do not mean to take anything away from Galston's achievement. What he says about the importance of family, civic education, and the meaning of liberal virtues should be persuasive to many citizens, perhaps for a variety of reasons. Nonetheless, the project of providing adequate foundations for liberal virtues may still, in the final analysis, point beyond the political philosophy of modern liberalism itself.

GALSTON'S THOUGHT IN THE 1990s

Throughout the 1990s William Galston has continued to write about the requisite conditions for the viability of the liberal state. His fundamental principles have not changed. He still believes that a liberal regime is "a community of subcommunities," which is unified on the basis of core principles inculcated by public and private education and enforced by law.[69] He does, however, seem more optimistic about the capacity of religion to shore up the moral foundations of liberal democracy, and he is intent on defending the presence of religion in the public square, except in a few noteworthy instances.

While allowing considerable diversity in the subcommunities, a liberal community, Galston admits, does have a distinctive influence on the lives of most individuals, families, groups, and churches. In other words, individuals are free in principle to choose a way of life, but liberal public principles exercise a gravitational pull on people's day-to-day life. Galston's description of liberalism's influence is imaginative and, in my mind, quite accurate.

> To understand this dimension think of the social space constituted by liberal political principles as a rapidly flowing river. A few vessels may be strong enough to head upstream. Most, however, will be carried along by the current. But they still choose where in the river to sail and where along the shore to moor. The mistake is to think of the liberal regime's public principles as constituting either a placid lake or an irresistible undertow. Moreover, the state may seek to mitigate the effect of its public current on the navigation of specific vessels whenever the costs of such corrective intervention are not excessive.[70]

For example, the shape of liberalism today inclines people to think more about their rights than their duties. In cultural matters liberalism pulls people to "embrace an expansive notion of personal autonomy." Galston observes that the "idea of autonomy becomes a hyper-expansive notion of individual choice, which is the closest thing to an inviolable norm that now exists in American culture."[71] Galston even notes that liberal public principles contribute to the generation of pluralism *within* various churches.[72] For example, even Catholicism, once known for great unity among believers, now has to deal with individual Catholics deciding that "x" number of Catholic teachings (such as those on divorce, assisted-suicide, and same-sex marriage) are not compatible with their thinking or way of life.

Galston points out that some liberal theorists, such as Amy Gutmann and Stephen Macedo, want to intensify the pull of liberal principles through law, political rhetoric, and civic education. For example, they argue that public education should induce all students to engage in a Socratic questioning of the way of life handed on to them by their parents. Galston opposes this approach, arguing that public education should inculcate only the core beliefs and virtues needed for the viability of the liberal state. Galston's guiding principle is "maximum feasible accommodation of diverse ways of life, limited only by the minimum requirements of civic unity."[73] In one of his major scholarly articles Galston says that "liberal societies can and must make room for individuals and groups whose lives are guided by tradition, authority, and faith."[74] For example, Catholic hospitals should not be forced to do abortions; the Boy Scouts should remain free to choose their own leaders; and the Amish rightfully enjoy the government-granted privilege of keeping their children out of school after the eighth grade.[75] Galston calls the attempt to impose liberal norms on individuals and groups "exclusionary liberalism" or "liberal imperialism."[76] "At the heart of the liberal democratic settlement," Galston argues, "is a principled refusal to allow religions to engulf the political order, or politics to invade and dominate religion."[77] Acceptance of the core liberal beliefs and virtues by all groups prevents religious tyranny and the renunciation of liberal imperialism creates breathing space for individuals and groups.

Maximum feasible accommodation not only carves out space for revealed religions but also serves to benefit the liberal state in the long run. Galston believes that the beliefs and virtues taught by the revealed religions will, for the most part, contribute to the viability and unity of the liberal state by supporting its core principles and requisite virtues. Galston welcomes opposition to such tendencies as individualism, egoism, and unthinking conformity to reigning public opinions. He even says that Catholics "must reject . . . versions of liberalism" that "embrace skepticism or relativism about the human good; . . . downplay the role of the state or seek to exclude faith-based arguments from public discourse; [or]

. . . emphasize the prerogatives of the state at the expense of family and associ-
ational autonomy."[78] Galston is willing to tolerate even teachings he thinks
might unduly burden liberal regimes, all the while trying to persuade groups and
faiths not to oppose core liberal principles. He specifically urges Catholic social
thinkers both to critique "the expansive and unnuanced account of personal autonomy that is the long pole in a number of liberal theoretical tents these days"
and to oppose "exclusionary liberalism."[79] But he also urges Catholics not to use
theology or natural law to "impose" on non-Catholics their views on abortion,
assisted suicide, or homosexuality. He reasons, "Catholics may be affronted by
a legal code that permits acts they view as abominable. But in circumstances of
deep moral diversity, the alternative to enduring these affronts is even worse."[80]
Galston does not advert to the fact that Catholic social thinkers may see, for example, the legalization of physician-assisted suicide as just one more improper
use of choice, and consequently may rightfully attempt—arguably on the basis
of Galston's principles—to "persuade" their fellow Americans not to go the way
of Oregon and legalize it. At any rate, Galston believes the advantages of "maximum feasible accommodation" will outweigh the disadvantages by a wide mar-
gin, despite the problems that may arise from improper advocacy on the part of
the Churches or anyone else.

As a second major theme, Galston addresses the requirements of civic
unity in a good liberal community. Galston never tires of reiterating his conviction that a liberal community must be established and maintained. It cannot be a good community if citizens abuse their liberty, think only of their
rights, and fail to maintain strong bonds in the family, neighborhoods and voluntary associations. Galston is especially worried about the relativism gaining a foothold in the lives of so many citizens.

> This new morality—do what you choose, when you choose, without fear of le-
> gal coercion or social disapproval—is an experiment without precedent in hu-
> man history. Perhaps it will succeed; I doubt it. At some point, we will be called
> upon for sacrifices that we can't pay others to make on our behalf. And then we
> will see whether the self-protective nonjudgmentalism Wolfe so ably describes
> constitutes an adequate basis for a free society.[81]

Galston is referring to the work of sociologist, Alan Wolfe, who published his
findings about America's moral condition several years ago in *One Nation,
After All.* From his conversations with middle-class Americans over a two-
year period Wolfe found that they are willing to be personally accountable but
reluctant to make judgments about what anyone else is doing or to assume responsibility for righting what they see as wrong in society. On the basis of the
evidence presented by Wolfe, Galston says that the sociologist "pulls his
punches" in not raising "far more serious questions."

A choice-based conception of social life leads to instrumental bonds, a cult of conflict avoidance, an absence of real engagement, and a loss of seriousness. Worst of all it is hard to see how this new morality provides any basis for sacrifice, in either personal or civic life. Marriages are ended when they become inconvenient; religions are selected like new fashions in the mall and then cast aside when they cease to meet our personal needs.[82]

In Galston's mind this level of morality is insufficient to build and maintain a good liberal community. Consequently, Galston addresses America's moral deficiencies in many of his writings and proposes helpful solutions.

Like a growing number of other public intellectuals, Galston argues that families, public schools, voluntary associations, and churches can become more effective seedbeds of good habits, virtues, and salutary beliefs.[83] To that end he advocates public support for the two-parent family, public discouragement of divorce and teen pregnancy, parents taking responsibility for giving a moral education to their children, a limited character formation in the public schools (as needed by a good liberal community), respect for religion, including its contribution to the public square, and a reinvigoration of civic associations. Galston would like to see marriage preparation mandated by the state and carried out by faith-based institutions.[84] He would further welcome the repeal of no-fault divorce laws, which have contributed to the high rate of divorces. And Galston would like all citizens to understand the difference between asserting a right and doing what is right. In his mind there has been too much "rights talk" and not enough talk about personal and social responsibilities. He also expresses "grave doubts" about the encouragement of gambling by the state. Galston believes that the rising popularity of gambling "not only reflects but also reinforces a loss of confidence in hard work as a source of social advancement."[85] Doing productive work is one of the ways citizens contribute to the viability of the liberal state.

Galston's expectations of colleges and universities reveal still another facet of his sustained effort to shore up a liberal community. He wants all colleges to transmit "the principles, beliefs, and virtues that liberal societies (indeed, all societies) require for their perpetuation."[86] He also wants them to make a "gentlemanly liberal education" available, which "equips talented individuals to exercise farsighted and public spirited leadership within the framework of an established order."[87] Those capable of such an education are the "natural aristoi," men and women of talent and virtue. Galston himself, of course, is one of those men who has received such an education and has dedicated his life to promoting the good of civil society and the liberal state.

Galston admires and cherishes the liberal state because it enables people of different points of view to live together in relative peace and harmony. But there is an even more profound reason for his admiration and affection. Galston describes himself as a value pluralist and a political liberal. According to value pluralism, "there is no summum bonum that enjoys a rationally grounded priority for all individuals."[88] Otherwise stated, "Contrary to the teachings of classical philosophical and theological traditions, human nature does not prescribe a single, generally valid model of human flourishing or perfection."[89] Therefore, it would never be right for the state to impose on citizens any one model of a dominant good. On the other hand, value pluralism "is not the same as relativism. Philosophical reflection supports what ordinary experience suggests—a non-arbitrary distinction between good and bad."[90] Hence, Galston believes that the minimal perfectionism of the liberal state can be defended on objective grounds: it is a true account of human beings in society. Galston is really saying that reason can arrive at a certain number of basic truths valid for all human beings, but is incapable of discerning a *summum bonum* for all. In other words, Galston claims to know that neither reason nor faith can legitimately say that human nature "prescribe[s] a single, generally valid model of human flourishing or perfection."[91] Of course, Galston's definitive position on the limits of reason and faith presupposes a philosophical vision as grand as that of Kant. To say that neither reason nor faith can discern a *summum bonum* is implicitly a claim to possess an extraordinary degree of knowledge.

CONCLUSION

While continuing to admire what Galston is trying to do for liberal society, I am not at all persuaded that he has made good arguments for his assertions about the limits of faith and reason. I am surprised that he does not confess an inability to evaluate the claims of the classical theological traditions or argue that faith would be required to accept the teachings of Revelation about the highest good. He has only shown that his view of a smooth-running liberal polity requires the avowal of an incapacity to know the *summum bonum* on the part of philosophers, theologians, Church authorities, and political leaders. Galston seems to believe that lives lived without aspirations for a *summum bonum* would offer protection against religious and political tyranny. Second, Galston's public commitment to the Democratic Party may generate some blind spots (as would a similar commitment to the Republican Party). For example, he really has nothing significant to say about "the culture of death" in America. On the other hand, his political principles led him to break with the mainstream of the Democratic Party on, at least, two significant issues. Galston deplored the Democratic Party's decision not to allow Governor Robert Casey to speak at the 1992 Democratic Convention. "I

protested against it to no avail. I believe the Democratic Party has made a serious and indeed historic mistake in turning *Roe v Wade* into a litmus test for
party leadership."[92] Recently, Galston also pointed out that he "published
an article . . . recommending a carefully monitored national voucher experiment."[93] This position, contrary to the platform of the Democratic Party, does
fit in with his belief that faith-based groups can serve public purposes.

Galston is very aware that prominent political theorists, such as John
Rawls, want to keep religion out of the public square in order to promote
peace and harmony. To counter this undue narrowing of religious liberty Galston argues for maximum feasible accommodation of religion in liberal
regimes. He makes this argument both to show respect for religion and to promote the good of liberal regimes. Galston knows that religions generally promote the practice of the virtues necessary for the survival of liberal regimes.
But even this most accommodating liberal wants the Catholic Church to be
silent in public on abortion, assisted suicide, and homosexuality.

NOTES

1. William A. Galston, "Moral Personality and Liberal Theory: John Rawls's
'Dewey Lectures,'" *Political Theory* 10 (1982): 511.

2. Galston, "Moral Personality," 512.

3. William A. Galston, "Pluralism and Social Unity," *Ethics* 99 (1989), 725.

4. Galston, "Moral Personality," 515.

5. William A. Galston, "Defending Liberalism," *American Political Science Review* 76 (1982): 622.

6. Galston, "Defending Liberalism," 622.

7. William A. Galston, "Public Morality and Religion in the Liberal State," *PS* 19
(1986): 804.

8. Galston, "Public Morality," 804.

9. Galston, "Public Morality," 810.

10. Galston, "Defending Liberalism," 627.

11. Galston, "Public Morality," 818.

12. Galston, "Defending Liberalism," 627.

13. Galston, "Defending Liberalism," 627.

14. William A. Galston, *Liberal Purposes: Goods, Virtues, and Diversity in the
Liberal State* (New York: Cambridge University Press, 1991), 173.

15. Galston, *Liberal Purposes,* 174–77.

16. Galston, *Liberal Purposes,* 177.

17. Galston, *Liberal Purposes,* 179.

18. Galston, *Liberal Purposes,* 177.

19. Galston, "Defending Liberalism," 628.

20. William A. Galston, "Equality of Opportunity and Liberal Theory," in *Justice, Equality, Here and Now,* ed. Frank Lucash (Ithaca, N.Y.: Cornell University Press, 1986), 93.

21. William A. Galston, "On the Alleged Right to Do 'Wrong': A Response to Waldron," *Ethics* 93 (1983): 320–21.

22. William A. Galston, *Justice and the Human Good,* 127–42.

23. William A. Galston, *Justice and the Human Good,* 137.

24. William A. Galston, "False Universality: Infinite Personality and Finite Existence in Unger's Politics," *Northwestern Law Review* 81 (1987): 761

25. Galston, *False Universality,* 761–62.

26. Galston, *False Universality,* 763.

27. Galston, *False Universality,* 764.

28. Galston, *Liberal Purposes,* 292.

29. Galston, *Liberal Purposes,* 292.

30. William A. Galston, "Tocqueville on Liberalism and Religion," *Social Research* 54 (1987): 517.

31. Galston, "Tocqueville," 517.

32. Galston, *Liberal Purposes,* 292.

33. Galston, *Liberal Purposes,* 292.

34. Galston, *Liberal Purposes,* 292.

35. Galston, "Pluralism and Social Unity," 712.

36. Galston, *Liberal Purposes,* 293.

37. Galston, *Liberal Purposes,* 100, 146, 290, 291.

38. Galston, *Liberal Purposes,* 293.

39. I would add that the Supreme Court has allowed some minority religious groups to engage in religious practices contrary to the law, from *Sherbert v Verner,* 374 U.S. 398 (1963) to *Wisconsin v Yoder,* 406 U.S. 205 (1971). That may be history, however, in the light of *Employment Division, Department of Human Resources of Oregon, et al. v Smith et al.* 108 L.Ed.2d 876 (1990).

40. Galston, *Liberal Purposes,* 293–94.

41. Galston, *Liberal Purposes,* 294.

42. Galston, *Liberal Purposes,* 295–96.

43. Galston, *Liberal Purposes,* 295.

44. Galston, "Tocqueville," 501–18.

45. Galston, *Liberal Purposes,* 295.

46. Galston, *Liberal Purposes,* 298.

47. Galston, "Public Morality and Religion in the Liberal State," 820.

48. William A. Galston, "Liberal Virtues," *American Political Science Review* 82 (1988):1281–82.

49. Galston, "Liberal Virtues," 1282.

50. William A. Galston, "Civic Education in the Liberal State," in *Liberalism and the Moral Life,* ed. Nancy L. Rosenblum (Cambridge, Mass.: Harvard University Press, 1989), 93.

52. Galston, "Liberal Virtues," 1284.

52. Galston, "Liberal Virtues," 1285
53. Galston, "Civic Education," 90.
54. Galston, "Civic Education," 91.
55. Galston, "Civic Education," 95.
56. Galston, "Civic Education," 99.
57. Galston, "Civic Education," 101.
58. Galston, "Tocqueville," 511.
59. Galston, "Liberal Virtues," 511.
60. Galston, "Liberal Virtues," 1286.
61. Galston, "Liberal Virtues," 1286.
62. Galston, "Liberal Virtues," 1287.
63. Galston, *Justice and the Human Good,* 279.
64. Galston, "Liberal Virtues," 245–46.
65. Galston, "Tocqueville," 518.
66. Galston, "Tocqueville," 517.
67. Galston, "Tocqueville," 517.
68. Galston, of course, does not attempt to reform Christianity. But his remarks about the inevitable negative influence of liberal principles on religious belief and practices can be highly instructive to religious leaders. They might be able to learn what kinds of precautions must be taken to preserve religious integrity. For example, church leaders need to keep in mind the American tendency to place such an emphasis on autonomy and rights that the authoritative character of the Bible, tradition, and church authority is weakened. It is ironic that a secular liberal theorist such as Professor Galston is more aware of the gravitational pull of liberal principles on Christianity than many leading theologians.
69. For example, Galston argues that the liberal state properly aims to protect human life, to ensure the development of every citizen's basic capacities, and to promote social rationality, "the kind of understanding needed to participate in the society, economy, and polity." In the name of these goals the state would rightly prohibit human sacrifice by the Aztecs (but not abortion) and mistreatment of the young by any individual or group. It could also prevent any kind of private or public education from hindering the development of "social rationality." Cf. "Two Concepts of Liberalism," *Ethics* 105 (April 1995): 525.
70. Galston, "Two Concepts of Liberalism," 530.
71. William Galston, "Contending with Liberalism: Some Advice for Catholics," *Commonweal* 127, no. 7 (2001): 13.
72. William Galston, "Expressive Liberty, Moral Pluralism, Political Pluralism: Three Sources of Liberal Theory," *William and Mary Law Review* 40 (1999): 880.
73. Galston, *Expressive Liberty*, 902.
74. Galston, *Expressive Liberty*, 889–90.
75. Galston, "Two Concepts of Liberalism," 516.
76. Galston, "Contending with Liberalism," 14.
77. Galston, *Expressive Liberty*, 905.
78. Galston, "Contending with Liberalism," 15.
79. Galston, "Contending with Liberalism," 15.

80. Galston, "Contending with Liberalism," 15.

81. Review of Alan Wolfe, *One Nation, After All,* in *The Public Interest,* 133 (fall 1998): 116–20.

82. Review of Alan Wolfe, *One Nation, After All,* in *The Public Interest,* 133 (fall 1998): 116–20.

83. William A. Galston, "A Public Philosophy for the 21st Century," *The Responsive Community* (summer 1998): 21.

84. Cf. William A. Galston, "Divorce American Style," *The Public Interest* 124 (summer 1996): 12–26.

85. William A. Galston, "Gambling Away Our Moral Capital," *The Public Interest* 123 (1996): 58–71.

86. William A. Galston, "Moral Inquiry and Liberal Education in the American University," *Ethics* 110 (July 2000): 814.

87. Galston, "Moral Inquiry," 816.

88. William A. Galston, "Value Pluralism and Liberal Political Theory," *American Political Science Review* 93 (1999): 770.

89. Galston, "Value Pluralism," 772.

90. Galston, "Value Pluralism," 770.

91. Galston, "Value Pluralism," 772.

92. Galston, "Contending with Liberalism," 15.

93. Galston, "Contending with Liberalism," 14.

11

The New Natural Law Theory of John Finnis

Joseph R. Reisert

Until recently, most contemporary political theorists condescendingly regarded natural law theories as little more than quaint but faintly embarrassing relics of a naïve past they were glad to have outgrown. Guilty, as it seemed, of fallaciously inferring "ought" from "is," natural law theories were deemed incapable of supplying the foundation for any truly philosophical ethics or politics. For this reason, contemporary moral and political philosophers have taken their inspiration not from the works of natural lawyers like Saint Thomas Aquinas but, rather, from the works of other theorists with different philosophical approaches—above all, in recent years, from the deontological ethics of Immanuel Kant.

The new natural law theory of John Finnis, however, poses a serious and fundamental challenge to the broadly Kantian theories, articulated by John Rawls and others, now ascendant in moral and political philosophy. Although it is based on Aquinas's work, Finnis's contemporary account escapes the traditional objections to natural law theory and directly engages the main currents of recent philosophy. We may begin by observing the striking, if perhaps surprising, similarities between the intellectual aspirations of Finnis and Rawls: both thinkers argue against utilitarianism and other consequentialist theories; both seek to establish the inviolability of certain basic human rights; and both formulate an account of legitimate political authority grounded in a conception of public reason.

Indeed, if Finnis did not so strongly argue against the use of such labels,[1] one would be obliged to classify his theory as *liberal*, since it asserts the existence of absolute constraints on government action. In Finnis's case, however, the traditional labels are unusually unhelpful. His normative prescriptions are both "conservative" and "liberal": he opposes abortion and the expansion of homosexual rights beyond the decriminalization of sodomy, but he also opposes the threat to kill innocent civilians implicit in the nuclear deterrent and has recently come to oppose capital punishment as well.[2] At the theoretical level, Finnis's conception of natural law is likewise difficult to pigeonhole, blending deontological and teleological elements in such a way that neither label adequately describes his theory.[3]

Building from Thomistic premises but aiming to fill lacunae remaining in Aquinas's account, Finnis has developed (in collaboration with Germain Grisez and Joseph M. Boyle, Jr.) a freestanding account of natural law–the new natural law theory, as it has come to be known[4]–which appears in his books, *Natural Law and Natural Rights*[5] and *Fundamentals of Ethics,*[6] but important subsequent developments of the theory appear in two works jointly authored by the three men, *Nuclear Deterrence, Morality, and Realism*[7] and "Practical Principles, Moral Truth, and Ultimate Ends."[8] In more recent papers, including "Is Natural Law Theory Compatible with Limited Government?"[9] and "Natural Law and Legal Reasoning,"[10] Finnis has refined his own positions yet further and sharpened his critique of John Rawls's political liberalism. Finnis's latest volume, *Aquinas: Moral Political and Legal Theory,* presents a sophisticated reconstruction of Aquinas's social thought, but it contributes to the development of the new natural law theory as well, since Aquinas's philosophy is, according to Finnis's interpretation, substantially consistent with that theory.[11]

As Finnis uses it, the term "natural law" denotes "the set of principles of practical reasonableness in ordering human life and human community."[12] In other words, the principles of natural law are objectively true *normative* principles, indicating the kinds of action that are practically reasonable and hence permitted and those that are practically unreasonable and hence forbidden. Thus the heart of Finnis's theory is its account of practical reasoning, which will be presented in the next section of this chapter. The second half of the chapter will examine Finnis's practical conception of the social sciences, his critique of Rawls's political liberalism, and his own defense of limited government and inviolable human rights.

A SKETCH OF THE NEW NATURAL LAW THEORY

Finnis's new natural law theory is erected upon avowedly Thomistic foundations, but his interpretation departs in some key respects from the conventional, neo-Scholastic account of Aquinas. The crucial departure was suggested in a seminal 1965 article by Germain Grisez, which proposed a novel reinterpretation of Aquinas's first principle of practical reason, "good is to be done and pursued, and evil is to be avoided."[13] According to the conventional view, the first principle of practical reason is itself a *moral* principle. [14] Its content—our knowledge of moral good and evil—is discerned by observing human nature scientifically, in order to discover the objects of our natural inclinations. What we are found to desire by nature is good; evil is defined by its opposition to the good. Because human beings desire to live, to know, to form families and political communities and the like, it is morally good for us to live, to know, to form families and political communities, and so on, and evil to impede these things. The inferences from facts to norms required by this approach will be valid only if a teleological conception of nature is true. In other words, this approach to moral reasoning presupposes that everything in the physical world, including man, has been oriented by divine providence toward the attainment of some end or ends. But the success of modern natural science has made a return to such a teleological conception of nature almost unthinkable: hence, the widespread contemporary disdain for natural law theories.

According to Finnis and Grisez, however, Aquinas's moral theory does not depend on a teleological conception of nature because it does not seek to derive moral norms from facts about what human beings happen to desire by nature. They reject the conventional reading of Aquinas because it is inconsistent with a key methodological insight, central to Aquinas's mature philosophy: that human reason can perceive four different sorts of order (or "sets of unifying relationships") in the world, and that each is to be studied and understood in its own distinctive way.[15] The four orders are: (1) a *natural order,* which human beings can perceive but do not create and which we study in the natural sciences; (2) an *epistemological order,* an "order we can bring into our own thinking,"[16] which we study, for example, in logic; (3) an *existential* or *moral order,* which we "bring into our own actions and dispositions by intelligently deliberating and choosing,"[17] the order we study in moral and political philosophy and related fields; and (4) a *technical order,* the order we "can impose upon whatever matter is subject to our powers,"[18] studied in the applied sciences, the arts and crafts, and so forth. The power of this fourfold conceptualization of human reason has not as yet been sufficiently appreciated, and in reviving it Finnis has made an important contribution to the philosophy of the social sciences. Far from being some antiquarian curiosity, Finnis's Thomistic account of reason both resembles and challenges the account of human understanding proposed by that quintessentially modern thinker, Jürgen Habermas.[19]

We can now see why Finnis thinks the neo-Scholastic reading of Aquinas summarized above must be wrong and why, in any case, he rejects the conception of natural law it suggests. That account must be rejected because it conflates inquiry into the *natural* order with inquiry into the *moral* order. It obscures the difference between theoretical and practical reasoning, and in so doing fails to acknowledge the significance of the fact that human actions and associations have their origins in the free choices of human beings.[20] While it is true that our biological, human nature is relevant to practical reasoning (how could it not be?), Finnis rejects the idea that the requirements of morality can be *derived* from knowledge of this sort.

Finnis and Grisez avoid the difficulties to which the conventional account is subject by denying that the first practical principle is itself a moral principle.[21] They hold, rather, that just as the principle of noncontradiction makes possible theoretical reasoning by giving it a certain form, so too does the first practical principle make possible practical reasoning by giving its own, distinctive form. The principle, "good is to be done and pursued, and evil is to be avoided," indicates the necessary structure of practical principles as *directive*. The goods "to be done" are not discovered by the scientific observation of human beings; rather, they are identified by *practical* reason itself. The goods practical reason identifies as rationally worthwhile human ends generate *basic practical principles* of the form: " X (say, human life) is a good, to be pursued and preserved . . . , and what damages X is a bad, to be avoided."[22] The basic goods are, claims Finnis, *self-evident* and include the following: life (including health and safety as well as procreation), knowledge, play (or skillful performance), aesthetic experience, sociability (in his later works, Finnis writes instead of the distinct goods of friendship and marriage[23]), practical reasonableness, and religion ("the establishment and maintenance of proper relationships between oneself . . . and the divine").[24]

The basic practical principles corresponding to the basic goods make possible all our practical reasoning by disclosing to us the variety of goods we might seek to realize in our actions. The basic practical principles do not, by themselves, generate any *moral* norms because they do not specify by what means these goods may rightly be pursued. Rather, they guide our practical reasoning by enabling us to see the intelligible point of freely chosen actions—even of those that are morally evil. For example, one might choose to steal in order to acquire the financial resources needed to secure one's own material well-being, or one might plan and carry out a murder as an aesthetic experience. Those actions are intelligible in light of the goods they advance, though they are wicked. The basic practical principles do no more than to preclude as irrational any choice to act without reason or to pursue the bad for the sake of the bad. To be able to rule out certain choices as *immoral,* one or more specifically moral premises must be added to the basic practical principles. Here is the gap Aquinas's moral theory failed to bridge with sufficient clarity.[25] Finnis calls the additional required premises "intermediate moral principles," "requirements of practical reasonableness," and "modes of responsibility" at different places in his body of work, but the terms are interchangeable.

These modes of responsibility (as I shall refer to them) include the following requirements: (1) To have a "coherent plan of life." (2) Not to discount arbitrarily any of the basic goods in one's practical reasoning. (3) Not to discount arbitrarily the interests of any persons in one's practical reasoning; the force of this prescription is captured in the common demand that moral reasons be *universalizable*. (4) To avoid fanaticism and dilettantism. (5) To use efficient means to advance one's purposes, that is, to advance the good as effectively as possible, taking appropriately into account the likely consequences of one's actions. When it is unreasonably overextended, this requirement yields the method of utilitarianism in practical reasoning. (6) Not to act directly contrary to any of the basic human goods. Finnis suggests that the force of this mode is largely captured by the humanity formula of Kant's categorical imperative ("Act so that you treat humanity, whether in your own person or in that of another, always as an end and never as a means only").[26] (7) To advance the common good of the communities of which one is a part. (8) Not to act contrary to one's conscience.[27] These principles, "requirements of *method* in practical reasoning," will all be familiar to students of the history of ethics, as each one has been taken by some thinker at some time to have been the master principle of ethics.[28]

These modes of responsibility are all specifications of the *first principle of morality,* which, like the first principle of practical reason and the basic practical principles corresponding to the basic human goods, is held by Finnis to be self-evident.[29] He articulates the principle as follows: "In voluntarily acting for human goods and avoiding what is opposed to them, one ought to choose and otherwise will those and only those possibilities whose willing is compatible with integral human fulfillment."[30] The central idea of morality, as Finnis conceives it, is both simple and powerfully appealing: morality is nothing other than the requirement that our actions be fully reasonable.[31] We are not to be deflected from the path of the reasonable by any passion or emotion, but we are instead to act wholly in accordance with the directions supplied by the basic practical principles.

The idea of integral human fulfillment plays a role in Finnis's theory of practical reasoning akin to that played by the idea of the kingdom of ends in Kant's practical philosophy: each represents the conception of an ideal community that is the "orienting ideal" of the good will.[32] Although the two ideas are formally similar, their content differs significantly. Kant's kingdom of ends is "a systematic union of rational beings under common objective laws," whose content is derived from the requirements of pure practical reason itself.[33] Finnis objects to Kant's formulation on the ground that it is incomplete: it mistakes one basic human good—practical reasonableness—for the whole of human good.[34] Thus Finnis's conception of ideal community embraces all of the basic goods: integral human fulfillment is an ideal of reason corresponding to an ideal community in which all human persons realize, so far as is possible, all of the basic goods.[35]

Although Finnis claims that the basic principles are self-evident, specific moral norms—like the absolute prohibition on directly killing another human being—are emphatically *not self-evident*. They are reached by arguments that link one or more of the specifications of the first principle of morality with one or more of the basic human goods. Thus, for example, the principle prohibiting the direct killing of human beings is the valid consequence of the following practical premises: life is a basic form of human good, and, according to the sixth mode of responsibility enumerated above, we ought never to act in a way directly destructive of any one of the basic forms of human good. By now it should be clear that Finnis's new natural law theory neatly evades Hume's objection to traditional natural law theories. In Finnis's account, practical reasoning proceeds solely on the basis of practical premises, and so oughts are derived only from other, more basic oughts—never from any purely factual statements.

I have skipped lightly over two issues that require further elaboration before we can proceed further. First is the matter of self-evidence; next is the problem of identifying goods as basic. Once we have seen that the new natural law theory can satisfactorily answer its critics on these vital points, we will be better positioned to see the force of Finnis's critique of utilitarianism.

Self-evidence

Finnis claims that the first principle of practical reason, the first practical principles corresponding to the basic goods, and the first principle of morality are all *self-evident*. Although, as he acknowledges, there appears to be "something fishy about appeal to self-evidence," a careful examination of what Finnis means will dispel the ichthyic odor.[36] Let us begin by observing what self-evidence does not imply: self-evidence is not a function of our subjective certainty about some proposition, nor are all self-evident principles simply intuitions—insights unrelated to data."[37] It follows that self-evident principles need not be known by everyone and that one can be mistaken about a putatively self-evident principle. Self-evident principles "cannot be verified by experience or deduced from any more basic truths through a middle term"; they are known, rather, by "understanding what is signified by their terms"— an understanding that can be acquired only by someone with experience of the relevant sort.[38] That the truth of principle cannot be proved, however, does not entail that it cannot be rationally *defended*. Any putatively self-evident principle can be defended dialectically, by showing, on the basis of its relation to other knowledge, that it cannot be denied (or alternatives to it cannot be affirmed) without yielding unacceptable conclusions.[39]

To illustrate that there is nothing truly fishy about treating the first principles of practical reasoning as self-evident, Finnis observes that every sort of ordinary empirical inquiry presupposes some "principles or norms of sound judgment"—methodological principles—whose truth cannot be demonstrated or observed, but whose truth is known by any experienced investigator, and is indeed presupposed in any ongoing inquiry.[40] For example, any empirical inquiry must adhere to the maxim that the "principles of logic, for example the forms of deductive inference, are to be used and adhered to in all one's thinking."[41] No proof of this proposition can be given, since no proof could proceed without using the principle in question. But no proof is necessary, since its truth is evident to any experienced researcher into questions of fact. The same holds true for a whole range of methodological principles governing scientific inquiry, and, claims Finnis, it holds true as well for the basic principles governing practical reasoning.

In any case, no normative political theory can escape the need for underived foundational principles of some sort. Ronald Dworkin, for example, bases his political and legal philosophy on the foundational premise that "human beings must be treated as equals by their government . . . because that is what is right"—a claim that he nowhere attempts to prove or seems to regard as requiring proof. In short, he treats the claim as if it were self-evident, but without saying so.[42] Finnis's claim that the basic principles of his practical philosophy are self-evident may be jarring to some modern readers, but there is nothing fishy about it; in fact, it has the merit of drawing explicit attention to his most basic premises and of indicating the sorts of argument that can most effectively be deployed to dispute them.

Basic Goods

Now let us consider Finnis's claim that there are seven basic, incommensurable forms of human good. Since these goods are self-evident, according to Finnis, their goodness cannot be proved by reference to any further good. Finnis claims instead that the basic human goods are grasped directly by practical reason. Critics have found this claim puzzling and have suggested that Finnis's enumeration of basic goods is not based on any acts of practical understanding but rather simply reflects his strongly held opinions about what is good and bad for human beings. To see that the basic goods are perceived by practical reason, however, consider how we understand human action—our own and those of others. We

understand actions by reference to the intelligible end or purpose the actor is trying to bring about by that action. The effort to understand actions would be fruit-
less if there were no basic goods that serve as ultimate reasons for action, for if
there were no ultimate reasons for action, any inquiry into purposes would yield
an infinite regress.

It will be helpful to illustrate this point with an example.[43] Let us suppose
that we see our neighbor getting into her car. Let us further suppose that she
is a friend and, knowing our interest in practical philosophy, is pleased to answer our eccentric, prying question into her reasons for acting. We ask her
why she is getting into her car. She replies that she is going to the local high
school, and she is in a hurry, so she is driving rather than walking. In a sense,
our question has been answered: given her desire to get to the school quickly,
it may well make sense for her to drive rather than walk (depending on traf-
fic and distance, and so on). But her action still has not fully been explained;
we may still reasonably ask why she is going to the school at all. Suppose she
answers that she is going to hear a lecture about some topic of interest to her
or to see an exhibition of fine artwork. These answers do answer our question, and upon hearing either of them, there would be nothing more to ask: it
simply makes sense for someone to want to learn or to appreciate fine art. Her
action would be fully explained. We may wonder how these goals fit in with
other plans we know our neighbor to have, but in any case there would be
nothing mysterious or unintelligible about her (or anyone) having discovered
an interest in learning or in the arts.

Now let us suppose that she had answered instead that she has taken a part-
time job at the school. Again, this makes a certain degree of sense: we know
well the usefulness of money. Money is required to purchase the whole variety of goods needed to sustain life; it can be spent on gifts to express our
friendship with others; it can be used to purchase books or fine art; it can be
saved, and so on. But to see that the good of money cannot provide an ultimate reason for action, let us suppose further that our neighbor had made a
fortune on the stock market and has far more money than she could ever
spend. "I'm not working for the money," she tells us. "All right," we answer,
"you're doing it because the work is challenging and satisfying to you or to
have the companionship of fellow-employees." "No and no," she says. "I just
want the money, not to spend it, nor for the security or reputation of having
savings (since I already have plenty of money for those things); I am not interested in the skills I exercise or the people I work with, nor do I have any
reason for working other than to get money." At this juncture, we would be
thoroughly baffled. Her interest in money simply for its own sake makes no
sense: it cannot provide an ultimate (question-stopping) reason for action and
hence cannot be a basic good. But the goods Finnis identifies: life, health,

knowledge, play, aesthetic experience, sociability, practical reasonableness, and religion do supply just such answers.

We may also identify goods as basic by means of dialectical arguments that show the unacceptable consequences attendant upon denying the goodness of one or other of the basic goods. Consider the good of knowledge. The goodness of knowing is evident to anyone with experience of both ignorance and knowledge: it is better to know and to understand than to be confused, unaware, ignorant. It is self-evidently good. But let us suppose that a skeptic seeks to deny the goodness of knowledge. Can he coherently do so? No, argues Finnis; the skeptic's denial is "operationally self-defeating."[44] Seriously to assert that knowledge is not a basic good is to make a contribution to a philosophical discourse that aims to discern the truth (in this case, about the goodness of knowledge). In making his denial, the skeptic demonstrates in action his commitment to the proposition that knowledge is a good—in trying to find out the truth about this proposition, our skeptic is acting for the sake of knowledge, treating it as a basic good—which is just what he had sought in words to deny. Dialectical arguments can be constructed to defend the other basic goods as well.

One might still object at this point that all actions are really motivated by the desire for pleasure: we do what pleases us and avoid what pains us. Finnis responds to this reductivist objection by invoking Robert Nozick's famous thought experiment about an "experience machine."[45] The experiment asks us to imagine a device that could, by directly stimulating a person's brain, enable someone who had plugged into it to experience any and all sensations he had chosen; but there is a catch: one must connect for life or not at all. Ought one to choose a life of inactivity accompanied by a host of agreeable feelings, attached to the experience machine? One would taste the pleasure of (say) making friends, of scientific discovery, or great achievements in business or the arts, or experience the sense of having attained spiritual enlightenment—without, of course, having actually done any of those things. Plainly, it is not reasonable to choose such a life. And if that is so, it is because there is more to life than subjective experience, than feelings; real actions and real achievements are what we, as reasonable creatures, in fact desire. The basic goods that orient our practical reasoning cannot be reduced to pleasure.

Morality versus Utilitarianism

On the basis of the account of practical reason just developed, Finnis concludes that utilitarian or consequentialist ethical theories must be rejected as wholly irrational. Generally speaking, such theories propose some form of maximizing rule as the basic principle of ethics, for example, that we ought to act in order to bring about the greatest net good for the greatest number of people, in the long run. Of course there are a host of difficulties—arguably insurmountable difficulties—in ascertaining with sufficient certainty the future consequences of any action, such that it is not even clear whether we can ever practically carry out anything at all resembling the consequential calculus that utilitarian theories require. But even were it possible to know the future with the requisite certainty and in the requisite detail, Finnis discerns a different, but no less fatal, difficulty inherent in the utilitarian method. If there exist a multiplicity of equally basic and incommensurable goods, there can be no coherent way of maximizing the good or minimizing harm: under these circumstances, the whole idea of maximizing becomes utterly *senseless.*

We may often *feel* that consequentialist weighing can yield a determinate conclusion about how we should act, but this feeling of certainty by itself tells us nothing. Our sense that the consequences of one course of action are better than those of another course of action are, Finnis observes, made possible by our having already chosen for ourselves some purpose or commitment which forms the basis of our judging. Finnis does not, of course, deny that cost-benefit analysis can intelligibly be applied in certain, technical contexts, but he does insist on its limited applicability. Cost-benefit analysis can tell us how most efficiently to accomplish some given end, but it cannot determine for us which ends we should pursue.[46] Thus Finnis, like Kant before him, rejects utilitarianism as a system of moral reasoning on the grounds that it is no more than a sophisticated form of rationalizing conclusions one desires to reach on other grounds.[47]

A PRACTICAL SCIENCE OF POLITICS

According to Finnis, the social sciences, including political science and analytical jurisprudence, are *practical* sciences. In other words, the social sciences are fundamentally normative and prescriptive, and even the task of describing social reality logically depends upon a prior normative account of how human persons ought to relate to one another. Finnis thus inverts the conventional modern understanding of the relationship between description and prescription. This inversion is required, however, by the recognition that the objects of social scientific inquiry—states, firms, households, legal systems, and the like—are not natural objects like stars or planets but are constituted by the choices of the persons who comprise them. In the terms introduced earlier, the objects of social scientific inquiry are part of the *moral-existential* order, not the *natural* (or any other) order, and thus must be understood in the appropriate terms.

As we have already seen, human actions can be understood only by reference to their point—the intelligible good or goods they seek to realize; this is true not only of individual actions but also of actions undertaken by groups as well. In order adequately to describe a social practice, then, reference will have to be made to the internal, practical perspective of the participants, as Max Weber long ago perceived and the great legal positivist H. L. A. Hart more recently also understood.[48] But which perspective should inform our study of, say, a state or legal system? Finnis answers that the perspective of full practical reasonableness enables us to identify focal cases of, say, political communities, so that other polities would emerge as departures from (or corruptions of) the focal case.[49] Without a central or focal case to orient our descriptive account, a social theorist could do no more that to catalogue the different practices of different peoples or to indicate what concepts were of interest to himself.

We are now in a position to understand the sense in which natural law theory does indeed assert that "unjust laws are not law" but, despite the claims of some legal positivists to the contrary, the assertion does not involve natural law theory in any sort of absurdity. Finnis contends that "the central case of law is coordination of willing subjects by law which by its fully public character (promulgation), clarity, generality, stability, and practicability, treats them as partners in public reason."[50] Unjust laws, at least insofar as they are practically unreasonable, obviously cannot treat citizens as partners in public reason. Thus, unjust laws cannot be laws in the focal sense of law, but are laws only in a secondary, analogical sense, in much the same way as the natural law is not a focal case of law. Notice that to observe that unjust laws are not focal cases of law is not to reach any definitive conclusion about one's obligation to obey any given unjust law, but it does enable us to see clearly and to articulate with more precision the differences between, say, a tyrant's edicts and the legislative enactments of a reasonably just constitutional democracy. Conceived in this way as practical, the social sciences become better able to give a faithful portrait of the world of human affairs as it is understood by the human agents whose actions constitute it.

Normative Political Theory

In order to understand Finnis's normative political theory, it will be helpful to compare it to Rawls's political liberalism, which it resembles in two key respects (beyond their shared rejection of utilitarianism, which we have already noted). Like Rawls, Finnis maintains both that there exist inviolable human rights and that, to be legitimate, political power must be exercised in accordance with public reason. Finnis disagrees with Rawls, however, about what basic rights all persons have and about what kind of reasons are to count as public.[51] Because the latter disagreement is the more fundamental of the two, we will examine it first.

In *Political Liberalism,* Rawls maintains that political legitimacy requires that a society's fundamental law be justifiable to all its citizens in terms of public reasons. In other words, its basic, constitutional principles must be such that "all citizens as free and equal may reasonably be expected to endorse [them] in light of their common human reason."[52] Finnis agrees that legislators "are entitled to impose as requirements only those practical principles which are accessible to all people whatever their present religious beliefs or cultural practices," but in his view those universally accessible practical principles are the principles of the natural law—which are *natural* precisely because they are based on reason alone, not on revelation. Although the change from Rawls's insistence that public reasons are those *that free and equal citizens may reasonably be expected to endorse* to Finnis's claim that public reasons are those *that are accessible to all people, whatever their present religious beliefs or cultural practices* may appear to be slight, much in fact turns on this difference.

The root of Finnis's objection to Rawls's conception of public reason is that he rejects the method of political constructivism from which that conception is derived. Simply put, Finnis rejects Rawls's reliance on the idea of a social contract to identify principles of political justice. Working in the tradition of Locke, Rousseau, and Kant, Rawls argues that the most reasonable principles of justice are those that would be unanimously chosen by citizens in a suitably constructed hypothetical situation of choice, the "original position."[53] As a "device of representation," the original position models a set of restraints on the reasons that may be introduced in support of any putative principle of justice. These restraints are derived from conceptions of society and of the person that are "implicit in the public culture of a democratic society;" they are explicitly not derived from any particular comprehensive moral or religious tradition.[54] Rawls's aspiration is to generate principles of justice that all reasonable citizens can endorse—even when they disagree vigorously about which comprehensive religious or moral doctrine is true.

Finnis objects that Rawls's political constructivism is at once too modest and too presumptuous. It is too modest in that in seeking only to formulate a political conception of justice based on premises derived from the public political culture, it despairs too quickly both of attaining any genuine moral knowledge and of justifying the liberal conception of justice to anyone who does not already approve of the practices of liberal-democratic regimes. Conversely, it presumptuously expels from constitutional-political discourse some number of true practical principles in order to gain unanimous assent to a political conception of justice. These two objections both stem from a still more fundamental critique: at bottom, Finnis objects to the conception of legitimate authority implicit in the ideal of political autonomy at the heart of Rawls's constructivist project. According to Rawls, all (reasonable) citizens are to be able to affirm the political principles of justice for themselves; by living in accordance with those principles, they will be politically autonomous—subject only to a (basic, constitutional) law they have given themselves.[55]

Finnis rejects this Kantian conception of political autonomy entirely and the priority of (political) right upon which it is based. It is no accident that Rawls's unsatisfactory remarks about abortion rights provide the occasion for Finnis's most forceful critique of the Rawlsian conception of public reason.[56] The question of abortion is a hard case from a contractarian perspective because it raises a question about whom to include within the social contract: are the interests of fetal human beings to be taken directly into account or not? Rawls excludes fetuses from the contract and attempts to justify this exclusion by appealing to political values—"respect for human life, the ordered reproduction of political society over time, . . . and . . . the equality of women."[57] He does so in order to preserve his political liberalism as a freestanding political conception, so that it may receive the universal assent of all reasonable and rational citizens. But, charges Finnis, the appeal to political values here is just a covert appeal to the conclusions authorized by the comprehensive doctrines Rawls himself favors. By itself, this objection is not decisive: Rawls freely admits that only a range of comprehensive moral views are compatible with political liberalism. That is why Rawls judges any comprehensive moral doctrine that excludes a first trimester abortion right to be "to that extent unreasonable."[58]

The harder question for Rawls is this: on the basis of what criteria are comprehensive views that reject abortion (like Finnis's) deemed to be unreasonable? The appeal to public values here turns out to be nothing more than an appeal to majority preferences, restated a high level of generality. These are "our" values, Rawls in effect says to Finnis; anyone who wants to be part of "our" society must accept them. Finnis rightly replies that this is not an argument, but an appeal to political power—and one that has the effect of excluding rational, moral argument about the status of fetal human life. Rawls's contractarianism thus shares the central problem of social contract theories generally: it cannot give an adequate account of whom to include within the contract and whom to exclude. (Hobbes and Rousseau were very clear about the moral arbitrariness of the scope of the contract, and Kant's political theory runs into serious difficulties at just this point). To avoid circularity, any account of the scope of the contract must be formulated in terms other than those authorized by the contract itself; but any appeal to external principles undermines the point of the contractarian procedure, since it suggests that the underlying principles, rather than those generated by the contractarian procedure, are ultimately determinative.

The latter is Finnis's view; therefore, he rejects the contractarian approach and the aspiration to discover principles of political right that can be affirmed independently of claims about the good. We are instead to examine political societies and legal systems from the perspective of the account of practical reasonableness developed above. Our first question therefore must be: *What good or goods does the political community (the state) aim to realize?* Although much of the classical tradition from Aristotle forward seems to suppose that the political community aims to realize a distinct form of good—that is, one choice worthy for its own sake—Finnis disagrees. Some communities do indeed find their intelligible point in an intrinsic common good that can be attained in no other way. The friendship of close friends is one such good, the *fides* of husband and wife is another, claims Finnis, and so too is the communion of religious believers participating in an act of communal worship.[59] The political community, however, aims at none of these; rather, it aims at a purely instrumental common good. Peace, public order, prosperity, the rule of law—these are great goods, but they are all valuable because and only insofar as they make possible the attainment of other, truly basic goods.

To see that the political community must be understood as instrumental to the attainment of other, intrinsic goods, it will be helpful to see why one of the most influential accounts of an intrinsic good at which the polity might be thought to aim must fail. Aristotle claims that the polity aims to make possible a self-sufficient life for its members—a way of life lacking in nothing. But, says Finnis, this aspiration is impossibly high for any real political community to meet. As we have seen, only the idea of integral human fulfillment can fully satisfy this aim; only where all persons participate so far as is possible in all of the basic goods can there be nothing more to desire. This ideal community, however, necessarily transcends the limits of any real community. Second, there are important limits to what the political authorities can in fact accomplish; were the government expected to make people good in the hopes of creating a perfectly self-sufficient community, it would be bound to fail because people cannot be made good against their will. Law may command and forbid external actions, but it cannot directly operate on the will. By our own choices and our own actions, we constitute ourselves: if we are fully reasonable, fully responsive to the demands of natural law, we make ourselves good; if not, we make ourselves wicked.

To be sure, the political community is more than an association for the physical protection of its members; the political community aims to create the ensemble of conditions that would facilitate the living of practically reasonable, genuinely worthwhile, good lives by its members. Writes Finnis:

> The political community's rationale requires that the state should deliberately and publicly identify, encourage, facilitate, and support the truly worthwhile (including moral virtue), should deliberately and publicly identify, discourage, and hinder the harmful and evil, and should by its criminal prohibitions and sanctions (as well as its other laws and policies) assist people with parental responsibilities to educate children in virtue and to discourage their vices.[60]

This instrumental conception of the state implies that, although the state has an obligation to foster a public culture conducive to the living of good lives, there will also be a sphere of private activity in which the criminal law should not intervene. For this reason, Finnis supports the outcome of *Griswold v Connecticut*,[61] which invalidated a state law criminalizing the *use* of contraceptives by married couples, but disagrees with the Court's opinion in *Eisenstadt v Baird*,[62] which struck down a Massachusetts law prohibiting the *distribution* of contraceptives to the unmarried. The Connecticut statute regulated conduct outside the state's proper sphere of concern and so was rightly invalidated. In contrast, the Massachusetts statute regulated the public activities of the suppliers of contraceptive devices, and so it was a potentially permissible exercise of state power (if it is true that the use of artificial contraceptives is practically unreasonable and if the statute satisfies other, more general, requirements of political prudence). Whether or not Finnis is right that the use of artificial contraceptives is practically unreasonable,[63] he is surely right that an important line was crossed between *Griswold* and *Eisenstadt*, although the Court failed to perceive it.

Because political power may be legitimately exercised only on the basis of good (practical) reasons, the state is limited in a second way also. Not only must the government recognize that the goods it may advance are instrumental goods but also it is limited in its choice of means to pursue its ends: the state is bound by the requirements of practical reasonableness, just as are the individuals who constitute the political community. As we have seen, practical reasoning generates a series of moral absolutes which "constitute the most basic human rights." These absolutes include (but are not limited to): "the exclusion of intentional killing, of intentional injury to the person . . . of deliberate deception for the sake of securing desired results, of enslavement which treats a human person as an object of lower rank of being than the autonomous human subject."[64] Just as no individual may ever reasonably intend the death of another person, so too is the state forbidden from intending to kill. Hence, the death penalty is impermissible, and war—though sometimes legitimate—is extremely problematic.

Finnis suggests that the armed combat of soldiers at war may be distinguished from the application of capital punishment because soldiers need not intend the death of any hostile combatants (though the deaths of many will be the foreseeable consequence of one's legitimate efforts to repel the enemy's attacks), whereas the infliction of the death penalty requires precisely the intent to kill.[65] Nonlethal but effective weapons (the stun-rays of science fiction) would presumably be welcomed by the armed forces, but a nonlethal death penalty is simply oxymoronic. Finnis does not shrink from following his principles to their logical, though discomfiting, conclusions. The norm that forbids intentional killing also rules out as immoral the policy of nuclear deterrence, since it is based on the threat to kill vast numbers of innocent persons, should an enemy government threaten our vital interests.

HUMAN RIGHTS AND FAITH IN GOD

Although Finnis's new natural law theory is the most prominent contemporary development of a tradition to which Aquinas was perhaps the most noteworthy contributor, it must be emphasized that it is a secular theory, based on reasons in principle accessible to all—not on any sort of revelation. We can all examine our own processes of practical reasoning to discern the role of basic human goods and the corresponding basic practical principles in our deliberations. We can all examine the dialectical arguments used to support Finnis's claim to have identified correctly the basic human goods and the first principle of morality ("be fully reasonable"). And we can, of course, all question the validity of any practical argument before accepting as true any particular moral claim.

Finnis does argue, however, that his account of practical reasonableness points beyond itself, suggesting a need for an account of the "last things"— whether there is a personal God, whether the soul is immortal, and if so what its fate might be. Although few political theorists today pursue these questions, our neglect of such issues is quite recent: Kant, for example, pursued them with utmost seriousness, as did nearly every other great political thinker of the past. In the closing chapter of *Natural Law and Natural Rights,* Finnis sketches an argument for the existence of God and provides some further reasons (not intended to be taken as conclusive) for affirming the existence of a personal God, such as is revealed in the Jewish and Christian scriptures.[66] He concludes by showing how such a further account deepens and completes the account of practical reasonableness accessible to natural reason alone— though he stresses that his own moral theory remains the most plausible such theory, even if his religious claims should fail.

Finnis's own writings in political theory and jurisprudence thus model his conception of public reason he favors. His major moral and political claims are grounded in reasons accessible to all, but they are subsequently supported and deepened by appeal to religious sources—including the Christian scriptures and the teachings of the Roman Catholic Church. Many liberals may be tempted to dismiss Finnis's work on account of its openness to traditional religion, but that would be a mistake. In these days of Kantian liberalism ascendant, good liberals should value few things more than perceptive criticism and the forceful statement of a clear alternative—precisely what we find in the works of John Finnis.

NOTES

1. John Finnis, "Is Natural Law Theory Compatible with Limited Government?" in *Natural Law, Liberalism, and Morality: Contemporary Essays*, ed. Robert P. George (Oxford: Oxford University Press, 1996), 9. Further references to this work will be indicated by the abbreviation NLLG.

2. John Finnis, *Aquinas: Moral, Political, and Legal Theory* (Oxford: Oxford University Press, 1998) IX.2 and note C, 293. Cf. John Finnis, *Fundamentals of Ethics* (Washington, D.C.: Georgetown University Press, 1983), 129–30, where he defended capital punishment. I will refer to this work as FOE.

3. See, e.g., FOE 84, NLLG 9.

4. The label seems to have originated with the theory's critics. See, for example, Russell Hittinger, *A Critique of the New Natural Law Theory* (Notre Dame, Ind.: University of Notre Dame Press, 1987); and Stephen Macedo, "Against the Old Sexual Morality of the New Natural Law," in NLLG, 27–48.

5. John Finnis, *Natural Law and Natural Rights* (Oxford: Oxford University Press, 1980). Hereafter NLNR.

6. See n. 2, above.

7. John Finnis, Joseph M. Boyle, Jr., and Germain Grisez, *Nuclear Deterrence, Morality, and Realism* (Oxford: Oxford University Press, 1987). Hereafter NDMR.

8. Germain Grisez, Joseph Boyle, and John Finnis, "Practical Principles, Moral Truth, and Ultimate Ends," *American Journal of Jurisprudence* 32 (1987): 99–151. Hereafter PP.

9. See n. 1, above.

10. John Finnis, "Natural Law and Legal Reasoning" in *Natural Law Theory: Contemporary Essays*, ed. Robert P. George (Oxford: Oxford University Press, 1992), 134–57. Hereafter NLLR.

11. Finnis, *Aquinas*, ix.

12. Finnis, NLNR, 280.

13. Germain Grisez, "The First Principle of Practical Reason: A Commentary on the *Summa Theologiae*, 1–2, Question 94, Article 2," *Natural Law Forum* 10 (1965): 168–201.

14. For a representative version of the traditional account, see Ernest L. Fortin, "St. Thomas Aquinas," in *History of Political Philosophy,* 3rd ed., ed. Leo Strauss and Joseph Cropsey (Chicago: University of Chicago Press, 1987), 264.

15. Finnis, *Aquinas,* 21–22. See also NLLR, 139–40 and NLNR, 136–39.

16. Finnis, *Aquinas,* 21.

17. Finnis, NLNR, 137–38.

18. Finnis, NLNR, 137.

19. See generally Jürgen Habermas, *The Theory of Communicative Action,* 2 vols., trans. Thomas McCarthy (Boston: Beacon Press, 1984 and 1987), esp. vol. 1, 3–4.

20. Finnis, *Aquinas,* 22.

21. Finnis, *Aquinas,* 86–87, 95–96, 99.

22. Finnis, *Aquinas,* 86.

23. Compare NLLR III-IV (treating sociability as a basic good) to NLLG, 4 and *Aquinas,* V.4 (where marriage is treated as a basic good).

24. Finnis, NLNR, 89, and see generally NLNR, 86–90.

25. Finnis, FOE, 69.

26. Finnis, NLNR, 122, quoting Kant, *Foundations of the Metaphysics of Morals,* trans. Lewis White Beck (Indianapolis: Bobbs-Merrill, 1959), 47.

27. Finnis, NLNR, chap. V. See also FOE, III.6.

28. Finnis, NLNR, 102.

29. On the relationship between the modes of responsibility and the first principle of morality, see PP, 127–29.

30. Finnis, NDMR, 283 (emphasis in original). The same formulation appears at PP, 128, and NLLG, 7, but without the emphasis. See also FOE, 72–73.

31. Finnis, NLLR, 137.

32. See Immanuel Kant, *Groundwork of the Metaphysics of Morals,* trans. H. J. Paton (New York: Harper & Row, 1953), 100–102.

33. Kant, *Groundwork,* 101.

34. Finnis, FOE, 122.

35. Finnis, Boyle, and Grisez, PP, 131–32.

36. Finnis, NLNR, 67.

37. Finnis, Boyle, and Grisez, PP, 106.

38. Finnis, Boyle, and Grisez, PP, 106.

39. Finnis, Boyle, and Grisez, PP, 111.

40. Finnis, NLNR, 68.

41. Finnis, NLNR, 68.

42. Ronald Dworkin, "Liberalism" in *A Matter of Principle,* 203. Compare Dworkin, "Do We Have a Right to Pornography?" in *A Matter of Principle,* 370.

43. The following example is not exactly Robert George's, but it draws freely from his discussion in "Recent Criticism of Natural Law Theory," *University of Chicago Law Review* 55 (1988): 1390–1394.

44. Finnis, NLNR, 74.

45. Finnis, FOE, 37–42; NLNR, 95–96. Nozick's version of the thought experiment can be found in Robert Nozick, *Anarchy, State, and Utopia* (New York: Basic Books, 1974), 42–45.

46. Finnis, FOE, 90–93, and NLLR 146.

47. Finnis, FOE, 120.

48. Finnis, *Aquinas,* 38; NLNR 12–16.

49. Finnis, NLNR, 15, *Aquinas,* 48.

50. John Finnis, "Seegers Lecture: Public Reason, Abortion, and Cloning," *Valparaiso Law Review* 32 (spring 1998): 364 (internal references omitted). Hereafter abbreviated PR. This is the focal case because it identifies the conditions under which "legal obligation is . . . at least presumptively a moral obligation" and "the establishment and maintenance of legal as distinct from discretionary or customary order is regarded as a moral ideal." NLNR, 14.

51. Finnis, PR, 363–64.

52. John Rawls, *Political Liberalism* (New York: Columbia University Press, 1993), 137, 217. Hereafter PL.

53. John Rawls, *Theory of Justice* (Cambridge: Harvard University Press, 1971) sec. 3; compare PL I.4.

54. Rawls, PL, 15, 34.

55. Rawls, PL II.6, 78; PL III.1, 98.

56. John Finnis, PR 372–75.

57. Rawls, PL, 243 n. 32.

58. Rawls, PL, 243 n. 32.

59. Finnis, NLLG, 5.

60. Finnis, NLLG, 8. Finnis embraces the principle of "subsidiarity," the norm directing governments to aid their citizens in living well by respecting the independence of subordinate associations.

61. 381 U.S. 479 (1965).

62. 405 U.S. 438 (1970).

63. For Finnis's argument on this point, see NLLG, 14–16 and *Aquinas,* V.4 and note e.

64. Finnis, NLLR, 148.

65. Finnis, *Aquinas,* 286–87.

66. Finnis, NLNR, 405–420.

Index

abortion, 36, 90, 192, 209
academic moralism, x, 78–81, 91–93
Achieving Our Country, 154
Ackerman, Bruce, 63
activism, 89
After Virtue, 121, 122–23, 125, 134–35
altruism, 4
American Constitutional Law, 142
American Public Philosophy Institute, xix
anarchy, 61
Anarchy, State, and Utopia, 61, 70–71
ancient philosophy, xiii–xiv
animals, 134–39
antiperfectionist liberalism: alternatives to, xi, xix; egalitarianism and, xvi, xvii; good and, xvi, xix; libertarianism and, xv–xvi; life and, xvii; minimal state and, xvii; morality and, xvi, xviii, 161–63, 172; pragmatic liberalism and, xviii; rights and, xvi; social contract theory and, xvi; tradition and, xviii, 128. *See also specific kinds*
Aquinas, Thomas, Saint, 114, 115, 135–36, 167. *See also* Thomism
Aristotle: Alasdair MacIntyre and, 122; biology and, 135–36; challenge

model and, 38; morality and, 124–25, 126, 131, 134, 135; perfectionist liberalism and, 2; transcendence and, 177
Athens, 126
Augustine, Saint, 126
autonomy: bad and, xix, 164, 169–70; belief and, 171–72; deontological liberalism and, 99–100; family and, 165; good and, xviii–xix, 164, 165–66, 169–70; government and, xix, 164, 166, 167–68; harm principle and, 166–69; legal pragmatism and, x, 142; liberalism and, 182, 188; marriage and, 164–65; morality and, 162–66; perfectionist liberalism and, xviii–xix, 162–66; pluralism and, 163–66, 167; politics and, 209; reason and, 169–70, 171–72; religion and, 53, 54; self-respect and, 171–72; value and, 163–64, 165–66, 169–70. *See also* libertarianism; liberty

bad: autonomy and, xix, 164, 169–70; cruelty, xviii, 153; harm principle, xix, 166–69; killing, 197–98, 211–12; new natural law and,

217

About the Contributors

Christopher Wolfe is professor of political science at Marquette University, and president of the American Public Philosophy Institute. He received his B.A. from the University of Notre Dame in 1971 and his Ph.D. from Boston College in 1978. He is the author of *The Rise of Modern Judicial Review* (1986), *Judicial Activism* (1990), and editor (with Robert George) of *Natural Law and Public Reason* (2000).

Michael Pakaluk received his A.B. from Harvard, M.Litt. from Edinburgh, and Ph.D. in philosophy from Harvard in 1988. He is currently associate professor of philosophy at Clark University in Worcester, Massachusetts. The editor of *Other Selves: Philosophers on Friendship* (1991), he is currently writing an introduction to Aristotle's *Nicomachean Ethics* and a commentary on Plato's *Phaedo.*

Celia Wolf-Devine, an associate professor at Stonehill College, holds a B.A. from Smith College and a Ph.D. in philosophy from the University of Wisconsin at Madison. She is the author of *Descartes on Seeing: Epistemology and Visual Perception* and *Diversity and Community in the Academy: Affirmative Action in Faculty Appointments,* and coeditor, with her husband Philip Devine, of *Sex and Gender: A Spectrum of Views.*

R. George Wright holds an A.B. from the University of Virginia and a Ph.D. in political science and J.D. from Indiana University. He is professor of law at Indiana School of Law. He has taught constitutional law, legal philosophy, environmental law, torts, and administrative law.

Jack Wade Nowlin is assistant professor of law and Jessie D. Puckett, Jr., Lecturer in Law at the University of Mississippi School of Law, where he teaches constitutional law, civil rights, and criminal law. He received his J.D. from the University of Texas School of Law and his M.A. and Ph.D. in politics from Princeton University. His articles have appeared in the *Oklahoma Law Review,* the *Kentucky Law Journal,* and *Vera Lex.*

Terry Hall is director of the Honors Program and associate professor of philosophy at the University of St. Thomas (Houston). He has also taught at the University of Notre Dame and served as a professional staff member in the U.S. House of Representatives.

David M. Wagner is associate professor at Regent University School of Law. He received his B.A. in history and his M.A. in medieval studies from Yale, and his J.D. from George Mason University. He has also served as an editorial writer, government speechwriter, and director of legal policy at the Family Research Council. He is the author of the monograph *Defining Deviancy Up: How the Child Protection System Harms Families* (1994).

Gerard V. Bradley is professor of law at the University of Notre Dame Law School. He is the author of *Church-State Relationships in America* (1987) and other articles on constitutional theory and legal philosophy.

Robert P. George holds the McCormick Chair of Jurisprudence at Princeton University. He received his B.A. from Swarthmore College, his M.Div. and J.D. from Harvard University, and a D.Phil. from Oxford University. He is author of *Making Men Moral* (1993), *In Defense of Natural Law* (1999), and *The Clash of Orthodoxies* (2001).

J. Brian Benestad is professor of theology and religious studies at the University of Scranton. He is editor of a three volume collecton of Ernest Fortin's essays, published by Rowman & Littlefield, and author of numerous articles on the subject of virtue and the common good.

Joseph R. Reisert is the Harriet S. and George C. Wiswell, Jr., Assistant Professor of American Constitutional Law in the Department of Government at Colby College. He received his Ph.D. from Harvard University and his A.B. from Princeton University. He is the author of *Jean-Jacques Rousseau: A Friend of Virtue* (Cornell University Press, 2003).